Charles Frederick Millspaugh, Lawrence William Nuttall

Flora of West Virginia

Charles Frederick Millspaugh, Lawrence William Nuttall

Flora of West Virginia

ISBN/EAN: 9783337107826

Printed in Europe, USA, Canada, Australia, Japan

Cover: Foto ©Andreas Hilbeck / pixelio.de

More available books at **www.hansebooks.com**

FIELD COLUMBIAN MUSEUM.

PUBLICATION 9.

Botanical Series.   Vol. 1, No. 2.

FLORA

OF

WEST VIRGINIA

BY

CHARLES FREDERICK MILLSPAUGH,
Curator, Department of Botany,

AND

LAWRENCE WILLIAM NUTTALL

CHICAGO, U. S. A.
January, 1896.

PUBLICATIONS OF THE MUSEUM.

For the convenience of scientific workers it has been deemed expedient to issue the publications of the Museum in separate series for each of the sciences represented. The following series thus far have been established: Historical, Geological, Botanical, Zoölogical, Ornithological and Anthropological.

A consecutive number has been given the entire set of publications to indicate the order of issue. Each departmental series, however, has its own volume number and individual consecutive pagination, making the literature of the science, or general subject, independent and complete for separate binding; or they may be bound in order of publication without relation to subject. Proceedings, memoirs, monographs, bulletins, and hand-books and catalogues of collections, are included within the scope of the publications.

Full lists of the publications of the Museum may be found in the Annual Report of the Director.

Publications are sent to societies and institutions of a public character that reciprocate with their own literature and to a limited number of scientists who are able to exchange.

Two publications have been issued of the Botanical series: Contribution to the Flora of Yucatan (Pub. 4); and The Flora of West Virginia (Pub. 9). Contribution II to the Flora of Yucatan is in preparation.

FREDERICK J. V. SKIFF,
Director.

CONTENTS.

	PAGE
Introductory,	69
Botanical History,	70
Special Features of the Flora,	71
The Sylva,	76
Summary of the Flora,	80
Catalogue of the Species,	81
Host Index of the Fungi,	234
Local Plant Names,	261
Generic Index,	264

ILLUSTRATIONS.

Pl. V.	River Birches at Sutton, West Virginia,	FRONTISPIECE
Pl. VI.	Map of West Virginia,	169
Pl. VII.	Rhus radicans, Linn.,	215

The Flora of West Virginia.

BY

C. F. MILLSPAUGH AND L. W. NUTTALL.

The State of West Virginia comprises about 24,780 square miles of territory lying between 37°30' and 40°30' north latitude, and 0°45' and 5°30' west longitude from Washington. Its outline of varied boundaries has become a synonym for irregularity, as a glance at the accompanying map will show; it might also comprise the topography, suggesting as it does an immense field over which a gigantic plow has left a confused maze of deep and irregular furrows. This topographical condition is mainly due to the great number of mountain ranges and a vast network of rapid streams, that, rising in the higher altitudes of the eastern and southern borders, pass in varied and tortuous courses through the State, to augment the Ohio on the west and northwest, and the Potomac on the northeast.

Along the low, as well as the lofty mountain ranges, there is comparatively little tableland, and in the wedge-like valleys there is a like absence of extensive bottoms, except along Tygart's Valley River in Randolph County, the Great Kanawha and the Ohio. Although there are many mountain glades, some nearly dry and others swampy, plainly indicating their late occupancy by small lakes, there is to-day neither pond nor lake within the limits of the State, and very little if any stagnant water.

As the major portion of the State lies west of the Alleghanies, the prevailing climate is much like that of western Pennsylvania, partaking little indeed of that southern atmosphere that we are wont to associate with the name Virginia.

The prevailing soil of the hills and valleys is stiff clay, and sandy and clayey alluvium, over which there is in general but little loam. The clay of the more open steep hillsides is so unctuous and unstable that frequent landslides occur during Spring, sometimes of great extent. This subsidence renders the valley streams muddy throughout the year. The rocks are principally sandstone and limestone, with some outcroppings of shales on the northeastern heights. The special features of the now very fertile and then quite sterile soils, with the varied differences in altitude, as well as the vast areas of primitive forests, yield a flora of great variety, and often widely differing at points only a few miles apart.

The amount of exploration necessary under such conditions to gain a full knowledge of the flora, becomes an arduous undertaking, though the interest in searching an almost virgin field is so deep as to greatly lighten the labor.

BOTANICAL HISTORY.

The early botanical explorers, Pursh. and Nuttall, found many of their novelties among the eastern mountains of this State, and the old Dutch gardener, Kin, here sought oddities for horticulture, but either on account of their limited knowledge regarding the geography of this section, or from the undeveloped condition of the area they traversed, the localities of their collecting are in most cases but imperfectly detailed. Since their time, with the exception of a few transient botanists who have incidentally worked over the neighborhood of some vacation resort, the work done on the flora may be summarized as follows :

In 1867 and 1871, Dr. A. S. Todd, as chairman of a committee of the Medical Society of West Virginia, published a list of the "Medicinal Plants of West Virginia." This list contains an enumeration of nine trees, seven shrubs and sixty herbs.

In 1870, Mr. DissDebarr, State Commissioner of Immigration, in his "Handbook of West Virginia," compiled a list of the timber trees of the State, in which he enumerated fifty-two species and added twelve species of shrubs.

In 1876, Professor Fontaine in compiling his portion of the Centennial volume upon the "Resources of West Virginia," listed more carefully the forest trees, shrubs and medicinal plants of the State, drawing the last from the publication of Dr. Todd. This work contains an enumeration of sixty-nine trees and sixteen shrubs.

In 1878, Profs. H. N. Mertz and G. Guttenberg manifolded a check list of the "Flora of West Virginia," being an account of work done along the upper Ohio bottoms, and in the mountains of the northeastern portion of the State, the latter while located at Harper's Ferry. This list enumerates fifty-nine trees, thirty-seven shrubs and four hundred ninety-four herbs.

In 1888 and 1889, Miss Verona Mapel, Preceptress of the High School at Glenville, Gilmer County, quite thoroughly worked over her immediate vicinity in connection with her school duties. She reports in manuscript forty-two trees, twenty-three shrubs and two hundred ninety herbs. Her list includes neither the commoner weeds and herbs, nor the grasses and sedges.

In 1890, '91 and '92, the present authors began a systematic survey of the State, publishing the results of their work in 1892 under the title of "A Preliminary Catalogue of the Flora of West Virginia." This catalogue included all known previous work and enumerated 1,645 species, giving localities, numerous critical notes, and descriptions and plates of several new forms.

In 1892, Mr. John K. Small and Miss Anna Murray Vail spent some time in Greenbrier County, exploring the vicinity of White Sulphur Springs. The results of their work are included in their "Report of the Botanical Exploration of Southwestern Virginia," published as one of the Memoirs of the Torrey Botanical Club.

From 1892 to the present, the authors have continued their investigation of the flora, adding the knowledge of over one thousand species to their preliminary list, and detecting many new localities for previously published species. This additional work forms the basis of the present publication. The small edition of the preliminary catalogue having been exhausted within a few months of its issue, and many institutions, libraries and personal workers being unable to secure copies of the work, it has been deemed expedient to include here all the species of that publication, without, however, repeating the body matter. These repeated species appear in small capitals, additional species new to the flora in black-faced type. As in the preliminary catalogue, all species that have been described from known West Virginia types are republished in full.

SPECIAL FEATURES OF THE FLORA.

The distribution of plants within the boundaries of the State is wonderfully comprehensive. Canada places representatives of her boreal flora upon its Alleghanian mountain tops, some that have even passed by the States of New York, New Jersey, Pennsylvania, Delaware and Maryland in the transit; the Southern States contribute to its flora through the influence of the mysterious New River on the southeast; the great trunk lines of railway, as well as the open condition of the western border line along the Ohio River, give entrance to individuals of a migratory character from the Western Plains; and from some not readily accountable reason, Eastern forms, and even coast line species stray within its limits.

Of the noteworthy species we connect in *Anemone trifolia*, L., Canby's and Curtiss' Virginian stations with Knipe's Pennsylvanian, and that in a direct and sequential manner through the State. Our elevations for this species range from 850 to 2,300 feet. *Trautvetteria Carolinensis* (Walt.,) Vail, is to be found along all such mountain rills as are deeply shaded, at altitudes above 1,000 feet. We extend the Manual distribution of *Caltha palustris*, L., southward nearly one degree, by finding it quite plentiful in the mountains of Randolph County, where *Isopyrum trifoliatum* (L.) Britt., keeps it company. *Helleborus viridis*, L., has its most western station on the north branch of the Potomac River, in Hardy County, whence it was first reported to Dr. Gray by Dr. Gamble, of Moorfield. *Aconitum uncinatum*, L., is at home all along the banks of Cheat River, at altitudes varying from 780 to 3,550 feet. Both species of *Actæa* are to be met with on the higher Alleghanies, where *Cimicifuga Americana*, Mx., is the principal representative of the tribe.

Magnolia Fraseri, Walt., is a striking vernal feature of the whole Alleghanian region, while *tripetala* and *acuminata* are common. *Berberis Canadensis*, Mill. becomes a veritable weed in many fields in the southern portion of the State, vying with *Papaver dubium*, L., and *Glaucium Glaucium* (L.), Karst, in the northeastern section. *Bicuculla eximina* (L.), Millsp., we have found only upon the highest peaks of the Alleghanies.

Of the rambling crucifers, *Sisymbrium Thaliana* (L.) Celak, finds a home in Fayette County, and *Lepidium campestre* (L.), R. Br., is the worst and most prevalent weed in the cultivated portions of the northeastern section.

Nearly all the violets lend their beauty to the adornment of the woods and meadows; *Viola pedata*, *var. bicolor*, Pursh., with flowers as large as the cultivated pansy and fully as beautiful, is frequent among the Devonian shales of the northeast; *Viola primulæfolia*, L., comes in from the coast as far as four degrees; and *Viola hastata*, Mx., is quite plentiful in the southern section.

Although *Sida hermaphrodita* (L.), Rusby, has not been found in the Alleghanies as yet, it is not at all rare along the New and Great Kanawha Rivers, from Quinnimont to the Ohio, and thence down that river to the limits of the State. *Hibiscus Moscheutos*, L., is found not only along the bottoms of the Great Kanawha, but also in the northeastern part of the State, while *H. Trionum*, L., is a quite common weed in gardens.

All of the native species of *Aesculus*, together with the var. *hybrida* of *octandra*, are found in the State. *Ailanthus glandulosis* is becoming a most troublesome weed in many sections, especially in the northern counties.

Among the Leguminals we have re-discovered *Astragalus Carolinianus*, L., which from our specimens is considered by Professor Britton to be indistinct from *A. Canadensis*, L., and as it has the priority of publication, the latter well-known name becomes a synonym. Another important discovery in this genus is that *A. distortus*, T. and G., habits the Devonian shales of Hardy County, the only station known for the species east of the Mississippi valley. This species is here associated with *Opuntia polyacantha*, Haw, in great quantity, giving this peculiar spot in the Alleghanies much the appearance of an arid waste in Arizona. *Stylosanthes hamata* (L.), Britt., here ventures farther east than has heretofore been supposed, and finds congenial soil along New River in Fayette County. *Lespedeza striata* (Thunb.), H. & A., spreads profusely throughout the southwestern portion of the State. A new clover, *Trifolium Virginicum*, Small, has been discovered in Greenbrier County, by Mr. J. K. Small.

The roses are striking in the many new forms they produce: *Rubus Millspaughi*, Britt., is so profuse in the mountains of Pocahontas and Pendleton Counties that, according to the mountaineers and hunters, it is upon it that the bears depend principally for fattening food prior to hibernation. *Rubus Canadensis roribaccus*, Baily, the Leucretia dewberry, came originally from Randolph County. Another peculiar Rubus (*R. Columbianus* Millsp., has 5 to 7-incised leaves of striking character. A new Spirea (*S. Virginiana*, Britt.) grows plentifully within half a mile of the University at Morgantown. Mercer County in the southern section of the State, presents a wonderful array of Crategi: *C. spathulata*, *C. cordata*, *C. apiifolia*, *C. coccinea*, *C. tomentosa*, *C. punctata*, *C. Crus-galli*, *C. flava* and its variety *pubescens*, and *C. uniflora* were all found during one day's botanizing in this section.

Of the Calycanths we have all, even the two species recorded "Virginia doubtful" in the Manual.

Of the saxifrages we have notably, *Astilbe decandra*, Don., *Saxifraga erosa*, Pursh., *Boykinia aconitifolia*, Nutt., *Heuchera villosa*, Mx., and *H. Americana*, L., and even the Laboradorian *Ribes prostratum*, L' Her.

Sedum Pulchellum, Nevii, ternatum, telephioides, and *telephium*, are with us. The beautiful *Liquidambar Styraciflua* extends limitedly down the Gauly and Great Kanawha. The Onagraceæ yield a new form in *Ludwegia alternifolia*, L., var. *linearifolia*, Britt. The purple and yellow passion-flowers (*P. lutea*, L., and, *incarnata*, L.) grace the thickets.

Passing many minor forms, the Compositæ gives us *Elephantopus Carolinianus*, Willd. and *tomentosus*, L. (called as a weed "The Devil's Grandmother"); *Eupatorium, cœlestinum*, L., profuse; *Solidago Curtisii, S. rupestris*, and *Riddellii, Silphium perfoliatum*, L.; *Rudbeckia speciosa*, Wend.; *Helianthus grosse-serratus*, Mart., *H. doronicoides*, Lam., and

H. laevigatus, T. and G., *Verbesina Virginica*, L.; *Cacalia suaveolens*, *reniformis*, and *atriplicifolia;* *Cnicus Virginianus*, and *pumilus*, Torr.; *Cichorium Intybus*, L.; *Tragopogon porrifolius*, L.; *Hieracium Canadense*, Mx., and *longipilum*, Torr. (extending both); and *Chondrilla juncea*, L., called as a weed "Naked-weed, Skeleton-weed."

The interesting bell-worts are: the white form of *Lobelia syphilitica*, L., and the rare *Campanula divaricata*, Mx.

Of the rarer heaths *Schollera erythrocarpa*, Mx., grows on the highest peak of the Alleghanies, alt. 4,800 ft.; *Chiogenes hispidula* at the Falls of Blackwater; *Menziesia globularis* Salisb., *Clethra acuminata*, Mx., *Moneses grandiflora*, Salisb... and all the Rhododendrons except *Rhodora* and *Lapponicum*; even the rare *R. canescens* (Mx.), Porter, being found along the Cacapon River.

Naumbergia thyrsiflora is found in Upshur County and *Mohrodendron Carolinum* (called Shittim-wood) is plentiful along the Gauly and New Rivers. *Polemonium Van-Bruntiæ*, Britt., comes south to our flora, as well as all the *Hydrophyllums*, together with *Phacelia Purshii*, Buck, and *parviflora*, Pursh.

The beautiful morning-glories, *Impomoea coccinea*, *hederacea*, *purpurea*, and *pandurata*, are all too plentiful as weeds here; and *Cuscuta glomerata*, *Gronovii*, and *Epithymum*, have been found sparingly. *Physalis viscosa*, L., steals away from "near the coast" and is found along the Ohio River, keeping company with *Lycium vulgare*, Dun., and *Physalodes Physaloides*, Gaertn.

The notable *Scropularias* are: *Collinsia verna*, Nutt., *Chelone obliqua*, L., and *Pentstemon Canescens*. Of the mints we have notably: *Kœllia verticilata*, *clinopodioides*, *pycanthemoides*, and *Montana*. The other mints worthy of remark are: *Meehania cordata*, *Clinopodium vulgare*, *Scutellaria saxatilis*, *serrata*, *incana*, *parvula*, and *nervosa*; *Marrubium vulgare*, *Galeopsis tetrahit*, and *Stachys palustris* and *cordata*.

Of the ten Euphorbias the most notable are *E. Darlingtonii* and *E. Glyptosperma*, *var.*, *pubescens*, Engl., the latter not having been previously found east of Iowa as far as we can learn.

The presence of *Quercus ilicifolia*, Wang, in Hardy Co., extends the Manual distribution southeastward; and the southing of *Q. macrocarpa*, Mx. is also extended by several stations in the State.

As to the conifers, we have about 470,000 acres of *Picea Mariana*, a few representatives of *Abies balsamea*, *Thuya occidentalis*, and several species of Pinus, as well as a few scant growths of *Taxus Minor*.

Among the sedges the principal item of interest is the re-discovery in Fayette County of what was doubtless the original type station of *Carex Fraseri*, And.

Of the *Equisetaceæ* the most notable form so far found is *E. lævigatum*, Braun., gathered in the southernmost part of the State thus extending its distribution southeastward.

Of the *Filices*, the rarer forms found with us are: *Polypodium polypodioides*; *Pellæa atropurpurea* in great quantities in the southern section; *Asplenium pinnatifidum, montanum* (plentiful) and *angustifolium*; *Dryopteris Goldieana*, and *marginalis*. *Cystopteris bulbifera; Dicksonia punctilobula;* and strange to say on the summit of Spruce Knob at an altitude of 4,800 ft. *Dryopteris fragrans*, in such great quantity that it is cut and stacked for fodder, this species being greatly relished by cattle.

Lycopodium lucidulum, L., *annotinum*, L., *obscurum* and its var. *dendroideum*, L. *clavatum*, and L. *complanatum* are all found in the forests of black spruce along the Alleghanies.

In the mosses, hepatics, and lichens, but little collecting has so far been done, no systematic searches having been made for specimens in these classes of plants. Among the lichens several new species have been discovered, the descriptions of which are still in manuscript with Professor Nylander. In the search for hepatics incidental to other exploration, in Mercer County, the dry bald face of a large limestone cave yielded a new species in *Plagiochila Virginica* Evans, as well as a rarity in the eastern flora of the United States, *Radula Xalapensis*, Mont. Among the mosses we have been rewarded in our itinerant work by finding two new forms *Dicranodontium Virginicus*, Britt. m. and *D. Millspaughi* Britt. m., as well as numerous noteworthy species.

The Fungi have been found to be of special interest, and it is to their collection and study that Mr. Nuttall has devoted most of his spare hours from business since 1893. His field of search for forms in this class of plants has been very limited, being almost wholly the immediate neighborhood of his home at Nuttallburg, in Fayette County, on New River. Even this small area has furnished the major part of the 980 fungi of this flora, and continues to present additional forms as well as unique hosts upon every search, no matter how casual the examination or short the time devoted to the trip. Fully two-thirds of the species collected have passed under the critical examination of Mr. J. B. Ellis, whose careful consideration of our numbers has been of incalculable assistance in this work.

The new species discovered in this area, and described in this Flora, are as follows:

Anthostoma micrœcium.	**Cercospora Chionanthi.**	Corticium leptaleum.
Aposphæria pezizoides.	Cercospora Œnotherae.	Coryneum cupulatum.
Aspergillus glaucus oblongisporus.	**Cercospora septorioides.**	Cyathicula quisquillaris.
Botryodiplodia acerina.	**Clasterosporium Cornutum.**	Cylindrocolla Dendroctoni.
Botrytis olivacea.	Cladosporium nigrellum.	**Cylindrocolla flagellaris.**
Camarosporium Linderæ.	**Corticium albo-flavescens.**	Cylindrosporium Cratægi.

Cytispora caryigena.
Cytispora Celtidis.
Cytispora exasperans.
Cytispora Halesiæ.
Cytispora Rhois-hirtæ.
Cytispora Sassafras.
Dermatella viticola.
Diaporthe Araliæ.
Diaporthe Halesiæ.
Diaporthe Hydrangeæ.
Didymella Physocarpi.
Diaporthe Tetrapteræ.
Diplodia caryigena.
Diplodia Cercidis.
Diplodia infuscans.
Dothiorella Asiminæ.
Dothiorella minor.
Eutypella densissima.
Fusicoccum ilicinum.
Gloeosporium Alni.
Gloeosporium rubicolum.
Gloeosporium Rumicis,
Gloeosporium Sanguinariæ.
Haplosporella Araliæ.
Haplosporella Celtidis.
Helminthosporium brachypus.
Helotiella Nuttallii.
Hypocrea tenerrima.
Hypocrea Virginiensis.
Hypoxylon atroviride,
Hymenula cerealis.

Hypoxylon Nuttallii.
Illosporium cæspitosum.
Isaria Virginiensis.
Lachnella Virginica.
Lophidium nitidum.
Macrosporium olivaceum.
Massaria Magnoliæ.
Microcera erumpens.
Myxosporium luteum.
Myxosporium platanicolum.
Myxosporium seriatum.
Pestalozzia Toxica.
Phlyctænā Ipomœæ.
Phoma Ascelepiadea.
Phoma negundinicola ramicola.
Phoma obscurans.
Phoma pedunculi.
Phoma Pennsylvanica.
Phyllosticta Araliæ.
Phyllosticta Castaneæ.
Phyllosticta Celastri.
Phyllosticta cercidicola.
Phyllosticta globifera.
Phyllosticta lindericola.
Phyllosticta macrospora.
Phyllosticta opaca.
Phyllosticta Oxydendri.
Phyllosticta Quercus-Prini.
Phyllosticta rhoicola.
Phyllosticta Ribis.
Phyllosticta Xanthorrhizæ.

Pilacre gracilipes.
Pleosphæria corticola.
Saccidium vitis.
Septoria Brassicæ.
Septoria hyalina.
Septoria Polymniæ.
Septoria Tecomæ.
Septoria Trautvetteriæ.
Septosporium Equiseti.
Sirococcus Halesiæ.
Sphæronæma infuscans.
Sphæronæma Physocarpi.
Sphæropsis Asiminæ.
Sphæropsis Asiminæ fructigena.
Sphæropsis Ipomœæ.
Sphæropsis Œnotheræ.
Sphæropsis Physocarpi.
Steganosporum pedunculi.
Stagonospora petiolorum.
Stagonospora Physocarpi.
Stachylidium caricinum.
Trematosphæria vitigena.
Trichægum nodulosum.
Tubercularia hamata.
Tympanis Oxydendri.
Valsa albo-puncta.
Valsa Chionanthi.
Valsa Diospyri.
Valsa etherialis.
Vermicularia Trautvetteriæ.
Verticillium osteophilum.

Of these those in black-faced type are here described for the first time.

Beside these unique forms, we report many species from our region that have not been before credited to the flora of North America, include many hitherto unpublished asci and spore measurements of species otherwise well described, and have transferred many not before well understood to their proper genera.

The host plants have proven also to be of special interest in that many of them yield certain species for the first time in the mycologic literature of this country, and many others pose as altogether new to Host Indices.

THE SYLVA.

The State is very happily located for the growth of forests, being in the favored belt of temperature between about 37° and 41° north latitude. Within its boundaries trending northeast and southwest, thus opening the country to the damp, warm winds from the Gulf, are numerous ranges of the great Appalachian, or Atlantic highlands, but by far the larger portion of the State lies on the westward slope of these mountains in the trans-Appalachian belt, the waters of which chiefly run northwestward and southwestward to the Ohio River. The altitude of the country descends from the Backbone or Alleghany range of the Appalachians, from an altitude of from 2,500 and 4,800 feet to 500 at the southwestern corner of the State on the Ohio, at Kenova, and about 600 on the same river at Wheeling. The altitude of the eastern corner of the State at Harper's Ferry is 272 feet; thus the range of altitudes in the State is from 272 feet to about 4,800, giving a climatic range of 3,728 feet, or the equivalent of about 16° of latitude; consequently West Virginia has extensive areas of adaptability for every variety of forest growth that is found within the limits of the northern States east of the Rocky Mountains.

The most elevated portion of the State is the great eastern border of the ridgy plateau from which the trans-Appalachian country descends, a territory some 200 miles in length from the headwaters of the Big Sandy to those of the North Branch Potomac, this region is in the main from 2,500 to 4,800 feet in altitude, and furnishes a congenial home to the black spruce, the white pine, and other evergreen trees peculiar to northern latitudes.

West Virginia has a greater amount of hardwood timber in its forests than any other State in the Union. A thorough examination convinces us that nearly or quite two-thirds of the State remains uncleared, and by far the greater portion of the uncleared land is still in virgin forests where the ax of man has never found its way, and where magnificent specimens of forest growth stand thickly side by side and reach a towering height, no finer view of standing timber may be had within the confines of the Union. These splendid forests covering over sixteen thousand square miles yield nearly every species found in the north. Here trees grow to such size that ordinary methods will not suffice to handle them, and are frequently so densely compact that the light of day scarce penetrates their shade, and pathways must be cut before the ax men can find room to work.

The following list of the trees of the State, giving the diameter of trunks and width of board yield, is that of the State exhibit in the Forestry Building at the World's Columbian Exposition, 1893. The specimens were all gathered during the winter of 1892–3.

Ash (white), *Fraxinus Americana*. Logs 40 in., 62 in., 93 in., planks 27 and 33 in., finished boards, plain, 20 and 21 in., mottled, 9, 13 and 16 in., figured 9 and 13 in.

Ash (black), *F. nigra*.

Ash (mountain), *Sorbus Americana*. Trunk 8 in.

Ash (prickly), *Xanthoxylum Americanum*. Trunk 12 in.

Alder (mountain), *Alnus viridis*. Trunk 4 in.

Beech, *Fagus atropunicea*. Trunks 24 in., 27 in. and 38 in., plank 27 in., finished boards 27 and 31 in., quartered boards 7 and 9 in.

Beech (water), *Carpinus Caroliniana*. Trunk 10 in.

Birch (red), *Betula lenta.* Trunks 34 in., 93 in., 61 in., 48 in., planks 15 and 30 in., finished boards 12 and 16 in., figured boards 8, 13, and 14 in.

Birch (yellow), *Betula lutea.* Trunks 34 in., 36 in., 42 in., 49 in., plank 26 in.

Birch (hybrid), *Betula lenta* x *lutea.* Trunk 2 in.

Basswood (white), *Tilia Americana.* Trunks 32 in., 36 in., 43 in., 51 in., plank 28 in., finished board 16 in.

Basswood (yellow), *Tilia heterophylla.* Trunk 26 in.

Buckeye, *Æsculus glabra.* Trunk 29 in.

Buckeye (purple), *Æ. octandra hybrida.* Trunk 29 in.

Box Elder, *Acer Negundo.* Trunk 27 in.

Butternut, *Juglans cinerea.* Trunk 12 in.

Balsam Fir, *Abies balsamea.* Trunk 13 in.

Chestnut, *Castanea dentata.* Trunks 53 in., 40 in., 62 in., 78 in. plank 40 in., finished boards 26 in.

Cherry (wild), *Prunus serotina.* Trunks 36 in., 39 in., 48 in., 53 in., plank 27 in., finished boards 6 and 18 in., blistered 13, figured 6 to 19 in., curly 9 to 21 in.

Cherry (wild), *Prunus Pennsylvanica.* Trunk 14 in.

Cucumber, *Magnolia acuminata.* Trunk 35 in., plank 26 in.

Cottonwood, *Populus monilifera.* Trunk 26 in.

Crab (wild), *Pyrus coronaria.* Trunk 8 in.

Dogwood, *Cornus florida.* Trunks 7 in., 13 in., 28 in.

Elm (White), *Ulmus Americana.* Trunks 23 in., 42 in., 61 in.

Elm (red, slippery), *Ulmus pubescens.* Trunk 16 in.

Fringe tree, *Chionanthus Virginica.* Trunk 3 in.

Gum (black), *Nyssa sylvatica.* Trunk 36 in., plank 27 in.

Gum (sweet), *Liquidambar styraciflua.* Block 19 in.

Grape (Fox), *Vitis Labrusca.* Trunk 22 in., branches 18 in.

Hackberry, *Celtis occidentalis.* Trunk 18 in.

Haw (black), *Viburnum prunifolium.* Trunk 5 in.

Hemlock, *Tsuga Canadensis.* Trunk 42 in., plank 30 in., finished boards 12 and 19 in.

Hercules Club, *Aralia spinosa.* Trunk 5 in.

Hickory (bitter), *Hicoria minima.* Trunks 9 and 12 in.

Hickory (red), *Hicoria glabra.* Trunks 11 and 17 in.

Hickory (shagbark), *Hicoria ovata.* Trunk 27 in., planks 14 and 18 in.

Holly (white), *Ilex opaca.* Trunk 10 in.

Holly (mountain), *Ilex monticola.* Trunk 6 in.

Ironwood, *Ostrya Virginiana.* Trunks 12 in., 24 in., 38 in.

Juniper, *Juniperus Virginiana.* Trunk 7 in.

Laurel, *Kalmia latifolia.* Trunk 8 in., root 24 in.
Locust (yellow), *Robinia Pseudacacia.* Trunks 18 in., 24 in., 38 in.
Locust (honey), *Gleditchia triacanthos.* Trunks 14 in., 28 in., 30 in., in thorn 10 in.
Magnolia, *Magnolia tripetala.* Trunk 15 in.
Magnolia (ear-leaf), *Magnolia Fraseri.* Trunk 12 in.
Mulberry, *Morus rubra.* Trunks 8 and 11 in.
Mulberry (paper), *Papyrius Papyrifera.* Trunk 9 in.
Maple (blistered), *Acer saccharum,* Marsh. Trunk 26 in., boards 9 and 11 in.
Maple (sugar), *Acer saccharum,* Marsh. Trunks 30 in., 40 in., 48 in., plank 28 in., finished boards 29 in., curly boards 13 to 16 in.
Maple (black), *Acer nigrum.* Trunk 16 in.
Maple (white), *Acer saccharinum* L. Trunks 35 in., 49 in., plank 26 in., birdseye boards 10 to 12 in.
Maple (red), *Acer rubrum.* Trunk 14 in.
Maple (striped), *Acer Pennsylvanicum.* Trunk 6 in.
Osage Orange, *Toxylon pomiferum.* Trunk 4 in.
Oak (black), *Quercus velutina.* Trunks 10 and 27 in., finished board 11 in.
Oak (Spanish), *Quercus digitata.* Trunks 13 and 18 in.
Oak (swamp), *Quercus palustris.* Trunk 15 in.
Oak (laurel), *Quercus imbricaria.* Trunk 10 in.
Oak (chestnut), *Quercus Prinus.* Trunks 14 in., 27 in., 36 in., finished board 21 in.
Oak (black jack), *Quercus nigra.* Trunks 18 in., 23 in.
Oak (white), *Quercus alba.* Trunks 50 in., 28 in., 32 in., 61 in., plank 37 in., boards (quartered) 5 to 13 in., quartered curly 10 in.
Oak (red), *Quercus rubra.* Trunks 42 in., 54 in., 84 in., plank 44 in.
Persimmon, *Diospyros Virginiana.* Trunk 12 in.
Poplar (yellow), *Liriodendron Tulipifera.* Trunk 48 in., trunk "wheels" 24, 36, 48, 60, 74, 90, and 138 in., the tree from which the last wheel came cut 25,000 feet of merchantable boards, plank 36 and 57 in., cube 36 in., finished boards 27 to 46 in.
Pine (white), *Pinus strobus.* Trunk 36 in.
Pine (yellow), *Pinus echinata.* Trunk 28 in.
Pine (pitch) *Pinus rigida.* Trunk 16 in.
Papaw, *Asimina triloba.* Trunk 8 in.
Rhododendron, *Rhododendron maximum.* Trunk 6 in.
Red Bud, *Cercis Canadensis.* Trunks 5½ and 9 in.
Scyamore, *Platanus occidentalis.* Trunks 52 in., 36 in., 40 in., finished board quartered 33 in.

Sassafras, *Sassafras Sassafras.* Trunk 22 in., finished board "wavy" 18 in.
  Silver Bell, *Mohrodendron Carolinum.* Trunk 8 in.
  Sourwood, *Oxydendron arboreum.* Trunk 15 in.
  Spruce (black) *Picea Mariana.* Trunks 31, 34, and 49 in., planks. 8 and 40 in., finished boards 18 and 20 in.
  Spicewood, *Benzoin Benzoin.* Trunk 2 in.
  Sumach, *Rhus typhina.* Trunk 8 in.
  Service, *Amalanchier Canadensis.* Trunks 8 and 9 in.
  Thorn, *Crategus coccinea.* Trunk 10 in.
  Tree of Heaven, *Ailanthus glandulosus.* Trunks 8 in., 24 in., 38 in.
  Witch Hazel, *Hamamelis Virginica.* Trunks 4 and 5 in.
  Walnut (black) *Juglans nigra.* Trunks 30 and 36 in., plank 29 in. finished boards "wavy" 20 in., "figured" 21 in.
  Willow (black), *Salix nigra.* Trunk 12 in.

SUMMARY OF THE FLORA.

	Genera	Species.		Genera	Species.
Fungi, etc.,	342	980	Equisitæ,	1	4
Lichens,	31	115	Filicinæ,	14	40
			Ophioglossæ,	2	7
Thallophyta, etc.,	373	1095	Lycopodæ,	1	5
			Selaginellæ,	1	1
Hepaticæ,	24	32			
Musci	42	90	Pteridophyta,	19	57
Sphagnæ,	1	1			
			Gymnospermæ,	7	13
Bryophyta,	67	123	Monocotyledons,	95	268
			Dicotyledons,	412	1028
			Anthophyta,	514	1309

Total number of species, varieties and forms detected in the State to the date of this Flora, - - - - - - - 2584.

CATALOGUE.*

Fungi.

PHALLACEÆ.
ITHYPHALLUS Fries.
I. impudicus (Linn.) Fr.
 In the juvenile, egg stage, June 15, 1893, Oct. 28, 1893, we find the veil under pileus about one-third its length and part of it encircling the stipe about the middle (*Nuttall*, 983).

NIDULARIACEÆ.
CRUCIBULUM Tul.
C. vulgare Tul.
 On sticks and leaves, open woods, and on old cotton cloth, July 6, 1893 (*Nuttall*, 1079).

LYCOPERDACEÆ.
TYLOSTOMA Pers.
T. mammosum (Mich.) Fr.
 On light soil on rock, March 24, 1893 (*Nuttall*, 880).

MITREMYCES Nees.
M. lutescens Schn.
 On wet mossy banks, alt. 2,000 ft., March 25, 1893 (*Nuttall*, 881).

GEASTER Mich.
G. mammosus Chev.
 On earth, Short Creek, July 6, 1893 (*Nuttall*, 1080).

BOVISTA Dill.
B. lepidophora (E. & E.) De Ton.
 In grass on lawn, Sept. 5, 1893. Clavate 8 cm. high, 12 cm. broad, sterile base 3.5 cm. thick, white cuticle 1.5 mm. thick, gleba pale yellow (*Nuttall* 1193).

B. PILA Berk. & Curt.
 Free on open ground. Monongalia Co., near Morgantown (*Millspaugh*).

---

*Unless otherwise stated, all my numbers in this Flora are from Fayette Co., near Nuttallburg.—L. W. Nuttall.

LYCOPERDON Tourn.

L. gemmatum Batsch.
  On ground in woods, alt. 2,000 ft., Aug. 24, 1893 (*Nuttall*, 1180).

L. furfuraceum Schæff.
  In grass on lawn, Sept. 3, 1893. Capillitium thicker than the spores, branches few, 2.5 to 4 cm. in diameter, outer coat pure white (*Nuttall*, 1188).

L. pedicellatum Peck.
  On moss on ground in pine woods, alt. 2,000 ft., March 10, 1893. Pedicels 20 μ long (*Nuttall*, 864).

L. PYRIFORME Schæff.
  Under bark of *Quercus palustris*, Monongalia Co., near Morgantown and near Little Falls (*Millspaugh*) on rotten wood, Feb. 2, 1893 (*Nuttall*, 832).

SCLERODERMA Pers.

S. VULGARE Hornem.
  On chips of *Picea Mariana*, Tucker Co. Falls of Blackwater (*Millspaugh*). Grant Co., on dead logs, Otter Fork of Cheat; and Monongalia Co., Tibbs Run, plentiful on clay of a path (*Millspaugh*). In laurel thickets, July 28, 1893. Spores 10 μ. (*Nuttall*, 1125).

S. Bovista Fr.
  On ground, March 21, 1893 (*Nuttall*, 876).

BOVISTELLA Morg.

B. Ohioense (Ell. & Morg.) Morg.
  In grass on lawn, June 26, 1893 (*Nuttall*, 1003).

MUCORACEÆ.

MUCOR Mich.

M. MUCEDO Linn.
  On open canned fruit left standing (*Millspaugh*). On dead dry fruit *Asimina triloba*, Oct. 1, 1895 (*Nuttall*, 1866, 754).

SPORODINIA Link.

S. Aspergillus (Scop.) Schroet.
  On dead *Agaricus* and *Boletus*, Sept. 10, 1893 (*Nuttall*, 1196).

PERONOSPORACEÆ.

CYSTOPUS Lev.

C. CANDIDUS (Pers.) Lev.
  On living leaves of *Dentaria diphylla*, Monongalia Co., at Little Falls (*Millspaugh*). On *Brassica nigra*, July 8, 1893 (*Nuttall*, 1082).

C. Portulacæ (DC) Lev.
   On *Portulacca oleracea*, July 8, 1893 (*Nuttall*, 1083).

C. Bliti (Biv.) DeB.
   On *Amaranthus retroflexus*, July 20, 1893. Spores 18 to 22 x 15 to 18 μ (*Nuttall*, 1615).

PLASMOPARA Schroet.

P. VITICOLA (B. & C.) Berl. & De Ton.
   On fruit of *Vitis Labrusca*, Monongalia Co., near Morgantown (*Millspaugh*).

PHYTOPHTHORA DeBary.

P. INFESTANS (Mont.) DeB.
   On living leaves and tubers *Solanum tuberosum*, Monongalia Co., near Morgantown (*Millspaugh*).

BREMIÀ Regel.

B. Lactucæ Regel.
   On *Lactucca Canadensis* and *L. hirsuta*, June 14, 1894 (*Nuttall*, 1549).

PERONOSPORA Corda.

P. OBOVATA Bon.
   On living leaves *Spergula arvensis*, Preston Co., near Terra Alta (*Millspaugh*).

ENTOMOPHTHORACEÆ Nowak.

EMPUSA Cohn.

E. MUSCÆ (Fr.) Cohn.
   On *Musca domestica*, Monongalia Co., at Morgantown (*Millspaugh*). Very prevalent on a species of *Tachina* found on maple leaves in great numbers in 1892 at Morgantown (*Millspaugh*).

E. GRYLLI Fr.
   On tufted caterpillars, on grasshoppers, and on the house fly, Monongalia Co., at Morgantown (*Millspaugh*).

SCHIZOMYCETACEÆ.

BACCILLUS Cohn.

B. TUBERCULOSIS Koch.
   In sputa of consumptive (*Millspaugh*).

B. ACIDI-LACTICI (Zopf) Schroet.
   In soured milk (*Millspaugh*).

B. SUBTILIS (Ehrenb.) Cohn.
   In infusion of hay and on exposed boiled potato (*Millspaugh*).

B. ULNA Cohn.
   On exposed coagulated egg albumen (*Millspaugh*).

SPIRILLUM Ehrenb.

S. UNDULA (Muell) Ehrenb.
: In infusion of hay (*Millspaugh*).

BACTERIUM Ehrenb.

B. LINEOLA (O. F. Muell) Cohn.
: In infusion of radish (*Millspaugh*).

B. TERMO (O. F. Muell.) Ehrenb.
: In various decomposing organic substances (*Millspaugh*).

MICROCOCCUS (Hall.) Cohn.

M. CREPUSCULUM (Ehrenb.) Cohn.
: Found associated with *Bacterium Termo* in decomposing vegetable infusions (*Millspaugh*).

M. AMYLOVORUS Burrill.
: On fruit of *Pyrus communis*, Monongalia Co., near Morgantown (*Millspaugh*).

M. AURANTIACUS, Cohn.
: Caught on sterilized potato in laboratory (*Millspaugh*).

M. LUTEUS Cohn.
: Caught on sterilized potato in laboratory (*Millspaugh*).

STREPTOCOCCUS Billr.

S. PYOGENES (Rosenb.) Zopf.
: *Micrococcus septicus*, Cohn. In blood of dead calf (*Millspaugh*).

S. UREÆ (Cohn.) Trev.
: *Micrococcus ureæ*, Cohn. In decomposing urine (*Millspaugh*).

SACCHAROMYCETACEÆ.

SACCHAROMYCES Meyen.

S. CEREVISIÆ Meyen.
: In Pasteur's liquid left uncorked in laboratory (*Millspaugh*).

S. MYCODERMA Reess.
: On same liquid as above at same date (*Millspaugh*).

DIATOMACEÆ.

CYMBELLA GASTROIDES, Kuetz.
CYMBELLA TURGIDA (Grun.) Greg.
STAURONEIS PHŒNICENTRON Ehrb.
NAVICULA VIRIDIS, Kuetz.
NAVICULA MAJOR, Kuetz.
NAVICULA NOBILIS (Ehrb.) Kuetz.

NAVICULA RHOMBOIDES, Ehrb.
NAVICULA BOREALIS (Ehrb.) Kuetz.
NAVICULA TRINODIS, Lewis.
ACHNANTHES LANCEOLATA, Breb.
SYNEDRA ULNA (Nitzsch.) Ehrb.
NITZSCHIA AMPHIOXYS INTERMEDIA, Grun.

MYXOMYCETEÆ.
PHYSARUM Pers.

P. citrinum Schum.
    On moss, alt. 2,000 feet, Aug. 2, 1893, (*Nuttall*, 1160).

P. pulcherrimum B. & R.
    On dead wood, July 25, 1893 (*Nuttall*, 1133).

P. psittacinum Ditm.
    On fruit cones of *Magnolia Fraseri*, alt. 2,000 ft., Aug. 12, 1893 (*Nuttall*, 1165).

P. sinuosum (Bull.) Rost.
    On bark of *Aralia spinosa*, Aug. 16, 1893 (*Nuttall*, 1154).

LEOCARPUS Link.

L. fragilis (Dicks.)
    On *Aspidium spinulosum* and twigs of *Tsuga Canadensis*, Nov. 25, 1895 (*Nuttall*, 1888).

TILMADOCHE Fr.

T. nutans (Pers.) Rost.
    On dead *Asparagus* leaves, and dead limbs *Magnolia Fraseri*, Nov. 4, 1893 (*Nuttall*, 1264).

T. gyrocephala (Mont.) Rost.
    On dry bark of *Hicoria ovata*, living leaves of *Hydrangea*, etc., Short Creek, alt. 1,300 ft., Aug. 21, 1893 (*Nuttall*, 1168).

T. viridis (Gmel.) ?
    On dead limbs *Magnolia Fraseri*, Sept., 1895 (*Nuttall*, 1856, 744?)

DIDYMIUM Schrad.

D. squamulosum (Alb. & Schw.) Fr.
    On new timber in mine near the entrance, Sept., 1893 (*Nuttall*, 1342).

DIACHÆA Fries.

D. leucopoda (Bull.) Rost.
    On dead wood and leaves in damp, shady place, June 23, 1893 (*Nuttall*, 998).

LAMPRODERMA Rost.

L. violaceum (Fr.) Rost.
    On very rotten wet log, Short Creek, alt. 1,300 ft., Oct. 25, 1893 (*Nuttall*, 1255).

COMATRICHA P. Hoyer.

C. Friesiana (DeB.) Rost.
On rotten log, Nov. 6, 1893 (*Nuttall*, 1237).

STREMONITIS Gled.

S. fusca Roth.
On rotten log, and on *Hydnum* sp., April 7, 1893 (*Nuttall*, 889).

S. ferruginea Ehrh.
On log, Keeney's Creek, June 9, 1893 (*Nuttall*, 973).

TUBULINA Pers.

T. cylindrica (Bull.) DeC.
On dead log. Spores brown, rough (reticulate?) approx. 6 μ diameter, Oct. 20, 1893 (*Nuttall*, 1230).

LINDBLADIA Fries.

L. effusa (Ehr.) Rost.
Forms large patches on dead *Tsuga Canadensis* at Short Creek Cliff and Masterson's Glade, July 15, 1893 (*Nuttall*, 1130).

CRIBRARIA Pers.

C. aurantiaca Schrad.
On dead wet log, July 25, 1895 (*Nuttall*, 1826, 712).

RETICULARIA Bull.

R. Lycoperdon Bull.
On dead log, Short Creek, April 6, 1893 (*Nuttall*, 888).

ARCYRIA Hall.

A. punicea Pers.
On rotten stump, June 15, 1893 (*Nuttall*, 979).

A. cinera (Bull.) Schum.
On damp dead wood and weeds in shade, July 24, 1893 (*Nuttall*, 1118).

A. nutans (Bull.) Grev.
On dead log, Short Creek. Spores 7.5 μ, July 24, 1893 (*Nuttall*, 1119).

LYCOGALA Mich.

L. epidendron Buxb.
On wet dead logs, June 15, 1893 (*Nuttall*, 995). On *Magnolia Fraseri*, Nov. 1895.

TRICHIA Hall.

T. fallax Pers.
On side of dead log, Oct. 19, 1893. Rich reddish-brown color when fresh, shining pale-brown when dry; elaters long and slender pointed, spores 10 to 12.5 μ (*Nuttall*, 1209).

T. CHRYSOSPERMA (Bull.) DeC.
  On decayed wood, Monongalia Co., near Morgantown (*Millspaugh*). On dead logs, Feb. 8, 1893 (*Nuttall*, 842).

T. proximella Karst.
  On *Liquidambar styraciflua*, Feb. 6, 1893 (*Nuttall*, 836).

HEMIARCYRIA Rost.

H. RUBIFORMIS (Pers.) Rost.
  Under bark of *Fraxinus Americana* and *Quercus alba*, Monongalia Co., near Morgantown (*Millspaugh*). On bark of dead *Quercus* sp. Feb. 13, 1893 (*Nuttall*, 843).

H. CLAVATA (Pers.) Rost.
  Under bark of wet decaying log *Quercus alba*. Monongalia Co., near Morgantown (*Millspaugh*). On dead log, June 15, 1893 (*Nuttall*, 831).

H. stipata Schw.
  On dead wet limbs of *Magnolia Fraseri*, Sept. 16, 1895 (*Nuttall*, 1847).

HYPHOMYCETACEÆ.

OOSPORA Wallr.

O. fasciculata (Berk.) Sacc.
  On decaying orange, Jan. 15, 1893 (*Nuttall*, 1134).

MONILIA Pers.

M. aureo-fulva C. & E.
  On under side dead log *Liquidambar styraciflua*, Aug. 29, 1893 (*Nuttall*, 1186).

M. FRUCTIGENA Pers.
  On ripe fruit *Prunus cerasus* cult. Monongalia Co., near Morgantown (*Millspaugh*). On fruit of *Prunus domestica* cult. and *Amygdalus Persica* cult., June 28, 1893 (*Nuttall*, 1006).

POLYSCYTALUM Riess.

P. sericeum Sacc.
  On *Quercus Prinus*, Nov., 1893 (*Nuttall*, 1335, 293).

OIDIUM Link.

O. erysiphoides Fr.
  On *Zizia cordata*, *Eupatorium purpureum* and *Rubus odoratus*, Nov. 18, 1893 (*Nuttall*, 1266, 210).

O. LEUCOCONIUM Desm.
  On leaves of *Rosa* cult., Cabell Co., near Huntington (*Millspaugh*).

O. MONILIOIDES Link.
  On living leaves *Poa pratensis*, Preston Co., near Terra Alta (*Millspaugh*). On same host, May 30, 1894 (*Nuttall*, 1512).

BOTRYOSPORIUM Corda.

B. pulchrum Corda.
On *Lactuca Canadensis*, Aug. 23, 1895. Tips of branches inflated. Spores 7.5 x 2.5 μ (*Nuttall*, 1844, 735).

TRICHODERMA Pers.

T. lignorum (Tode) Harz.
Under bark rotten *Hicoria ovata* Short Creek, alt. 1,250 ft., Dec. 8, 1893 (*Nuttall*, 1299, 248).

ASPERGILLUS Mich.

A. glaucus (Linn.) Link.
On *Crategus* sp., April 30, 1894 (*Nuttall*, 1474).

A. glaucus oblongisporus E. & E. n. var?
Found on *Lachnocladium semivestitum* after neglect in plant press (*Nuttall*, 1871, 760).
This is either a new species or a distinct variety of A. glaucus. The smooth oblong-elliptical conidia are quite different from the usual form. Spores 5 to 7.5 x 2.5 to 3 μ.

A. flavus Lk.
Also found on *Lachnoladium semivestitum* neglected in plant press (*Nuttall*, 1877, 760).
Conidia 4 to 6 μ diameter.

STERIGMATOCYSTIS Cram.

S. nigra v. Tiegh.
On dried peach in garden, Aug. 15, 1893 (*Nuttall*, 1170).

PENCILLIUM Link.

P. glaucum Link.
On *Hydnum* sp. and *Polyporus varians*, Aug. 16, 1893 (*Nuttall*, 1164, 136).

BOTRYTIS Mich.

B. olivacea E. & E. sp. nov.
TYPE HABITAT: On dead log. Short Creek, alt. 1,800 ft., Feb. 26, 1894 (*Nuttall*, discov. 1411, 381). Fungi Columbiana, 593. N. A. F., 3187.
Forming thin olivaceous patches 2 to 4 cm. in extent, composed of olive-brown, septate threads, about 4 μ thick, and dichotomously or oppositely branched above, and the short (15 to 25 μ) branches sub-attenuated above, and bearing the obovate or elliptical, olive-brown, 6 to 8 x 4 to 4.5 μ conidia at their tips.

B. torta E. & E., Proc. Phila. Acad., 1894, 375.
TYPE HABITAT: On dead leaves *Carex Fraseri*, Dec. 10, 1893 (*Nuttall*, discov. 1248, 257).

Hyphæ simple, sparingly branched, twisted above as in *B. streptothrix* or in *Streptothrix atra* B. & C., brown, 80 to 100 x 3 to 4 μ, forming numerous small brownish-black tufts, effused or gregarious, on both sides of the leaf. Conidia elliptical brown, 5 to 6.5 x 3 to 3.5 μ.

Differs from *B. streptothrix* (C. & E.) in its much smaller conidia and more dwarfish growth.

B. vulgaris Fr.
On leaves *Magnolia Fraseri*, alt. 2,000 ft., July 12, 1893; on burrs of *Xanthium Canadense*, Nov. 1, 1893; on pedicels of *Ipomœa pandurata*, Feb. 17, 1894; on decaying *Brassica oleracea*, Jan. 18, 1894; on *Cicuta maculata*, March 18, 1894 (*Nuttall*, 1116).

HYPHODERMA Fr.
H. Desmazieri Duby.
On living leaves *Pinus echinata*. Wood Co., near Lockhart's Run (*Millspaugh*).

VERTICILLIUM Nees.
V. osteophilum E. & E., sp. nov.
Type habitat: On jaw bone of calf, in woods, Nov. 27, 1894 (*Nuttall*, discov. 1761, 647.)

Prostrate sterile hyphæ yellowish-brown, distantly septate, rough, 6 to 7 μ diameter; fertile hyphæ, loosely cespitose, erect septate, smooth, yellowish-hyaline, 7 to 15 μ diameter, the primary branches alternate, and issuing at right angles, bearing opposite or ternately-verticillate branches, the ulmate division 12 to 15 x 4 μ 3 to 4 in a terminal verticil, with tips often curved and bearing 1 to 4 terminal, globose, hyaline, 3.5 to 4 μ; conidia.

V. puniceum (Cke. & E.) Grev.
On dead sticks, June, 1893 (*Nuttall*, 1115).

TRICHOTHECIUM Link.
T. roseum (Pers.) Link.
On dead dried peach on ground; on decaying leaves *Ilex verticillata*, Sept. 14, 1893 (*Nuttall*, 1199).

CEPHALOTHECIUM Corda.
C. roseum Corda.
On old *Polyporus pergamenus*, Short Creek, alt. 1,300 ft., Nov. 10, 1893 (*Nuttall*, 1260, 205).

DACTYLIUM Nees.
D. dendroides (Bull.) Fr.
On *Polystictus versicolor*, and apparently checking its development. Oct. 12, 1893 (*Nuttall*, 1206). Spores 28 x 10 μ.

RAMULARIA Ung.

R. Celastri Ell. & Mart.
On leaves of *Celastrus scandens* near the ground. Oct. 11, 1894. Conidia 15 to 28 μ (*Nuttall*, 1700).

R. Tulasnei Sacc.
On *Fragaria* cult., Oct. 27, 1894 (*Nuttall*, 1724).

R. Taraxaci Karst.
On *Taraxacum Taraxacum*, Oct. 20, 1894 (*Nuttall*, 1722).

DEMATIACEÆ.

CONIOSPORIUM Link.

C. harknessioides (Ell. & Holl.) Sacc.
On *Rumex acetosella*, Oct. 20, 1894 (*Nuttall*, 1727, 613).

TORULA Pers.

T. dimidiata Penz.
On *Rhus hirta*, alt. 1,300 ft.; Nov. 21, 1893 (*Nuttall*, 1273, 220).

T. herbarum Link.
On *Asparagus officinalis*, Nov. 1, 1893 (*Nuttall*, 1240, 186).

PERICONIA Bon.

P. pycnospora Fres.
On *Parthenocissus quinquefolia*, Feb. 20, 1894. Conidia 12.5 to 15 μ diameter. On *Rubus odoratus*. On *Polymnia Uvedalia*. On *Phytolacca decandra*, hyphæ 600 x 15 to 16 μ (*Nuttall*, 1413). On *Polymnia Uvedalia*, spores 12.5 to 15 μ Nov. 16, 1894 (*Nuttall*, 1743).

GONATOBOTRYUM Sacc.

G. maculiocolum (Wint.) Sacc.
On young sprouts *Hamamelis Virginica* 1 to 2 feet high; Short Creek, alt. 1,850 ft., Aug. 15, 1894 (*Nuttall*, 1656).

STREPTOTHRIX Corda.

S. atra B. & C.
On dead limbs on ground. Conidia 6 to 8 x 4.5 to 5 μ, Dec. 16, 1893 (*Nuttall*, 1329).

ZYGODESMUS Corda.

Z. graminicola E. & E.
On *Carex Fraseri*, spores 7.5 μ Feb. 11, 1894 (*Nuttall*, 1374, 334).

Z. pannosus B. & C.
On charred bark, May 28, 1894 (*Nuttall*, 1531, 502).

STACHYLIDIUM Link.

S. caricinum E. & E., Proc. Phila. Acad., 1894, 377.
    TYPE HABITAT: On dead leaves *Carex Fraseri* Feb. 11, 1894 (*Nuttall*, discov. 1375, 335).
    Hyphæ fasciculate brown, septate 600 to 700 x 3 μ simple or occasionally forked above towards the tip, with short cylindrical hyaline branches opposite or in whorls of three, bearing at their tips the elliptical, hyaline 4 to 5 x 1.5 to 2 μ conidia, collected into a globose head 10 to 12 μ diameter.

FUSICLADIUM Bonord.

F. DENDRITICUM (Waller.) Fckl.
    On living *Pyrus Malus* leaves and fruit. Monongalia Co., near Morgantown (*Millspaugh*).

F. Virginiense E. & E. sp. nov?
    TYPE HABITAT: On living leaves *Aster infirmus*, June 29, 1894 (*Nuttall*, discov. 1593, 541).

POLYTHRINCIUM Kunze & Schm.

P. Trifolii Kunze.
    On *Trifolium repens*, July 4, 1894 (*Nuttall*, 1588).

CLADOSPORIUM Link.

C. herbarum (Pérs.) Link.
    On *Polygonatum biflorum, Menispermum Canadense*, and leaves of *Rhus hirta*, June 28, 1894 (*Nuttall*, 1564).

C. herbarum fasciculare Corda.
    On *Reseda* cult., Jan. 28, 1894. Conidia 15 to 18 x 6 to 7.5 μ 1 to 2 septate (*Nuttall*, 1354).

C. nigrellum E. & E., Proc. Phila. Acad., 1893, 463.
    TYPE HABITAT: On inner bark of *Robinia Pseudacacia* railroad ties, Keeney's Creek, Oct. 1893 (*Nuttall*, discov. 1227, 172).
    Hyphæ densely tufted, septate, subequal, 150 to 200 x 5 to 6 μ, tufts effused, subconfluent, forming a black, velvety coat extending over the surface of the bark indefinitely, with the same habit as *Macrosporium nigrellum* C. & E. Conidia smoky-hyaline, becoming pale brown, variable in size, the smaller ones ovate, continuous or uniseptate, 6 to 8 x 5 μ, the larger ones oblong-elliptical or sub-cylindrical, 2 to 3-septate, 12 to 15 x 5 to 6 μ.

C. Triostei Peck.
    On living leaves *Triosteum perfoliatum*, alt. 1,200 ft., July 26, 1894 (*Nuttall*, 1824).

C. epiphyllum (Pers.) Mart.
    On dying leaves *Robinia Pseudacacia*, July 31, 1893 (*Nuttall*, 1139).

C. ———— sp.
On dead decorticated limb *Magnolia Fraseri*, Sept., 1895 (*Nuttall*, 1853, 739).
A most beautiful velvety black form.

C. epimyces Cooke.
On pileus *Polyporus varians*, Jan. 25, 1894 (*Nuttall*, 1341).

CLASTEROSPORIUM Sz.

C. Cornutum E. & E., sp. nov.
TYPE HABITAT: On decaying wood, Oct. 21, 1895 (*Nuttall*, discov. 1883).
Hyphæ prostrate, septate, branched, brown, about 6 μ diameter. effused in black velvety patches 1 to 2 cm. across. Conidia in pairs or threes, horn-shaped, 10 to 14 septate, 100 to 225 x 14 μ, broadest below, gradually tapering above to an obtuse point, curving outward at the base, rising and spreading out above like the horns of an ox. The conidia are but slightly constricted at the septa and are sessile on the hyphæ, appearing at first as a simple nodule or tubercle on the side of the thread.
Allied to *C. Hirudo* Sacc., but that has solitary multiseptate (55 to 65) conidia and evanescent hyphæ.

HELMINTHOSPORIUM Link.

H. persistens Cooke.
On branches of *Acer* in pine woods, alt. 2,000 ft., March 9, 1894. Conidia 75 to 150 x 10 to 15 μ (*Nuttall*, 1421, 392).

H. macrocarpon Grev.
On decorticated limbs *Platanus occidentalis*. Oct. 6, 1895 (*Nuttall*, 1887). On *Magnolia Fraseri*, Nov. 1895.

H. folliculatum Corda.
On *Zea Mays*, Aug. 2, 1895 (*Nuttall*, 1835).

H. attenuatum Peck & Cooke.
On dead log, Short Creek, alt. 1,800 ft., June 10, 1894 (*Nuttall*, 1547).

H. septemseptatum Peck.
On *Magnolia Fraseri*, June 20, 1894 (*Nuttall*, 1574, 534).

H. brachypus E. & E. sp. nov.
TYPE HABITAT: On dry wood of old log. Oct. 8, 1895 (*Nuttall*, discov. 1873, 757).
Effused in brownish-black patches of several centimeters in extent, velutinous, thin. Prostrate hyphæ only sparingly branched, obscurely septate, crooked; fertile hyphæ cespitose, erect, 40 to 50 x 4 to 6 μ, 2 to 3 septate, abruptly constricted at the tips and subtruncate. Conidia terminal, oblong-fusoid, 5-septate

brown, not constricted at the septa, 30 to 40 x 12 to 14 μ, with a short (8 to 10 μ) obconical, hyaline or pale-brown, persistent pedicel, which is sometimes prolonged into a hyaline thread as long as the spore. This prolongation may be something of the nature of a pith or medulla drawn out of the supporting hypha and remaining attached to the pedicel.

CERCOSPORA Fres.

C. Armoraciæ Sacc.
 On *Roripa Armoracia*. Conidia 175 x 5 μ, Aug. 26, 1894 (*Nuttall*, 1687, 593).

C. caulophylli Peck.
 On living leaves *Caulophyllum thalictroides*, Grant Co., near Bayard (*Millspaugh*).

C. Violæ Sacc.
 On *Viola obliqua*, Aug. 10, 1895 (*Nuttall*, 1841, 731).

C. granuliformis Ell. & Hol.
 On living leaves *Viola obliqua*, June 28, 1894 (*Nuttall*, 1565).

C. oculata E. & K.
 On leaves *Vernonia Noveboracensis*, Aug. 6, 1894 (*Nuttall*, 1682).

C. Vernoniæ E. & K.
 On leaves *Vernonia Noveboracensis*, Oct. 10, 1894 (*Nuttali*, 1698).

C. omphacodes Ell. & Hol.
 On *Phlox amœna*, July 14, 1894 (*Nuttall*, 1605).

C. Dirantherae E. & K.
 On leaves of *Dianthera Americana*. Oct. 23, 1895 (*Nuttall*, 1879).

C. avicularis Wint.
 On living leaves *Polygonum aviculare*, July 5, 1895 (*Nuttall*, 1815).

C. dubia (Riess) Wint.
 On *Chenopodium album viride*, July 4, 1894 (*Nuttall*, 1587).

C. beticola Sacc.
 On leaves *Beta vulgaris*, Oct. 4, 1894 (*Nuttall*, 1692).

C. Bœhmeriæ Peck.
 On leaves *Bœhmeria cylindrica*, Oct. 5, 1894 (*Nuttall*, 1694).

C. Acalyphæ Peck.
 On leaves *Acalypha Virginica*, Oct. 3, 1894 (*Nuttall*, 1691).

C. Ampelopsidis Peck.
 On *Parthenocissus quinquefolia*. Conidia + 40 x 3 μ, June 30, 1894 (*Nuttall*, 1578).

C. Menispermi E. & H.
On leaves *Menispermum Canadense.* Conidia + 77 x 5 μ June 26, 1894 (*Nuttall*, 1562).

C. ageratoides E & E.
On *Eupatorium ageratoides*, Oct. 14, 1894 (*Nuttall*, 1706).

C. anthelmintica Atk.
On living leaves *Chenopodium anthelminticum*, Oct. 15, 1894 (*Nuttall*, 1713, 601).

C. Kalmiæ E. & E.
On leaves *Kalmia latifolia*, Aug. 15, 1893 (*Nuttall*, 1167).

C. Œnotheræ E. & E., Proc. Phila. Acad., 1894, 380.
TYPE HABITAT: On leaves *Onagra biennis*, Oct. 1894 (*Nuttall*, discov. 1704, 599).
Spots irregular, mostly elongated, grayish-brown, sub-angular, 3 to 5 x 2 to 3 mm. subconfluent. Hyphæ amphigenous, subhyaline, continuous or faintly 1 to 2 septate, 15 to 20 x 3 μ in minute scattered tufts, few in a tuft, spreading subundulate. Conidia linear or only slightly attenuated above, smoky-hyaline, nucleate and faintly 3 to 5 or more septate, 25 to 80 x 2 to 2.5 μ straight or only slightly curved.

C. Chionanthi E. & E., sp. nov.
TYPE HABITAT: On living leaves *Chionanthus Virginica*, Sept. 1895 (*Nuttall*, discov. 1852, 738).
Spots variable in shape, subindefinite, dark brown, grayish above, 2 to 4 mm. diameter. Hyphæ epiphyllous, cespitose, 75 to 150 x 3.5 to 5 μ, brown, septate, and subgeniculate or subundulate above. Conidia fusoid or clavate, becoming brown, 3 to 5-septate, 30 to 60 x 4 to 4.5 μ.

C. septorioides E. & E. sp. nov.
TYPE HABITAT: On leaves *Rubus Canadensis*, Oct. 16, 1894 (*Nuttall*, discov. 1725, 610).
Spots dirty-brown, irregular, subangular, more or less limited by the veinlets, 2 to 3 mm. diameter, definite, but without any differently colored border. Hyphæ epiphyllous, cespitose on a small tubercular base, simple, sub-entire, continuous, brownish, 20 to 25 x 3 μ. Conidia cylindrical, slightly curved, hyaline, nucleate, 35 to 63 x 2 to 2.5 μ.
Differs from *C. Rubi* Sacc. in its narrower conidia without septa, and its shorter hyphæ.

C. Rubi Sacc.
On leaves *Rubus Canadensis*, Nov. 1894 (*Nuttall*, 1785, 676).

C. depazeoides (Desm.) Sacc.
On *Sambucus Canadensis*, July 26, 1894 (*Nuttall*, 1626).

C. SMILACIS Thum.
On living leaves *Smilax rotundifolia*, Monongalia Co., near Camp Eden (*Millspaugh*). On *Smilax rotundifolia* (*Nuttall*, 1573, 533).

C. smilacina Sacc.
   On leaves *Smilax glauca*, Aug. 26, 1894 (*Nuttall*, 1653, 573).

C. columnaris E. & E.
   On *Phaseolus vulgaris* cult. Oct. 13, 1895 (*Nuttall*, 1870).

SPORODESMIUM Link.

S. toruloides E. & E.
   On dead twigs *Cornus florida*, June 10, 1894 (*Nuttall*, 1548, 514).

S. ——————— sp.
   TYPE HABITAT: On *Tsuga Canadensis*, Feb. 3, 1894 (*Nuttall*, discov. 331).

S. moriforme Peck.
   On *Opulaster opulifolius*, May 12, 1894. Spores 25 to 40 x 25 μ (*Nuttall*. 1503, 483).

S. aurantiacum B. & C.
   On a dead stick, Short Creek, July 25, 1893 (*Nuttall*, 1132, 115).

S. concinnum Berk.
   On wet dead sticks in association with *Clavaria mucida*, Oct. and Nov., 1893. Conidia 112 to 115 x 30 to 32 μ 65 to 100 x 30 μ (*Nuttall*, 1233).

SPEIRA Corda.

S. minor Sacc.
   On *Pinus Virginiana*, Dec. 15, 1894. Conidia 30 x 10 μ (*Nuttall*, 1775, 664).

MACROSPORIUM Fr.

M. commune Rabh.
   On dead stems of garden *Asparagus officinalis*, conidia+40 x 15 μ Nov. 1, 1893 (*Nuttall*, 1222). On petioles of *Aralia spinosa*, conidia 75 x 20 μ (*Nuttall*, 358). On *Rumex obtusifolius*, *Rhus radicans* and *Cicuta maculata*? (*Nuttall*).

M. ——————— sp.
   TYPE HABITAT: On dead stems *Polymnia Uvedalia*, Nov. 3, 1893 (*Nuttall*, discov. 1736, 623).

M. Abutilonis Speg.
   On *Abutilon Abutilon*, July 21, 1895 (*Nuttall*, 1836).

M. ——————— sp.
   TYPE HABITAT: On decayed fruit *Diospyros Virginiana*, April 25, 1895 (*Nuttall*, discov. 1825, 711).

M. asclepiadeum Cooke?
   On *Asclepias Syriaca*, Nov. 3, 1894 (*Nuttall*, 1730).

M. caudatum C. & E.
   On dead flowers of *Yucca* cult., Sept. 5, 1894 (*Nuttall*, 1680, 587). On stems of *Phytolacca decandra*, conidia 88 x 20 μ.

M. Saponariæ Peck.
On *Saponaria officinalis*, Oct. 6, 1894 (*Nuttall*, 1695).

M. olivaceum E. & E., Proc. Phila. Acad., 1894, 383.
TYPE HABITAT: Parasitic on *Sphæropsis Asiminæ* on dead limbs of *Asimina triloba*, March, 1894 (*Nuttall*, discov. 1418, 388).

Forms a light olive velutinous coat over the pustules of the *Sphæropsis*. Hyphæ tufted, yellowish brown (under the microscope), septate, erect, nearly straight or subundulate, 80 to 100 x 4 to 5 μ. Conidia obovate or obpiriform, 3 to 5-septate and muriform, brown, 24 to 38 x 15 to 20 μ terminal, sessile. Conidia also occur subcubical or subglobose 15 to 20 μ diameter with 2 septæ crossing each other at right angles.

M. antennæforme B. & C.
On *Celtis occidentalis*, Aug. 11, 1894 (*Nuttall*, 1652). Conidia + 95 x 15 μ.

M. ——————— sp.
TYPE HABITAT: On pods of *Datura Stramonium*, Feb. 10, 1894 (*Nuttall*, discov. 1369, 326).

M. TOMATO Cooke?
On ripe fruit *Lycopersicum esculentum* cult. Spores shorter than described. Sept. 9, 1893 (*Nuttall*, 1195). Same host Monongalia Co., at Morgantown, prevalent 1891 (*Millspaugh*).

M. Maydis C. & E.
On leaves *Zea Mays* cult., with conidia smaller than described, Nov. 1893 (*Nuttall*, 1334, 292).

TRICHÆGUM Corda.

T. nodulosum E. & E., Proc. Phila. Acad., 1894, 385.
TYPE HABITAT: On dead leaves *Carex Fraseri*, Feb. 11, 1894 (*Nuttall*, discov. 1373, 333).

Erumpent, tufted, becoming subeffused, black, tufts gregarious, forming subvelutinous patches 2 to 4 mm. across, or when standing singly the hyphæ and conidia forming a compact mass .5 to 1 mm. diameter, and resembling somewhat the sorus of a *Puccinia*. Hyphæ simple sparingly fasciculate, brown, septate, often swollen at the septa, about 4 μ thick and 200 to 300 μ long. Conidia near the base of the hyphæ, at first elliptical, yellowish-hyaline, uniseptate, 8 to 10 x 6 to 7 μ, soon becoming 4 to 6-septate, muriform and opaque, 10 to 25 μ diameter, subglobose, obovate, or elliptical.

SEPTOSPORIUM Corda.

S. EQUISETI PECK, Rep. State Bot. N. Y., 1892, 25.
TYPE HABITAT: Tips of living leaves *Equisetum arvense*, Doddridge Co., near Center Point, and Monongalia Co., on College campus, Morgantown (*Millspaugh*, discov. 1891).

Hypæ forming minute tufts, the fertile very short, bearing

acrogenous spores, the sterile longer, septate, colored; spores elliptical, usually with three transverse septæ and one or two longitudinal ones, colored, .001 in. long, .005 in. broad.

SARCINELLA Sacc.

S. heterospora Sacc.
On *Cercis Canadensis*, Oct. 16, 1894 (*Nuttall*, 1726, 610).

STILBACEÆ.
STILBUM Tode.

S. magnum Peck.
In cracks of bark, Nov. 6, 1893. Spores $2.5 \times 1.25\,\mu$ (*Nuttall*, 1278, 225).

S. flavipes Peck.
On dead driftwood *Platanus occidentalis*, Dec. 12, 1894 (*Nuttall*, 1767).

S. erythrocephalum Ditm.
On dung of Rabbit, Jan. 18, 1894 (*Nuttall*, 1345, 304).

S. vulgare Tode?
On fallen dead leaves, Short Creek, July 25, 1893 (*Nuttall*, 1137, 120).

PILACRE Fries.

P. gracilipes E. & E., Proc. Phila. Acad., 1894, 386.
TYPE HABITAT: On rotten wood, Short Creek, alt. 1,750 ft., Dec. 16, 1893 (*Nuttall*, discov. 1219, 274).
Scattered, stem slender, white-pruinose, 3 mm. long, .25 to .33 mm. thick. Head hemispherical, olivaceous, about 1 mm. diameter. Fertile hyphæ hyaline, dichotomously branched, 2 to $2.5\,\mu$ thick, bearing the conidia laterally. Conidia globose or subglobose, yellow-brown under the microscope, 4 to $5.5\,\mu$ diameter. Smaller and of a more slender growth than *P. Petersii* B. & C.

P. Petersii B. & C.
On *Acer saccharum* and *Ilex opaca*, Feb. 10, 1894 (*Nuttall*, 1371).
On *Magnolia Fraseri*, Nov. 1895.

ISARIA Pers.

I. Virginiensis E. & E., Proc. Phila. Acad., 1893, 465.
TYPE HABITAT: On the young stroma of *Hypoxylon rubiginosum?* June 30, 1893 (*Nuttall*, discov. 1109, 95, 102).
Stromata gregarious, simple, slender-clavate, 1.5 to 2 mm. high. Yellowish-white, obtuse and subcapitate at the apex, curved, often decumbent, clothed nearly to the base with spreading, hyaline, dendroid, 1.5 to $2\,\mu$ branching hyphæ (sporophores) 40 to $45 \times 2.5\,\mu$ their tips often toothed and bearing 1 to 4 elliptical or ovate, hyaline $3.5 \times 2.5\,\mu$ conidia.
Analogous to *I. umbrina* Pers (*Institale acariforme* Fr.), but differs in several respects.

I. clavata Ditm.
　　On dead sticks on ground, June, 1893 (*Nuttall*, 1110).

CERATIUM A. & S.

C. hydnoides (Jacq.) Alb. & Schw.
　　On rotten log, June 10, 1893 (*Nuttall*, 976).

SPOROCYBE Fr.

S. Rhois (B. & C.) Sacc.
　　On *Rhus copallina*, March 24, 1894, spores 7.5 x 2 to 2.5 μ.
　　On *Rhus hirta*, March 28, 1894, spores 10 x 2.5 μ (*Nuttall*, 1430).

S. Azaleæ (Peck) Sacc.
　　On capsules of *Rhododendron maximum*, Dec. 12, 1893. Conidia varying from globular through elliptical to cylindrical, dark brown, outer coat easily ruptured, 10x10, 8x5, 12x5, 15x7.5 μ (*Nuttall*, 1307).

TUBERCULARIACEÆ.

TUBERCULARIA Tode.

T. vulgaris Tode.
　　On twigs, Feb. 23, 1893. On *Robinia Pseudacacia*, Dec. 1, 1893. On *Aralia spinosa*, Dec. 13, 1893. On *Sambucus pubens*. On *Acer Negundo*, April 20, 1894 (*Nuttall*, 942). On limbs of dead *Rhus hirta*, Monongalia Co., near Morgantown, 1891 (*Millspaugh*).

T. hamata E. & E., Proc. Phila. Acad., 1894, 386.
　　Type habitat: On dead limbs of *Celtis occidentalis*. Feb. 2, 1894 (*Nuttall*, discov. 1357, 313).
　　Depressed hemispherical, umbonate, soon becoming black, .5 to 1.5 mm. diameter, Conidia oblong, slightly curved, hyaline, 5 to 8 x 1.5 to 2 μ on slender simple sporophores 30 to 40 μ long, incurved or involute at the tips.

T. ——— sp.
　　On *Asimina triloba*, Feb. 22, 1894. Flesh colored spores 18 to 22 x 3 μ (*Nuttall*, 1391, 361).

T. ——— sp.
　　Conidia of *Nectria verrucosa*. On dead twigs *Morus rubra* July 25, 1895 (*Nuttall*, 1827, 715).

T. Sambuci Corda.
　　On *Sambucus pubens*, Feb. 26, 1894 (*Nuttall*, 1409).

T. Celastri Schw.
　　On *Celastrus scandens*, April 25, 1895. Spores 5 to 6 x 2 μ (*Nuttall*, 1811).

DENDRODOCHIUM Bon.

D. affine Sacc.
　　On bark wet dead stumps, Oct. 24, 1893 (*Nuttall*, 1229, 174).

D. rubellum microsporum Sacc.
On dead limb *Magnolia acuminata*, Aug. 16, 1894, Short Creek, alt. 1,000 ft. On *Liriodendron Tulipifera* (*Nuttall*, 1659).

TUBERCULINA Sacc.

T. persicina (Ditm.) Sacc.
Parasitic on *Uredo* (Cæoma) *nitens*, that on *Rubus Baileyanus* June 10, 1894 (*Nuttall*, 1557, 527).

ILLOSPORIUM Mart

I. cæspitosum E. & E., Proc. Phila. Acad., 1894, 385.
TYPE HABITAT: On rotten log, Nov. 15, 1893 (*Nuttall*, discov. 1286, 231).

Sporodochia globose, 100 to 110 μ diameter, cespitose, forming tufts about 1 mm. diameter. Hyphæ 6 to 8 μ thick, branched, the branches curved or tortuous. Conidia globose or ovate 6 to 12 μ diameter.

Differs from *I coccinellum* Cke. in its color, and larger cespitose sporodochia.

HYMENULA Fr.

H. cerealis E. & E., Proc. Phila. Acad., 1894, 386.
TYPE HABITAT: On wheat straw *Triticum* sp. brought in from Painesville, Ohio, May 24, 1894 (*Nuttall*, discov. 1520, 495).

Sporodochia gelatinous, orbicular, yellowish-amber color becoming darker, at first sub-pulvinate, becoming depressed or flattened, .5 to .75 mm. diameter. Basidia slender, 25 to 30 x 1.25 μ simple or oftener branched. The branches erect. Conidia hyaline, oblong, minute, 3 to 4 x 1 to 1.25 μ.

CYLINDROCOLLA, Bon.

C. DENDROCTONI Peck, Flora, W. Va., 1892, 516.
TYPE HABITAT: On dead insects, *Dendroctonus frontalis*, beneath the bark of pine. Hampshire Co., near Romney, (*Millspaugh*).

The insects are probably killed by this fungus, as they lie dead in their burrows in the inner bark of the tree (*Pinus Virginiana*).

Sporodochia minute, forming irregular masses, soft, somewhat waxy, white or whitish; sporophores slender, abundantly branched above, often compacted below into a short stem-like base, spores catenulate, short cylindrical, subtruncate, colorless, .00016 to .0002 in. long, .00008 to .0001 in. broad.

On some of the insects there is a cottony or flocculent mass of white mycelium interwoven in a somewhat reticulate manner, and collected in strings or bundles. It bears no fruit but is probably a luxuriant growth of the mycelium of this fungus.

Occasionally the fungus seems to spread from the insect to bark immediately adjacent to it.

C. flagellaris E. & E. sp. nov.

TYPE HABITAT: On dead stem of *Helianthus decapetalus* Dec. 3, 1894 (*Nuttall*, discov. 1762, 650).

(*C. lactea* S. & E. partly, Sacc. No. 3550.)

Sporodochia gregarious, subglobose, subhyaline and gelatinous when fresh, lens-shaped, with a thin spreading margin, orbicular, .33 to .50 mm. diameter yellowish-amber color (whitish in the center) when dry. Sporophores densely fasciculate, flagelliform 2 to 3 times dichotomously branched, 80 to 100 μ long, separating into the short cylindrical, hyaline, 4 to 5 x 1 μ conidia.

This was included by Saccardo in Michelia II, p. 581, in C*ylindrocolla lactea*, S. &. E. (on rotten wood of *Kalmia*), but differs in the shape and color of the sporodochia and the sporophores only 2 to 3 times dichotomously branch. *C. lactea* retains its white color when dry, and resembles young *Lasiosphæria ovina*.

SCORIOMYCES Ell. & Sacc.

S. Cragini E. & S.

Under loose bark of dead *Hicoria* sp., Short Creek, alt. 1,250 ft., Nov. 21, 1893 (*Nuttall*, 1272, 219).

VOLUTELLA Tode.

V. ciliata (A. & S.) Fr.

On decaying leaves of *Prunus* cult. in grass, June 20, 1893 (*Nuttall*, 1010).

BACTRIDIUM Kunze.

B. FLAVUM K. & S.

Under decaying bark of *Quercus alba*, Monongalia Co., near Morgantown (*Millspaugh*).

HELISCUS Sacc.

H. Lugdunensis Sacc.

On dead limbs of *Ilex opaca*, thrown in wet places one year previously, March 16, 1894; sporodochia + 2 mm. diameter, conidia 30 to 33 x 5 μ (*Nuttall*, 1427, 400).

FUSARIUM Link.

F. CULMORUM Smith.

On heads of ripe living wheat. Monongalia Co., Laurel Point (*Millspaugh*).

"This specimen combines the characters of a number of so-called species, making it difficult to say which it really is. Probably they are all forms of one species." Professor Peck (in letter).

F. sarcochroum (Desm.) Sacc.

On *Acer Negundo*, April 24, 1894 (*Nuttall*, 1482, 462).

F. roseum Link.
On follicles of *Asclepias Syriaca*, May 31, 1894. Conidia 55 x 4 μ + 6-septate (*Nuttall*, 1530, 503).

F. SOLANI Mart.
Found associated with "black rot" on Tomato fruits that have fallen to the ground. Monongalia Co., at Morgantown, 1891 (*Millspaugh*).

F. roseum ―― Var. nov?
On dead fruit of *Diospyros Virginiana*, Aug. 1895 (*Nuttall*, 1831, 721).

F. ―――――― sp.
On stems of *Asparagus officinalis*, Oct. 28, 1893. Color, light pink. Conidia oblong to obovate 7.5 to 10 x 2.5 μ (*Nuttall*, 1239, 1248, 185).

MICROCERA Desm.

M. erumpens E. & E., Proc. Phila. Acad., 1894, 386.
TYPE HABITAT: On dead limbs of *Tsuga Canadensis*, March, 1895 (*Nuttall*, discov. 1398, 371).

Sporodochia scattered, depressed-globose, .5 mm. diameter, at first covered by the epidermis, raising it into little whitish pustules, then erumpent and closely embraced by the ruptured epidermis, at first orange-red, then becoming nearly black, and finally leaving subcupuliform cavities in the bark, when dry. Conidia falcate to fusiform, multinucleate, and finally three or more septate, 60 to 83 x 3 to 4.5 μ hyaline, narrowing to a slender point at each end, borne on short sporophores (20 to 35 μ), which are more or less branched above.

Differs from *M. coccophila* Desm. in the shape of the sporodochia and their subcuticular origin.

(The additional description, incorporated in this relation of the specific characters, is by E. & E.)

EPICOCCUM Link.

E. purpurascens Ehrenb.
On cardboard box in grass, April 13, 1894 (*Nuttall*, 1453).

E. NEGLECTUM Desm.
On living leaves of *Avena sativa* and *Catalpa Catalpa*, Monongalia Co., at Morgantown, 1891 (*Millspaugh*).

E. Duriæanum Mont.
Underside of outer bark of *Robinia Pseudacacia*, Nov. 10, 1893 (*Nuttall*, 1285, 229).

EPIDOCHIUM Fries.

E. melanochlorum Desm. ?
On *Carex Fraseri*, Feb. 11, 1894 (*Nuttall*, 1376, 337).

TRIMMATOSTROMA Corda.

T. Americana Thum.
On *Salix nigra*, March 21, 1894 (*Nuttall*, 1437, 410).

HYPHELIA Fries.

H. terrestris Fr.
On damp ground. June 18, 1893 (*Nuttall*, 1016).

SPHÆROPSIDEÆ.
SPHÆRIOIDAECÆ.
PHYLLOSTICTA Pers.

P. Paviæ E. & E.
On *Aesculus octandra hybrida* and *Hamamelis Virginica*, June 10, 1894 (*Nuttall*, 1539). (*P. sphæropsidea* E. & E.)

P. caryigena Sacc.
P. Caryæ E. & E. On living leaves of *Hicoria avata* and *H. microcarpa*, June 30, 1894 (*Nuttall*, 1580).

P. Celtidis E. &. K.
On living leaves of *Celtis occidentalis*, Oct. 10, 1894 (*Nuttall*, 1715, 603).

P. Hamamelidis Pk.
On living leaves of *Hamamelis Virginica*, June 10, 1894 (*Nuttall*, 1556).

P. Catalpæ E. & M.
On living leaves of *Catalpa Catalpa*, July 25, 1895 (*Nuttall*, 1623).

P. Sanguinariæ Wint.
On living leaves of *Sanguinaria Canadensis*, June 29, 1894 (*Nuttall*, 1567).

P. Ipomœæ E. & K.
On *Ipomœa pandurata*, Sept. 19, 1895. Spores 5 to 10 x 2 to 2.5 μ (*Nuttall*, 1861, 749).

P. Haynaldi Roum.
On *Ilex verticillata*. Oct. 5, 1895. Spores 5 to 8 x 2.5 to 3 μ (*Nuttall*, 1872, 756).

P. Ribis E. & E. sp. nov.
TYPE HABITAT: On leaves of *Ribes* cult. Oct. 21, 1895 (*Nuttall* discov., 1882, 768).
Spots large, irregular in shape, .5 to 1 cm., or often confluent along the margin of the leaf for 2 cm., rusty brown, becoming whitish or grayish, and mostly zonate, definite but without any differently colored border. Perithecia epiphyllous, scattered, 150 to 200 μ diameter, the apex prominent and black. Sporules oblong-elliptical, hyaline, granular and nucleate, 15 to 22 x 6 to 9 μ.

Distinguished from *P. ribicola* Fr., and *P. Grossulariæ* Sacc. by its much larger sporules.

P. Galacis (Cke).*
On leaves of *Galax aphylla*, May 4, 1894 (*Nuttall*, 1486, 474).

P. Ipomϙeæ E. & K.
On *Ipomϙa pandurata*, Sept. 19, 1895. Spores 5 to 10 x 2 to 2.5 μ (*Nuttall*, 1861, 749).

P. Haynaldi Roum.
On *Ilex verticillata*, Oct. 5, 1895. Spores 5 to 8 x 2.5 to 3 μ (*Nuttall*, 1872, 756).

P. Ampelopsidis E. & M.
On *Parthenocissus quinquefolia*, June 18, 1893 (*Nuttall*, 1014).

P. ASIMINÆ E. & K.
On living leaves *Asimina triloba*, Monongalia Co. near Camp Eden, 1891 (*Millspaugh*). On same host June 1, 1894, spores 8 to 10 x 6 μ (*Nuttall*, 1517).

P. Quercus-prini E. & E., Proc. Phila. Acad., 1894, 356.
TYPE HABITAT: On leaves *Quercus Prinus*, June 29, 1894 (*Nuttall*, discov. 1594, 542).
Spots orbicular, rusty brown, definite, with a very narrow border, 2 to 3 mm. diameter. Perithecia epiphyllous, scattered, erumpent, 90 to 110 μ diameter. Sporules ovate or oblong, hyaline, mostly a little curved, 5 to 6.5 x 2 to 2.5 μ.
This comes very near *Ph. Ludoviciana* E. & E., but in that species the spots are larger, perithecia more prominent below, and sporules rather larger. *Ph. marginalis* E. & E. also has similar sporules, but the perithecia are hypophyllous.

P. macrospora E. & E., Proc. Phila. Acad., 1894, 355.
TYPE HABITAT: On leaves of *Liriodendron Tulipifera*, Aug. 7, 1894 (*Nuttall*, discov. 1654, 574).
Spots few, suborbicular, ferruginous-gray, 3 to 5 mm. diameter, with a narrow, raised, darker border. Sporules oblong elliptical hyaline, nucleate, 15 to 30 (mostly 20 to 25) x 6 to 7 μ.

P. pirina Sacc.
On leaves *Pyrus Malus*, at Blue Sulphur Springs, July 25, 1894 (*Nuttall*, 1624).

P. Rosæ Desm.
On *Rosa humilis*. Spores 6 to 7.5 x 2.5 μ Sept. 18, 1895 (*Nuttall*, 1863).

P. gentianicola (DC).
On leaves of *Gentiana Andrewsii*, Sept. 19, 1895. Spores oval, 7.5 x 5 μ (*Nuttall*, 1857).

P. rhoicola E. & E., Proc. Phila. Acad., 1894, 356.
TYPE HABITAT: Rare, on leaves *Rhus radicans*, Aug. 18, 1894 (*Nuttall*, discov. 1668, 567 in part).

---
* *Phoma Galacis* Cke., Messrs. Ellis & Everhart decide from our specimens that this species belongs in Phyllosticta.

Spots 4 to 6 mm. diameter, deciduous, grayish-white, with a narrow black border. Perithecia epiphyllous, scattered, 100 to 110 μ diameter, convex-prominent above, visible also below. Sporules narrow-elliptical, hyaline, 2-nucleate, 5 to 6 x 2 to 3 μ.

Differs from *P. toxica*, E. & M., in its larger deciduous spots with a narrow border, and its narrow-elliptical sporules.

P. lindericola E. & E., Proc. Phila. Acad., 1894, 354.

TYPE HABITAT: On leaves *Benzoin Benzoin*, Aug. 26, 1894 (*Nuttall*, discov. 1688, 593).

Spots various; punctiform and minute without any definite border, often irregular in shape 1 mm. to 1 or 1.5 cm. diameter, or marginal, forming a narrow strip along the edge of the leaf for half its length, pale brown, nearly the color of weather-beaten wood, with a dark (almost black) border. Perithecia epiphyllous, hemispherical, 100 to 120 μ diameter, covered by the blackened epidermis which is raised into pustules barely pierced at the apex. Sporules oblong-elliptical, hyaline, 4 to 7 x 2 to 3 μ.

This differs in almost every respect from *Ph. Linderæ* E. & E.

P. Smilacis subeffusa E. & E.

On *Smilax rotundifolia*, Sept. 21, 1894 (*Nuttall*, 1701, 594). Perithecia scattered over surface of dead dry leaves of the host.

P. Oxydendri E. &. E., sp. nov.

TYPE HABITAT: On leaves of *Oxydendron arboreum*, Oct. 10, 1894 (*Nuttall*, discov. 1717, 605).

Spots suborbicular or elliptical, reddish-gray, 3 to 8 mm. diameter, with a narrow, slightly raised dark red border, beyond which the leaf is generally shaded reddish-purple. Perithecia epiphyllous, subapplanate, 100 to 120 μ diameter. Sporules oblong-elliptical, 2-nucleate, hyaline, 7 to 8 x 2.5 to 3 μ. The spots finally become of a lighter, dirty-white color.

P. Celastri E. & E., sp. nov.

TYPE HABITAT: On leaves *Celastrus scandens*, Oct., 1894 (*Nuttall*, discov. 1718, 606).

Spots mostly marginal, 8.5 to 1 cm. diameter, ferruginous, definite, with a narrow, darker border. Perithecia epiphyllous, subapplanate, 150 μ diameter. Sporules oblong, 7 to 10 x 2 to 2.5 μ, hyaline, 2-nucleate.

P. globifera E. & E., sp. nov.

TYPE HABITAT: On leaves *Cornus florida*, Oct. 24, 1894 (*Nuttall*, discov. 1728, 615).

Spots marginal, light-brown, continuous, extending across the tip of the leaf and partly down each side, 5 to 1 cm. wide, separated from the green part of the leaf by a narrow, purple margin. Perithecia amphigenous, discoid, black, 100 to 112 μ diameter. Sporules globose or short-elliptical, hyaline, granular, 6 to 8 x 5 to 6 μ.

P. Negundinis Sacc.

On *Acer Negundo*, July 5, 1894. Sporules 5 to 10 x 3 to 7.5 μ (*Nuttall*, 1631, 560, 561).

P. —————— sp.
On *Geum Canadense*, Oct. 24, 1894 (*Nuttall*, 1733). Spores irregular 4 to 7.5 x 1.5 to 2.5 µ 2-nucleate.

P. Acericola E. & E.
On living leaves *Acer saccharinum*, Putnam Co., near Buffalo, 1891 (*Millspaugh*). On leaves *A. rubrum*, June 24, 1894 (*Nuttall*, 1561).

P. Xanthorrhizæ E. & Nuttall, sp. nov.
TYPE HABITAT: On leaves *Xanthorrhiza apiifolia*, Nov. 3, 1893 (*Nuttall*, discov. 1738, 625).
Spots subelliptical, dirty-white in the center with a dark shaded margin, 3 mm. to 1 cm. long x 2 to 8 mm. wide, finally more or less deciduous. Perithecia seated on the white part of the spots, epiphyllous, subdiscoid, perforated above, 60 to 75 µ diameter. Sporules oblong-elliptical, hyaline, 2-nucleate, 5 to 6 x 2.5 to 3 µ.
Accompanied by a Macrosporium on the same spots.

P. —————— sp.
On leaves *Rubus Canadensis*, Nov. 3, 1894. Sporules variable in form, 5 x 1.25 to 2 µ (*Nuttall*, 1747, 627).

P. cercidicola E. & E., sp. nov.
TYPE HABITAT: On leaves *Cercis Canadensis*, Nov. 21, 1894 (*Nuttall*, discov. 1751).
Spots suborbicular, .5 to 1 cm. diameter, rusty-brown, becoming lighter, paler below, margin narrow reddish-purple. Perithecia epiphyllous, convex, suberumpent, but covered (except the apex) by the epidermis, 110 to 150 µ diameter. Sporules oblong, slightly narrowed and rounded or obtusely pointed at the ends, hyaline, 2 to 3-nucleate, 15 to 20 x 6 to 7 µ.
Differs in the character of the spots, and in the presence of a perithecium, from *Glœosporium Cercidis*, E. & E.

P. Araliæ E. & E., Proc. Phila. Acad., 1894, 355.
TYPE HABITAT: On leaves *Aralia spinosa*, Sept. 20, 1895 (*Nuttall*, discov. 1703, 598, 588?).
Spots suborbicular, light-brown with the margin a little darker, .5 to 1 cm. diameter. Perithecia epiphyllous, somewhat flattened, 100 to 150 µ diameter. Sporules oblong-elliptical, hyaline, 2-nucleate, 10 to 15 x 5 to 6 µ.

P. Sassafras Cooke.
On leaves *Sassafras Sassafras*, June 28, 1894. Sporules 5 to 7 x 2 to 3 µ (*Nuttall*, 1566).

P. Sambuci Desm.
On leaves *Sambucus Canadensis*, July 20, 1894 (*Nuttall*, 1614).

P. Labruscæ Thum.
On living leaves *Vitis* cult. (Concord), Wood Co., near Lockhart's Run, 1891 (*Millspaugh*). On leaves of *V. æstivalis* and *rupestris*, June 29, 1894 (*Nuttall*, 1569).

P. cornicola (D. C.) Rabh.
  On *Cornus florida*, Nov. 5, 1894 (*Nuttall*, 1748, 638).

P. Cookei Sacc.
  On leaves *Magnolia acuminata*, Aug. 9, 1894. Sporules 15 to 20 x 6 to 7.5 µ (*Nuttall*, 1655, 577).

P. Tiliæ Sacc.
  On leaves *Tilia Americana*, Aug. 10, 1894. Sporules 7 to 8 x 2.5 to 3 µ (*Nuttall*, 1672, 579).

P. Chionanthi Thum.
  On *Chionanthus Virginica*, Aug. 10, 1895. Spots darker than in type (from Portugal). Spores round or oval, 5 µ or 7.5 x 5 µ (*Nuttall*, 1833, 724).

P. liriodendrica Sacc.
  On leaves *Liriodendron Tulipifera*, June 16 and Oct. 29, 1894. Sporules 7.5 to 10 x 2 to 3 µ (*Nuttall*, 1571). *P. Liriodendri,* Cke.

P. Ulmi West?
  On leaves *Ulmus pubescens*, July 9, 1894. Sporules + 16 x 7.5 µ (*Nuttall*, 1631, 563).

P. phomiformis Sacc.
  On leaves *Quercus Prinus* and *Q. alba*, July 4, 1894. Sporules 15 to 30 x 6 to 8 µ (*Nuttall*, 1585).

P. Castaneæ E. & E., Proc. Phila. Acad., 1894, 357.
  TYPE HABITAT: On leaves *Castanea pumila* (not on *Castanea vesca* as originally published), July 26, 1894 (*Nuttall*, discov. 1639, 570).
  Spots orbicular, rust-color, with narrow dark-shaded margin. Perithecia epiphyllous, scattered on the spots, dark, semierumpent, 100 µ diameter, often collapsing. Sporules oblong, hyaline, 5 to 7 x 2 to 2.5 µ.

P. Lappæ Sacc.
  On *Arctium Lappa*, July 20, 1894 (*Nuttall*, 1613).

P. Dioscoreæ Cooke.
  On leaves *Dioscorea villosa*, June 29, 1894 (*Nuttall*, 1570).

P. opaca E. & E. sp. nov.
  TYPE HABITAT: On leaves of *Ilex opaca*. Oct. 5, 1895 (*Nuttall*, discov., 1881).
  Spots mostly marginal or terminal, of irregular shape, 1 to 2 cm. across, dirty-white, with a raised subferruginous narrow border. Perithecia evenly scattered, subepidermal, sublenticular, black, raising the epidermis into pustules, 200 µ diameter. Sporules elliptical, hyaline, 3 x 1.5 µ.
  Differs from *P. Ilicis* E. & E. only in its minute sporules.

PHOMA Fries.

P. ——————— sp.
  On *Opulaster opulifolius*, May 7, 1894 (*Nuttall*, 1510, 494). Spores 7 to 10 x 2.5 to 3 µ.

P. negundinicola ramicola E. & E., Proc. Phila. Acad., 1894, 357.
   TYPE HABITAT: On dead twigs *Acer Negundo*, April, 1894 (*Nuttall*, discov. 1483; 465, 466?).
   Perithecia evenly but not thickly scattered, globose, small, .25 to .33 mm. diameter, covered by the slightly ruptured epidermis, but distinctly prominent. Sporules oblong, elliptical, or ovate, hyaline, with a single large nucleus, 10 to 13 x 4 to 5.5 μ.
   Differs from the typical form, on the dead peduncles, in its broader sporules, the former being but 2.5 to 3 μ.

P. Pennsylvanica E. & E., Proc. Phila. Acad., 1894, 357.
   TYPE HABITAT: On dead limbs *Acer Pennsylvanicum*, Feb. 2, 1894 (*Nuttall*, discov. 1361, 318).
   Perithecia numerous, evenly scattered, subepidermal, .33 to .5 mm. diameter, whitish inside, raising the epidermis into minute pustules, but scarcely rupturing it. Sporules subglobose, 6 to 7.5 μ diameter, nearly hyaline.

P. Asclepiadea E. & E., sp. nov.
   TYPE HABITAT: On dead stems of *Asclepias Syriaca*, Oct. 10, 1894 (*Nuttall*, discov. 1717, 604).
   Perithecia thickly but evenly scattered, subelliptical, 110 to 120 μ in the longer diameter, subcuticular, covered by the blackened epidermis, which is raised into minute pustules but scarcely ruptured. Sporules oblong-elliptical, 2-nucleate, hyaline, 5 to 6 x 2 to 2.5 μ. On curved (almost hooked) basidia 12 to 15 μ long.
   Differs from the next form which occurs with it on the same stems, in its larger perithecia and sporules and its curved basidia.

P. ———— sp.
   On dead stems *Asclepias Syriaca*, Oct. 10, 1894 (*Nuttall*).

P. melaleuca B. & C.
   On petioles *Aralia spinosa*, April 25, 1895 (*Nuttall*, 1810).

P. leucostoma Lév.
   On *Opulaster opulifolius*, May 13, 1894. Sporules 2.5 to 4 x 1 μ (*Nuttall*, 1506, 487).

P. mixta B. & C.
   On fire-killed *Liriodendron Tulipifera*, Oct. 16, 1894. Sporules appendiculate at each end, 2-nucleate, 7 to 10 x 2 to 3 μ, oblong fusoid; the accompanying filiform process hooked at the apex, 20 x .75 to 1.5 μ (*Nuttall*, 1709).

P. scabra Sacc.
   On *Platanus occidentalis*, March 30, 1894 (*Nuttall*, 1459, 434).

P. obscurans E. & E., Proc. Phila. Acad., 1894, 357.
   TYPE HABITAT: On leaves of *Fragaria* cult., July 8, 1894 (*Nuttall*, discov. 1600, 554).
   Spots 5 to 8 mm. diameter, with a ferruginous center and broad purple border, paler below. Perithecia few, scattered, convex prominent. Sporules oblong-elliptical, hyaline 2-nucleate, 4.5 to 5.5 x 1.5 to 2 μ. Basidia simple, lanceolate-fusoid, 8 to 12 x 1.5 μ.

Phyllosticta fragaricola Desm. has similar sporules, but the spots are much smaller, with a white center. The basidia also indicate *Phoma* and not *Phyllosticta*.

P. ilicicola (C. & E.) Sacc.
On leaves of *Ilex opaca*, June 18, 1893 (*Nuttall*, 1017).

P. Spiræeæ Desm?
On *Opulaster opulifolius*, May 13, 1894. Sporules 10 to 13 x 2 µ (*Nuttall*, 1508, 489).

P. herbarum West.
On *Onagra biennis*, March 18, 1894 (*Nuttall*, 1435, 406).

P. Phytolaccæ B. & C.
On stems *Phytolacca decandra*, July 31, 1893 (*Nuttall*, 1140).

P. pedunculi E. & E., Proc. Phila. Acad., 1894, 357.
TYPE HABITAT: On old peduncles *Magnolia Fraseri*, Jan., 1894 (*Nuttall*, discov. 1339, 297).
Perithecia scattered, flattish pustuliform, .5 to .75 mm. diameter, with a prominent papilliform ostiolum. Sporules fusoid-oblong, hyaline, 2 to 3 nucleate, 7 to 11 x 2 to 2.5 µ ends acute.
Differs from *Stagonospora pedunculi* in its larger, flatter perithecia and fusoid-oblong (not cylindrical), rather shorter sporules.

P. uvicola B. & C.
On *Vitis* cult. (Concord), July 4, 1893 (*Nuttall*, 1108, 94).

P. nyssæcarpa Cooke.
On dead limbs *Nyssa aquatica*, April 15, 1895 (*Nuttall*, 1809, 696). Sporules 10 x 3 µ.

P. samararum Desm.
On samaras *Acer Pennsylvanicum*, Feb. 2, 1894 (*Nuttall*, 1363, 321).

P. smilacina (Peck) Sacc.
On *Smilax rotundifolia*, Aug. 17, 1894. Sporules about 18 x 6 to 7.5 µ (*Nuttall*, 1660).

APOSPHÆRIA Berk.

A. pezizoides E. & E., Proc. Phila. Acad., 1894, 358.
TYPE HABITAT: On decorticated trunks of *Platanus occidentalis, Salix nigra falcata, Betula nigra, Fraxinus sp.*, and *Liquidambar Styraciflua*, on abrasions made by driftwood and ice, where it seems to grow exclusively and always below high-water mark, April, 1894 (*Nuttall*, discov. 1458, 432).
Perithecia erumpent-superficial, seriate-aggregate, hemispherical, about .75 mm. diameter, with a distinct papilliform ostiolum, at length collapsing and pezizoid or discoid. Sporules elliptical or ovoid, 4 to 6 x 2.5 µ ends obtuse.

DENDROPHOMA Sacc.

D. Therryana Sacc. & Roum.
On *Platanus occidentalis*, April 19, 1894 (*Nuttall*, 1463).

SPHÆRONÆMA Fries.

S. Physocarpi E. & E., Proc. Phila. Acad., 1894, 358.
TYPE HABITAT: On dead stems *Opulaster opulifolius*, May, 1894 (*Nuttall*, discov. 1504, 484).
Perithecia gregarious, erumpent-superficial, hemispherical, 150 μ diameter, with a straight, stout beak 90 to 115 μ long. Sporules narrow-elliptical, hyaline, 2 to 3-nucleate, 7 to 9 x 2.5 μ.

S. infuscans E. & E. sp. nov.
TYPE HABITAT: On dead dry wood *Juglans cinerea.*, Dec. 5, 1894 (*Nuttall*, discov. 1766, 661).
Perithecia gregarious, erumpent-superficial, hemispherical, brownish-black, about .25 mm. diameter, with a short cylindrical (.33 mm.), shining-black, obtuse, perforated ostiolum. Sporules abundant, elliptical, continuous, hyaline 3 to 4 x 1.5 μ on basidia simple or branched below, about 12 μ long and .5 μ thick at the base, narrowed above.
The surface of the wood is blackened.

S. acerinum Peck.
On *Acer rubrum*, June 12, 1894 (*Nuttall*, 1543).

S. corneum C. & E.
On *Onagra biennis*, Jan. 21, 1895 (*Nuttall*, 1791, 682 in part).

S. Magnoliæ Peck.
On *Magnolia acuminata*, Short Creek, alt. 1,000 ft., Aug. 16, 1894 (*Nuttall*, 1658). Sporules 10 x 6 μ nucleus large.

SIROCOCCUS Preuss.

S. Halesiæ E. & E., Proc. Phila. Acad., 1894, 358.
On dead limbs *Mohrodendron Carolinum* (*Halesia tetraptera*), Feb. 26, 1894 (*Nuttall*, discov. 1407, 377, 376?).
Perithecia scattered, or 2 to 3-cornate, erumpent, subglobose, about .33 mm. diameter, black, with a minute papilliform ostiolum. Sporules subglobose, about 3 μ diameter, greenish-hyaline, 3 to 6-concatenate, the terminal sporule oblong and paler. Chains simple or sparingly branched, arising directly from the proliferous layer without any distinct basidia, collected in stellate clusters.

VERMICULARIA Fries.

V. phlogina Fairm.
On dead leaves *Phlox amœna*, Sept. 15, 1894 (*Nuttall* 1606).

V. compacta C. & E.
On *Rubus odoratus*, May 30, 1894; sporules 20 to 25 x 30 μ (*Nuttall*, 1513). On *Caulophyllum thalictroides* (552).

V. petiolorum Schw.
On *Aralia spinosa*, and on *Robinia Pseudacacia?* Feb. 17, 1894 (*Nuttall*, 1388, 356).

V. Toxica E. & E., sp. nov?
On *Rhus radicans*, Aug. 18, 1894 (*Nuttall*, 1669, 569).

V. Dematium (Pers.) Fr.
On *Cassia Marilandica*, Oct. 28, 1893 (*Nuttall*, 1251, 193). On *Heuchera Americana*.

V. Dematium ——————— var.
On *Onagra biennis*, March 9, 1894 (*Nuttall*, 1434, 405).

V. Arctii Schw.
On dead leaves and petioles *Arctium Lappa*, on ground, July 21, 1894. Sporules fusiform slightly curved + or — 20 x 3 μ. Setæ 35 to + 125 x 3 to 5 μ (*Nuttall*, 1617).

V. subeffigurata Schw.
On fruit peduncles *Magnolia Fraseri* in association with STAGONOSPORA PEDUNCULI E. & E., July 25, 1893 (*Nuttall*, 1136).

V. subeffigurata scapincola Schw.
Bases of dead leaves *Yucca filamentosa* cult., Feb. 19, 1894. Sporules 18 x 2.5 μ, largest setæ 200 μ (*Nuttall*, 1367).

V. Trautvetteriæ Nuttall, sp. nov.
TYPE HABITAT: On dead leaves *Trautvetteria Carolinensis*, July 15, 1894 (*Nuttall*, discov. 1633).
Perithecia very small, scattered. Sporules curved, sharp pointed, 18 to 25 x 2.5 to 3 μ. Setæ + 100 x 10 μ.

V. liliacearum West.
On *Asparagus officinalis, Vagnera racemosa, Clintonia umbellulata* and *Iris cristata?* Nov. 1, 1893 (*Nuttall*, 1241, 188).

DOTHIORELLA Sacc.

D. Asiminæ E. & E., sp. nov.
On *Asimina triloba*, Feb. 2, 1894 (*Nuttall*, 1392, 362).
Sporules 5 to 7 x 2 to 3 μ oval or oblong, some of them slightly curved. Perithecia suberumpent, seriate, .25 mm. diameter, white inside and out, ovoid, in series of 3 to 5, raising the epidermis into short ridges split along the top so as to expose the pallid white apices of the perithecia. Sporules oval or elliptical, hyaline, 5 to 7 x 2 to 3 μ.

D. minor E. & E., sp. nov.
TYPE HABITAT: On dead limbs *Liriodendron Tulipifera* April 11, 1895 (*Nuttall*, discov. 1804, 691).
Perithecia seriate-subconfluent, .5 to .75 mm. diameter, irregularly ruptured above, white inside, erumpent, splitting the epidermis into short (2 to 4 mm.) longitudinal cracks. Sporules elliptical, hy-

aline continuous, 5 to 7.5 x 3 to 3.5 μ. Differs from *D. Lirioden-dri*, Cke. in its much smaller sporules.

D. glandulosa (Cooke) Sacc?
On *Robinia Pseudacacia*, March 14, 1894 (*Nuttall*, 1423, 395).

FUSICOCCUM Corda.

F. ilicinum E. & E., Proc. Phila. Acad., 1894, 359.
TYPE HABITAT: On dying, transplanted, *Ilex opaca* (transplanted Dec. 28, 1893), May 24, 1894 (*Nuttall*, discov. 1521, 496).
Stromata cortical, convex, about 1 or 1.5 mm. diameter, multilocular, whitish inside, the tuberculiform apex pierced with a single pore, rupturing the epidermis and slightly raising it. Sporules fusoid, hyaline, nucleate 15 to 22 x 2.5 to 3 μ.

CYTISPORA Ehrenb.

C. Celtidis E. & E., Proc. Phila. Acad., 1894, 360.
TYPE HABITAT: On dead limbs *Celtis occidentalis*, Feb. 2, 1894 (*Nuttall*, discov. 1358, 314).
Stroma valsoid, flat, thin, 1.5 to 2 mm. diameter, only penetrating the surface of the bark, multilocular, gray inside, raising the bark into small pustules, and finally rupturing it, cells resembling perithecia. Sporules allantoid, 6 to 7 x 1 to 1.5 μ.

C. Halesiæ E. & E., Proc. Phila. Acad., 1894, 361.
TYPE HABITAT: On dead limbs of *Mohrodendron Carolinum* (*Halesia tetraptera*), June 7, 1894 (*Nuttall*, discov. 1540).
Stromata convex-conical, sunk in the bark, orbicular, about 1 mm. diameter, white inside, unilocular, the inner surface of the cavity lined with simple, straight basidia about 15 μ long, bearing the oblong-fusoid, hyaline, 2-nucleate, straight, 5 to 7 x 1 to 1.5 μ sporules, which are expelled through a single orifice perforating the raised epidermis.
This probably is the spermogonial stage of *Diaporthe Halesiæ* or *D. tetraptera*, both of which are found in company with it.

C. leucostoma (Pers.) Sacc.
On cultivated *Prunus domestica* and *Amygdalus Persica*, Dec. 12, 1894 (*Nuttall*, 1769).

C. exasperans E. & E., Proc. Phila. Acad., 1894, 360.
TYPE HABITAT: On dead limbs *Acer Pennsylvanicum*, Feb. 2, 1894, Short Creek, alt. 1,300 ft. (*Nuttall*, discov. 1366).
Stroma buried in the bark, orbicular, about 1 mm. diameter, 4 to 6-celled (at length one-celled), prolonged above into a stout, conical beak opening by a single round pore at the apex. Sporules oblong or allantoid, hyaline, 5 to 7 x 1.25 μ.

C. ——————sp.
On *Chionanthus Virginica*, March 28, 1894 (*Nuttall*, 1455, 427).

C. Persicæ Schw.
On *Amygdalus Persica* cult. "Early Rivers," June 30, 1893 (*Nuttall*, 1106).

C. ———— sp.
On *Cercis Canadensis*, April 10, 1894 (*Nuttall*, 1471, 447). Spores 5 to 6 x .75 μ.

C. rhoina Fr.
On *Rhus hirta*, June 20, 1894. Sporules 5 to 8 μ (*Nuttall*, 1551, 636).

C. caryigena E. & E., Proc. Phila. Acad., 1894, 359.
TYPE HABITAT: On dead limbs *Hicoria ovata*, May 31, 1894 (*Nuttall*, discov. 1524, 513).
Stroma cortical, convex, 1.5 to 2 mm. diameter, slaty-black, 4 to 6-celled, cells yellowish-white, subglobose, small. Sporules allantoid, hyaline 3.5 to 4.5 x .75 to 1 μ.
(Spermogonia of *Valsa caryigena*, B. & C.)?

C. Rhois-hirtæ Nuttall, sp. nov.
On *Rhus hirta*, June 10, 1894 (*Nuttall*, 1533, 635).
This form is clearly distinct from *C. Rhoina* Fr. Cirrus reddish yellow. Perithecia very prominent. Spores 8 to 10 x 2 to 2.5 μ.

C. Sassafras E. & E. sp. nov.
TYPE HABITAT: On fire-killed twigs of *Sassafras Sassafras*, Dec. 20, 1894 (*Nuttall*, discov. 1766, 666). Jamaica, Long Island (F. C. Stewart).
Stromata thickly scattered, conical, rising from an orbicular base about 1 mm. diameter, the black, shining apices erumpent and roughening the bark, at first multilocular, becoming unilocular. Sporules allantoid, hyaline, only slightly curved, 4 to 5 x 1 μ borne on simple, straight basidia about 12 μ long.

C. betulina Ehr?
On *Betula nigra*, Feb. 20, 1894. Cirrus yellowish, sporules, 4 to 6 x 1 μ (*Nuttall*, 1396, 367).

C. Salicis (Corda) Rabenh?
On *Salix nigra*, March 22, 1894 (*Nuttall*, 1429).

C. Platani Fckl.
On *Platanus occidentalis*, March 14, 1894 (*Nuttall*, 1424, 396)

C. leucosperma (Pers) Fr.
On *Carpinus Caroliniana*, Nov. 17, 1893. Sporules 5 x 1 μ (*Nuttall*, 1257).

C. ceratophora Sacc.
On *Fraxinus Pennsylvanica*, Oct. 17, 1893 (*Nuttall*, 1234, 163).

C. Curreyi Sacc?
On *Pinus Virginiana*, Dec. 13, 1844; on *Tsuga Canadensis*, April 15, 1895 (*Nuttall*, 1771, 697).

C. coccinea (Reb.) Fr.
On *Robinia Pseudacacia*, Feb. 2, 1894. Sporules 3 x .75 μ (*Nuttall*, 1355).

C. ———— sp.
Spermogonia of *Valsa goniostoma* Sz.? On fire-killed *Liquidambar Styraciflua*, Oct. 21, 1895 (*Nuttall*, 1884).

C. orthospora B. & C?
On *Robinia Pseudacacia*, April 20, 1894. Sporules irregular in shape 12 to 18 x 2.5 to 3 μ (*Nuttall*, 1478, 458).

C. carphosperma Fr.
On *Asimina triloba*, Nov. 5, 1893 (*Nuttall*, 1292, 237).

SPHÆROPSIS Lév.

S. Linderæ Peck.
On dead twigs *Benzoin Benzoin*, April 8, 1895 (*Nuttall*, 1795).

S. Asiminæ E. & E., Proc. Phila. Acad., 1894, 361.
TYPE HABITAT: On dead limbs *Asimina triloba*, Feb. 24, 1894 (*Nuttall*, discov. 1397, 370).
Perithecia scattered or subseriate, buried in the bark which is raised into little pustules over them and soon ruptured. Perithecia small (.25 mm.) thick-walled, with an obscurely papilliform ostiolum. Sporules oblong-elliptical, brown, obtuse, 18 to 22 x 8 to 10 μ.

S. Asiminæ fructigena E. & E. var. nov.
TYPE HABITAT: On old dried-up fruits of *Asimina triloba*, Oct. 3, 1895 (*Nuttall*, discov. 1871, 755).
A fructigenous form of *S. Asiminæ* E. & E. Perithecia smaller than in the species (110 to 140 μ) and more abundant. Sporules a little larger (20 to 24 x 9 to 12 μ).

S. Ampelopsidis C. & E.
On *Parthenocissus quinquefolia*, March 30, 1894. Sporules 18 to 20 x 10 to 12 μ (*Nuttall*, 1460, 437).

S. cerasina Peck.
On *Prunus serotina*, alt. 1,200 ft., Nov. 22, 1894 (*Nuttall*, 1746).

S. Physocarpi E. & E., Proc. Phila. Acad., 1894, 361.
TYPE HABITAT: On dead *Opulaster opulifolius*, May 2, 1894 (*Nuttall*, discov. 1502, 482, 486).
Perithecia scattered, .33 mm. diameter, buried in the inner bark, with their apices and papilliform ostiola erumpent, white inside (at first), sometimes, as in the preceding species 2 to 3 confluent. Sporules varying from short-elliptical 12 to 15 x 10 μ to oblong or obovate-elliptical 15 to 20 x 10 μ.
Differs from *S. Nielliæ* E.& E. in its buried perithecia and much larger sporules.

S. celastrina Peck.
On branches *Celastrus scandens*, April 27, 1895 (*Nuttall*, 1812).

S. Œnotheræ E. & E., sp. nov.
   TYPE HABITAT: On dead stems *Onagra biennis*, Jan. 21, 1895 (*Nuttall*, discov. 1792, 683).
   Perithecia scattered, erumpent, superficial, globose, 200 to 225 μ diameter, with a papilliform ostiolum, occasionally subcollapsing above. Sporules oblong-elliptical, pale brown, 20 to 25 x 10 to 12 μ on stout basidia shorter than the sporules. There are indications that the sporules become finally uniseptate.

S. Sumachi (Schw.) C. & E.
   On branches *Rhus hirta*, March 29, 1894. Sporules 20 to 26 x 8 to 12.5 μ (*Nuttall*, 1439).

S. Sassafras C. & E.
   On *Sassafras Sassafras*, April 10, 1895. Sporules 23 x 10 μ (*Nuttall*, 1801, 688).

S. phomatella Peck.
   On *Fraxinus Americana*, March 31, 1894 (*Nuttall*, 1441).

S. Caryæ C. & E.
   On hickory barrel-hoop, April 9, 1894. Sporules 18 to 25 x 8 to 11 μ (*Nuttall*, 1448).

S. Ipomœæ E. & E., Proc. Phila. Acad., 1894, 362.
   TYPE HABITAT: On dead peduncles of *Ipomœa pandurata*, Dec. 9, 1893 (*Nuttall*, discov. 1305, 249).
   Perithecia scattered, ovate-globose, 250 to 300 μ diameter, the upper part prominent and closely covered by the shining black epidermis. Sporules elliptical, brown, 18 to 23 x 10 to 13 μ on pedicels of about the same length as the sporules.

S. Menispermi Peck.
   On *Menispermum Canadensis*, Jan. 17, 1894 (*Nuttall*, 1343, 302).

CONIOTHYRIUM Corda.

C. Fuckelii Sacc.
   On *Parthenocissus quinquefolia*, sporules globular, 2 to 2.5 μ March 31, 1894 (*Nuttall*, 1442).

C. concentricum (Desm.) Sacc ?
   On leaves *Yucca filamentosa*, Sept. 1, 1894 (*Nuttall*, 1187).

HAPLOSPORELLA Speg.

H. Celtidis E. & E., Proc. Phila. Acad., 1894, 362.
   TYPE HABITAT: On dead limbs *Celtis occidentalis*, Feb. 2, 1894 (*Nuttall*, discov. 1359, 315).
   Perithecia mostly in valsoid clusters of 3 to 10, small, 200 μ white inside, slightly sunk in the inner bark, their papilliform ostiola rupturing the epidermis. Sporules elliptical, brown, continuous, 18 to 22 x 10 to 12 μ on basidia of about the same length as the sporules.

H. Araliæ E. & E., Proc. Phila. Acad., 1894, 362.

TYPE HABITAT: On dead limbs *Aralia spinosa*, Feb. 26, 1894 (*Nuttall*, discov. 1406, 375).

Stromata seriate-connate, erumpent through longitudinal cracks in the bark, and extending from 4 to 5 mm. to 2 or more centimetres. Perithecia ovate-globose, buried in the black, subcarbonaceous stroma, 3 to 6 in each single stroma, about .33 mm. diameter. Sporules elliptical, brown, 20 to 25 x 10 to 12 μ.

This may be the pycnidia of *Botryosphæria fuliginosa* (M. & N.).

DIPLODIA Fries.

D. Liriodendri Peck.

On fire killed *Liriodendron Tulipifera*, Oct. 16, 1894 (*Nuttall*, 1710).

D. Salicina Lév.

On dead twigs *Salix nigra*, March 25, 1894 (*Nuttall*, 1457).

D. Cercidis E. & E., Proc. Phila. Acad., 1894, 363.

TYPE HABITAT: On dead limbs *Cercis Canadensis*, April 9, 1894. (*Nuttall*, discov. 1475, 449).

Perithecia subseriate, globose, .33 to .5 mm. diameter, slightly sunk in the inner bark and splitting the epidermis with short longitudinal clefts. Sporules elliptical, 20 to 23 x 10 to 15 μ on stout basidia, uniseptate.

D. infuscans E. & E., Proc. Phila. Acad., 1894, 363.

TYPE HABITAT: On bark of dead limbs *Fraxinus Americana*, April 27, 1894 (*Nuttall*, discov. 1492, 459).

Perithecia ovate-globose, small, 110 to 150 μ diameter, thickly scattered, blackening both the outer and inner surface of the bark. Ostiolum not conspicuous, obscurely papilliform. Sporules oblong-elliptical, 12 to 15 x 8 to 10 μ scarcely constricted.

In *D. inquinans* West, the sporules and perithecia are larger, and the bark is not blackened within.

D. atrata (Desm.) Sacc.

On dead limbs *Acer Negundo*, April 20, 1894 (*Nuttall*, 1465).

D. caryigena E. & E., Proc. Phila Acad., 1894, 363.

TYPE HABITAT: On dead limbs *Hicoria ovata*, May 31, 1894 (*Nuttall*, discov. 1525). Also Canada (Dearness).

Perithecia subseriate, sunk in the inner bark, covered by the epidermis, which is raised into pustules and ruptured, about .5 mm. diameter, black. Sporules elliptical, brown, uniseptate, scarcely constricted, 15 to 20 x 8 to 10 μ (Pycnidia of *Valsa caryigena* B. & C.)

D. viticola Desm.

On *Vitis*, March 26, 1894. No septum visible in sporules (*Nuttall*, 1443, 412).

D. ilicicola Desm.?

On *Ilex opaca*, Dec. 20, 1894. Sporules 22 to 25 x 11 to 13 μ (*Nuttall*, 1777, 667).

D. Rubi Fr.
On *Rubus* cult., Feb. 19, 1895. Sporules 20 x 8 to 12 μ (*Nuttall*, 1789).

D. inquinans West.
On *Fraxinus Americana*, April 27, 1894 (*Nuttall*, 1491, 459).

D. Juglandis Fr.
On *Juglans cinerea*, April 9, 1894 (*Nuttall*, 1449).

D. Maydis (Berk.) Sacc.
On *Zea Mays*, Aug. 10, 1895. Spores 30 x 4 μ (*Nuttall*, 1840, 729).

BOTRYODIPLODIA Sacc.

B. acerina E. & E., Proc. Phila. Acad., 1894, 363.
TYPE HABITAT: On dead limbs *Acer Pennsylvanicum*, Feb. 2, 1894 (*Nuttall*, discov. 1362, 319).
Perithecia erumpent in botryoidal clusters, often seriately confluent for 1 or more cm., about .5 mm. diameter, white inside, flattish above, with a broad papilliform ostiolum. Sporules elliptical, brown, uniseptate, 20 to 25 x 12 to 15 μ on basidia of about the same length.

B. ———— sp.
Stylosporus stage ? of *Pseudovalsa sigmoidea* (C. & E.). On dead limbs *Quercus Prinus*, with that species. Spores brown, 1-septate 25 x 12.5 μ (*Nuttall*, 1829).

ASCOCHYTA Lib.

A. clematidina Thum.
On *Clematis Virginiana*, Aug. 10, 1895 (*Nuttall*, 1842, 733).

ACTINONEMA Fries.

A Rosæ (Lib.) Fr.
On *Rosa* cult., June 27, 1894 (*Nuttall*, 1563).

HENDERSONIA Berk.

H. Lirella Cooke.
On *Salix nigra falcata*, April 23, 1894 (*Nuttall*, 1480, 460). Sporules 15 x 7.5 μ.

H. Desmazieri Mont.
On bark of limbs *Platanus occidentalis*, April 24, 1894. Sporules + 40 x 22 μ (*Nuttall*, 1466).

STAGONOSPORA Sacc.

S. petiolorum E. & E., Proc. Phila. Acad., 1894, 365.
TYPE HABITAT: On dead petioles *Aralia spinosa*, Feb. 17, 1894 (*Nuttall*, discov. 1389, 357).
Perithecia scattered, innate, small, slightly prominent and covered by the shining, blackened epidermis, 150 to 250 μ diameter,

mostly sub-elliptical. Sporules oblong, hyaline, nucleate, becoming one or more septate, 12 to 20 x 2 to 5 µ.

S. pedunculi E. & E., Proc. Phila. Acad., 1893, 457.
TYPE HABITAT: On old fruit peduncles *Magnolia Fraseri* (not LIRIODENDRON TULIPIFERA, loc. cit.). Short Creek, July 25, 1893 (*Nuttall*, discov. 1135, 119).
Perithecia gregarious, pustuliform, about .33 mm. diameter, covered by the blackened epidermis. Sporules cylindrical, 18 to 22 x 2 to 2.5 µ, multinucleate, hyaline, straight.

S. Physocarpi E. & E., Proc. Phila. Acad., 1894, 365.
TYPE HABITAT: On dead stems and limbs *Opulaster opulifolius*, May 12, 1894 (*Nuttall* discov. 1505, 485).
Perithecia scattered, depressed-hemispherical; 200 to 250 µ diameter, sunk in the bark, with the upper part prominent but covered by the epidermis, which is pierced by the papilliform ostiolum, white inside. Sporules linear, multiseptate, hyaline 25 to 35 x 3 to 4 µ.

S. collapsa (C. & E.) Sacc.
On *Acer saccharinum*, Jan. 26, 1894. Sporules 15 to 23 x 3 µ (*Nuttall*, 1353, 309).

S. ——— sp.
On *Chionanthus Virginica* (*Nuttall*, 1462, 440). Spores + 25 x 7 µ 4-septate. This may prove to be only a stylosporous stage of some Dothidaceous species—Ellis.

CAMAROSPORIUM Schulz.

C. Linderæ E. & E., sp. nov.
TYPE HABITAT: On dead limbs *Benzoin Benzoin*, April 15, 1895 (*Nuttall* discov. 1808, 694).
Perithecia scattered, semierumpent .75 mm. diameter, the upper part, except the papilliform, erumpent ostiolum, covered by the closely adherent epidermis, which is raised into distinct, hemispherical pustules. Sporules oblong, 3-septate with 1 to 2 cells divided by a longitudinal septum, brown, obtuse, not constricted 12 to 18 (mostly 12 to 15) x 5 to 7 µ. The perithecia are of a firm consistence and slaty-black inside.

SEPTORIA Fries.

S. Tecomæ E. & E., Proc. Phila. Acad., 1894, 367.
TYPE HABITAT: On leaves *Tecoma radicans*, Aug. 11, 1894 (*Nuttall*, discov. 1671, 580).
Spots light brown (wood color), irregular in shape, small, 1.5 to 2 mm., inconspicuous and indistinctly margined. Perithecia immersed, small (65 to 70 µ) barely visible with a lens. Sporules 40 to 50 x 2 to 2.5 µ, not strongly curved, *nucleate*, hyaline.

S. Brassicæ E. & E., sp. nov.
TYPE HABITAT: On leaves *Brassica nigra*, Nov. 26, 1894 (*Nuttall*, discov. 1759, 646).

Spots suborbicular or subangular, 3 to 4 mm. diameter, dull white with a narrow, darker and sometimes slightly raised border. Perithecia epiphyllous, numerous, sublenticular, pale brown, coarsely cellular, broadly perforated above, 100 to 115 μ diameter. Sporules numerous, curved, obtuse, continuous, hyaline, 25 to 45 x 2 to 3 μ.

Closely allied to *S. Sisymbrii* Ell., but that has the spots greenish at first and never becoming more than whitish and the sporules 1 to 3-septate.

S. Rubi West.
On living leaves *Rubus Canadensis*, Wood Co., Lockhart's Run, 1891 (*Millspaugh*). On same host July 26, 1894 (*Nuttall*, 1627).

S. Corni-maris Sacc.
On *Cornus florida*, alt. 1,700 ft., July 19, 1894 (*Nuttall*, 1612).

S. cornicola Desmz.
On *Cornus alternifolia*, Sewell Valley, Aug. 6, 1894 (*Nuttall*, 1647).

S. kalmiæcola (Schw.) B. & C.
On living leaves *Kalmia latifolia*, 1891, Monongalia Co., at Camp Eden (*Millspaugh*).

S. ochroleuca B. & C.
On leaves *Castanea dentata*, June 30, 1894. Maximum number of perithecia in a single macula 20 (*Nuttall*, 1579).

S. microsperma Peck.
On *Betula lenta*, alt. 1,200 ft., Oct. 24, 1894. Sporules + 18 x .25 μ (*Nuttall*, 1722).

S. Polymniæ E. & E., Proc. Phila. Acad., 1894, 368.
TYPE HABITAT: On leaves *Polymnia Uvedalia*, June 29, 1894 (*Nuttall*, discov. 1595, 543).

Spots, scattered, angular, limited by the veinlets, 2 to 4 mm. diameter, dirty green. Perithecia epiphyllous, minute, 75 μ diameter, scattered, innate, inconspicuous. Sporules filiform, continuous, 35 to 50 x 1 to 1.25 μ.

S. Trautvetteriæ E. & E., Proc. Phila. Acad., 1894, 368.
TYPE HABITAT: On *Trautvetteria Carolinensis*, July 20, 1894 (*Nuttall*, discov. 1632, 564).

Spots irregular, subangular, partly limited by the veinlets of the leaf, often elongated and acute at one end, brownish-black, with an irregularly shaped white center, which is well defined, angular, 3 to 5 mm. in the longer diameter. Perithecia epiphyllous, but also visible below, small (65 to 75 μ), scattered, dark. Sporules abundant, nearly straight or slightly curved, continuous, 22 to 30 x 2 μ.

Differs from *S. Anemonis* Desm. in its broad, dark-margined white-centered spots, and rather longer and thicker sporules.

S. hyalina E. & E., Proc. Phila. Acad., 1894, 368.
TYPE HABITAT: On *Viola primulæfolia*, July 26, 1894 (*Nuttall*,

discov. 1641, 572). Also on *V. blanda*, Michigan (Hicks); and on *V. lanceolata*, Massachusetts (Miss Clarke).

Spots minute (.5 to 1 mm.) white, with a dark purple-shaded border. Perithecia punctiform, black, epiphyllous, subglobose, 65 to 75 μ diameter, not abundant. *Sporules filiform, nearly straight, or slightly curved, hyaline, nucleate, not visibly septate, 20 to 40 (mostly 25 to 35) x 1 to 1.25 μ.

S. Violæ West, has yellowish-brown perithecia on pale zonate spots with a reddish-brown border.

S. aciculosa E. & E.
On *Fragaria* cult., Nov. 3, 1894. Sporules 15 to 25 x .75 μ (*Nuttall*, 1731).

S. Helianthi E. & K.
On *Helianthus decapetalus*, Oct. 29, 1894. Sporules 50 x 2 μ (*Nuttall*, 1723).

S. Leptostachyæ E. & K.
On leaves *Phryma Leptostachya*, July 4, 1894. Sporules 20 to 25 x 1 μ (*Nuttall*, 1584).

S. Nolitangere Thum.
On *Impatiens biflora*, Aug. 5, 1894. Sporules 20 to 25 x 1.5 to 2 μ (*Nuttall*, 1649).

S. Violæ West.
On *Viola sagittata*, June 30, 1893. Sporules + 25 x 1.25 μ (*Nuttall*, 1577).

S. Saxifragæ Pass.
On *Heuchera Americana*, June 10, 1894. Sporules 15 to 20 x 2.5 to 3 μ (*Nuttall*, 1544, 521).

S. Lobeliæ Peck.
On *Lobelia cardinalis*, June 22, 1894 (*Nuttall*, 1559).

S. Scrophulariæ Peck.
On *Scrophularia Marilandica*, June 10, 1894. Sporules 40 to 50 μ long (*Nuttall*, 1538).

S. Verbenæ Rob. & Desm.
On leaves *Verbena urticæfolia*, Jefferson Co., near Shenandoah Junction (*Millspaugh*).

S. psilostega E. & M.
On *Galium circæzans*, July 14, 1894 (*Nuttall*, 1604).

S. Nabali B. & C?
On *Prenanthes serpentaria*, June 8, 1894.(*Nuttall*, 1536).

S. atro-purpurea Peck.
On *Aster cordifolius*, Nov. 24, 1894. Sporules + 35 to 55 x 1 to 1.5 μ (*Nuttall*, 1757, 644).

S. polygonorum Desm.
On *Polygonum Hydropiper*, June 8, 1894. Sporules 25 to 40 x 1.5 μ (*Nuttall*, 1537).

S. Smilaciniæ E. & M.
On *Vagnera racemosa* (SMILACINA), Aug. 14, 1894. Maculæ suffused with the marginal color late in season (*Nuttall*, 1252).

RHABDOSPORA Mont.

R. kalmiarum (Schw.)*
Sphæria Kalmianum Schw. On *Kalmia latifolia*, Aug. 26, 1894 (*Nuttall*, 1685, 590).

PHLYCTÆNA Mont. & Desm.

P. vagabunda Desm.
On *Vernonia Noveboracensis*, *Phytolacca decandra* and *Onagra biennis*, March 18, 1894 (*Nuttall*, 1436, 408).

P. septorioides Sacc.
On *Phytolacca decandra*, May 25, 1894 (*Nuttall*, 1498).

P. Ipomœæ E. & E., Proc. Phila. Acad., 1894, 369.
TYPE HABITAT: On calyx lobes *Ipomœa pandurata*, Dec. 9, 1894 (*Nuttall*, discov. 1305, 250).
Perithecia scattered, subcuticular, 75 to 80 μ diameter, covered by the blackened, slightly raised epidermis. Sporules linear, hyaline, curved above, 15 to 20 x 1.25 μ.

P. arcuata Berk.
On *Onagra biennis*, March 18, 1894. Sporules 30 to 35 x .75 μ (*Nuttall*, 1433, 403).

GELATINOSPORUM Peck.

G. betulinum Peck.
On *Betula lenta*, April 12, 1895. Sporules subfiliform nearly semicircular, 32 to 40 x 2.5 μ (*Nuttall*, 1797).

SPHÆROGRAPHIUM Sacc.

S. hystricinum (Ell.) Sacc.
On *Azalea viscosa*, May 4, 1894. Sporules narrowly arcuate-falcate 34 x 3 μ (*Nuttall*, 1501, 481).

S. Fraxini (Peck) Sacc.
On dead limbs *Fraxinus Americana*, Short Creek, alt. 1,300 ft., July 16, 1894. Sporules 50 to 60 x 2.5 μ (*Nuttall*, 1609).

NECTRIOIDACEÆ.

ASCHERSONIA Mont.

A. ———— sp.
On *Cornus florida*. Spores 3 to 5 x .75 μ (*Nuttall*, 1800, 687).

---

*Transferred to *Rhabdospora* by E. & E.

LEPTOSTROMACEÆ.

LEPTOTHYRIUM Kunze & Schm.

L. ——————— sp.
On living leaves *Ilex opaca*, Aug., 1894 (*Nuttall*, 1679, 584). Maculæ white.

L. Liriodendri Cke.
On dead fallen leaves *Liriodendron Tulipifera*, April 17, 1895 (*Nuttall*, 1805).

L. dryinum Sacc.
On living leaves *Quercus rubra*, alt. 1,300 ft., June 29, 1894 (*Nuttall*, 1592, 540).

L. Castaneæ (Spr.) Sacc.
On fallen leaves *Castanea dentata*, April 17, 1895 (*Nuttall*, 1806).

L. petiolorum ——————— var.
On dead leaves *Magnolia Fraseri*, April 11, 1895. Sporules 5 x 1 μ (*Nuttall*, 1802, 689).

L? foraminulatum Sacc. & Ell.
On fallen leaves *Ilex opaca*, Aug. 16, 1894. Sporules 25 x 3 μ (*Nuttall*, 1657).

L. vulgare (Fr.) Sacc.
On *Dioscorea villosa*, on *Aralia spinosa*, and on *Onagra biennis*. Sporules 5 to 7 x .75 μ on each host, Feb. 8, 1894 (*Nuttall*, 1368, 323).

SACIDIUM Nees.

S. Vitis E. & E., sp. nov.
TYPE HABITAT: On *Vitis cordifolia*, Nov. 6, 1893 (*Nuttall*, 1254, 198). Fungi Columbiani 290, N. A. F., 3067.
Perithecia scattered; scutellate not perforated, 180 to 220 μ diameter. Sporules oblong-cylindrical, straight or curved, 15 to 20 x 4 to 5 μ, filled with small nuclei.
In the specimens of *Sacidium viticolum*, B. & C. in Rav. F. Am. the sporules are ovate or elliptical, 6 to 7 x 5 μ, and the perithecia are only 75 to 100 μ diameter.

DISCOSIA Lib.

D. Artoceras (Tode) Fr.
On *Castanea dentata*, Oct. 20, 1893. On *Epigæa repens*, Jan. 18, 1894. On *Betula lutea*, *Fraxinus Pennsylvanica*, *Magnolia Fraseri*, *Cornus florida*, *Sassafras Sassafras*, and *Cephalanthus occidentalis* (*Nuttall*, 1228, 173).

D. maculicola Ger.
On living leaves *Disporum lanuginosum*, Grant Co., near Bayard (*Millspaugh*). On *Smilax rotundifolia* and *Oxydendron arboreum*, July 8, 1894 (*Nuttall*, 1598).

D. rugulosa B. & C.
Parasitic on upper surface of the maculæ of *Phyllosticta caryigena*, July 2, 1894 (*Nuttall*, 1583).

ENTOMOSPORIUM Lév.
E. MACULATUM Lév.
On living leaves and fruits *Pyrus communis* cult., Monongalia Co., Morgantown (*Millspaugh*).

LEPTOSTROMELLA Sacc.
L. filicina (B. & C.) Sacc.
On *Dryopteris spinulosa*, May 4, 1894 (*Nuttall*, 1487).

EXCIPULACEÆ.

DINEMASPORIUM Lév.
D. hispidulum (Schrad.) Sacc.
On *Asimina triloba*, March 9, 1894. Sporules 14 to 18 x 2 to 2.3 μ (*Nuttall*, 1422, 394).

MELANCONIACEÆ.

HAINESIA Ell. & Sacc.
H. Rubi (West).
On leaves of *Rubus* cult. Oct. 28 1895 (*Nuttall*, 1880).

GLŒOSPORIUM Desm. & Mont.
G. ———— sp.
On leaves of *Cercis Canadensis* (*Nuttall*, 985). Sporules 18 x 7.5, + 20 x 7.5, 23 x 7, 25 x 6 μ.

G. Sanguinariæ E. & E., Proc. Phila. Acad., 1894, 371.
TYPE HABITAT: On leaves *Sanguinaria Canadensis*, July 8, 1894 (*Nuttall*, discov. 1601, 555).
Spots yellow, oblong or irregular, 3 to 5 mm. diameter, situated near the apex of the leaf which is more or less uniformly blackened. Acervuli epiphyllous, numerous, innate, yellow and conspicuous. Conidia oblong, hyaline, continuous, mostly a little curved, 8 to 15 x 3.5 to 5.5 μ.

G. aridum E. & H.
On *Fraxinus Pennsylvanica*, June 10, 1894 (*Nuttall*, 1545, 518).

G. Rumicis E. & E., sp. nov.
TYPE HABITAT: On leaves *Rumex obtusifolius*, Oct. 27, 1894 (*Nuttall*, discov. 1729, 617).
Spots reddish-brown, lighter in the center, more or less distinctly zonate 3 to 4 mm. diameter, margin darker. Acervuli innate, small. Sporules erumpent above, oblong, hyaline, continuous, 5 to 8 x 2 to 2.5 μ.
The spots resemble those of *Ovularia obliqua* Cke., on *Ramularia decipiens* E. & E.

G. Alni E. & E., sp. nov.
TYPE HABITAT: On living leaves *Alnus rugosa*, Nov. 24, 1894 (*Nuttall*, discov. 1737, 624).

Spots dirty drown, suborbicular, indistinctly zonate, .5 to 1 cm. diameter, paler in the center, border concolorous, rather indefinite; acervuli epiphyllous, numerous, small, 100 to 120 μ diameter, chestnut color, becoming darker; conidia oblong-elliptical, 12 to 16 x 6 to 8 μ.

Differs from *G. cylindrospermum* Bon., on the same host, in its much broader conidia, and from *G. rubicolum* E. & E. in the different character of the spots and rather broader conidia.

G. nervisequum (Fckl.) Sacc.
On leaves *Platanus occidentalis*, June 10, 1894. Sporules 12.5 to 18 x 4 to 6 μ (*Nuttall*, 1555,526).

G. Robergei Desm.
On *Carpinus Caroliniana*, July 16, 1894 (*Nuttall*, 1608).

G. betularum Ell & Mart.
On *Betula nigra*, sporules 10 x 7 μ, July 16, 1894 (*Nuttall*, 1607).

G. cylindrospermum Bon.
On leaves of *Alnus rugosa*. Spores 8 to 10 x 2 to 2.5 μ (*Nuttall*, 1875).

G. venetum Speg.
On living leaves of *Rubus strigosus*, Sept. 19, 1895 (*Nuttall*, 1859).

G. rubicolum E. E., sp. nov.
TYPE HABITAT: On leaves of *Rubus strigosus* (*Nuttall*, discov. 747).

Spots at first numerous, angular, small and yellowish or reddish-yellow, soon confluent forming large brown, dry, dead spots of irregular shape and indefinite outline, occupying a large part of the leaf. Acervuli not numerous, scattered, epiphyllous, prominent, resembling perithecia; conidia oblong-elliptical, 12 to 16 x 6 to 7 μ.

Differs from *G. Rubi* E. & E. in its larger, fewer black acervuli and broader conidia, which also are about twice as large as in *G. Venetum* Speg.

MYXOSPORIUM Link.

M. luteum E. & E., Proc. Phila. Acad., 1893, 458.
TYPE HABITAT: On bark *Hicoria ovata*, April to July, 1893 (*Nuttall*, discov. 1015, 79). E. & E. N. A. F. 2953. Fungi Columbiani 150.

Stroma globose-conical, light yellow, .75 to 1 mm. diameter, slightly sunk in the inner bark, unilocular and opening by a single pore. The surface of the inner bark around this pore is of a pale slate color, the colored portion definitely limited by a black line so as to form an irregular circle about 2 mm. across, but this line does not penetrate the bark. Sporules navicular-oblong, hyaline, obtuse, 10 to 11 x 4 to 5 μ with 1 to 2 large nuclei. Basidia slender-cylindrical 15 to 20 x 1.5 μ. Mass of exuded sporules flesh color.

M. Rhois (B. & C.) Sacc.
On fire killed *Rhus hirta*, June 20, 1895 (*Nuttall*, 1575, 537).

M. platanicolum E. & E., Proc. Phila. Acad., 1894, 372.
TYPE HABITAT: On limbs *Platanus occidentalis*, April 24, 1894 (*Nuttall*, discov. 1485, 467).
Acervuli subcutaneous, vesiculoid, pale, 1 mm. diameter, raising the ruptured epidermis into pustules but not erumpent. Sporules oval or oblong-ovate, hyaline, nucleate at first, 10 to 12 x 5 to 6 μ, on stout basidia.

M. seriatum E. & E., Proc. Phila. Acad., 1894, 372.
TYPE HABITAT: On bark of *Acer* sp., June, 1894 (*Nuttall*, discov. 1552, 523).
Nuclei pallid, orbicular, about 1 mm. diameter, seated on the surface of the inner bark; surrounded by a thin layer of smoky colored radiating hyphæ, from the inner extremities of which the botuliform or oblong, 6 to 8 x 2 to 2.5 μ hyaline conidia are produced. The nuclei are seriately arranged, and the pale flesh-colored, flattish cirrhi are erumpent through narrow, longitudinal cracks in the bark.

COLLETOTRICHUM Corda.

C. LINDEMUTHIANUM (S. & M.) Scrib.
On pods of *Phaseolus* cult. "Wax, Butter Bean." Monongalia Co., near Morgantown, 1891 (*Millspaugh*).

C. ———— sp.
On *Sassafras Sassafras*, Oct. 15, 1894. Sporules 8 to 18 x 4 to 7 μ (*Nuttall*, 1714, 602).

C. lineola Corda.
On *Zea Mays*, Aug. 10, 1895 (*Nuttall*, 1834, 726).

CYLINDROSPORIUM Ung.

C. Cratægi E. & E., Proc. Phila. Acad., 1894, 372.
TYPE HABITAT: On leaves *Cratægus* sp., July 26, 1894 (*Nuttall* discov. 1640, 571).
Leaves more or less mottled with rusty red, at length uniformly of this same color. Acervuli innate, erumpent on both sides, and whitening the surface of the leaf with abundantly discharged conidia, which are 75 to 100 x 3 to 3.5 μ, nearly straight or more or less undulate and curved, nucleate, and faintly 3 to 5 septate.

C. Toxicodendri (Curtis) E. & E. Proc. Phila. Acad., 1893, 460.
On leaves *Rhus radicans*, June 29, 1894. Sporules, largest, 50 x 3 μ (*Nuttall*, 1568).

LIBERTELLA Desm.

L. faginea Desm.
On bark of dead *Fagus atropunicea*, Grant Co., near Bayard (*Millspaugh*). On dead *Prunus* sp. cult. Aug. 10, 1895. Cirrus bright red. Sporules variously curved 15 to 25 x 1 μ (*Nuttall*, 1843, 734).

L. ———— sp.
On felled *Robinia Pseudacacia*, April 4, 1894. Sporules 15 to 20 x .75 to 1 μ (*Nuttall*, 1470, 446).

L. acerina Westend.
On *Acer rubrum* or *saccharinum*, April 4, 1894. Sporules hyaline, 15 to 18 x 1 μ (*Nuttall*, 1445).

MELANCONIUM Link.

M. pallidum Peck.
On dead limbs *Hicoria ovata*. Sporules + 20 x 5 μ, May 31, 1894 (*Nuttall*, 1514).

M. oblongum Berk.
On dead limbs *Juglans cinerea*. Sporules 20 x 10 to 2 μ, Dec. 5, 1893 (*Nuttall*, 1291, 236).

M. bicolor Nees.
On *Betula nigra*, May 2, 1894 (*Nuttall*, 1489).

THYRSIDIUM Mont.

T. hedericolum Carpini Sacc.
On dead shoots *Carpinus Caroliniana*, May 2, 1894 (*Nuttall*, 1486).

MARSONIA Fisch.

M. Juglandis (Lib.) Sacc.
On *Juglans cinerea*, June 22, 1894 (*Nuttall*, 1560).

M. Martini Sacc. & Ell.
On *Quercus alba, velutina, et Prinus*, Aug. 18, 1894 (*Nuttall*, 1674, 583).

CORYNEUM Nees.

C. cupulatum E. & E., Proc. Phila. Acad., 1894, 374.
Type habitat: On dead limbs *Tsuga Canadensis*, Short Creek, Dec. 16, 1893 (*Nuttall*, discov. 1317, 272).
Erumpent superficial. Acervuli tuberculiform, black, 1 to 1.5 mm. diameter, hollowed out so as to be cup-shaped above. Conidia clavate, sessile, 6 to 9 septate, brown, 60 to 80 x 12 to 15 μ.

C. pustulatum Peck.
On dead limbs *Castanea dentata*, Dec. 7, 1893 (*Nuttall*, 1383).

PESTALOZZIA De Not.

P. ———— sp.
On leaves *Geum Canadense*, Oct. 24, 1894 (*Nuttall*, 1734). Sporules 20 x 6 μ. Setæ 5 to 12 μ long.

P. funerea Desm.
On *Ipomœa pandurata*, Sept. 19, 1895. Spores 23 to 25 x 6 to 7.5 μ (*Nuttall*, 1862, 750).

P. Guepini Desm.
On leaves *Rhododendron maximum*, *R. Catawbiense* and *Azalia viscosa*. Spores 18 to 20 x 8 μ, Aug. 2, 1894 (*Nuttall*, 1149).

P. Jefferisii Ell?
On *Opulaster opulifolius*, sporules 10 to 15 x 4 to 5 and 25 x 5 μ May 7, 1894 (*Nuttall*, 1509).

P. Toxica E. & E., Proc. Phila. Acad., 1894, 374.
TYPE HABITAT: On leaves *Rhus radicans*, Aug. 18, 1894 (*Nuttall*, 1670, 567).

Spots and perithecia as in *Phyllosticta rhoicola* E. & E. Sporules clavate-oblong, 4-septate, 12 to 15 x 4 to 5 μ, 3 intermediate cells pale brown, end cells short, conical, hyaline, the upper cell with a crest of 3 short, spreading hyaline bristles 6 to 7 μ long. Distance between the two extreme cells 12 μ, pedicels shorter than the spores.

STEGANOSPORIUM Corda.

S Castaneæ Lib?
On *Castanea dentata*, Nov. 14, 1893 (*Nuttall*, 1275, 221).

S. piriforme (Hoffm.) Corda.
On dying *Acer rubrum*, June 12, 1894 (*Nuttall*, 1553).

S. muricatum Bon.
On dead limbs *Betula nigra* in drift-wood along river, Oct. 21, 1895. Spores 35 to 50 x 15 to 18 μ (*Nuttall*, 1878).

USTILAGINACEÆ.

USTILAGO Pers.

U. SEGETUM (Bull.) Dittm.
On living heads of wheat and oats, Monongalia Co., near Morgantown; Lewis Co., near Alum Bridge; Taylor Co., near Thornton (*Millspaugh*).

U? ——— sp.
On under surface of newly fallen leaves *Asimina triloba*, Nov. 20, 1893 (*Nuttall* discov. 1288; 233).

U. MAYDIS (DC.) Corda.
On living ears and tassels of sweet corn, prevalent in Monongalia Co., 1891; near Morgantown (*Millspaugh*). On garden corn, July 31, 1894 (*Nuttall*, 1636).

U. Avenæ lævis, K. & S.
On oats, Sewell Mountain, alt. 2,600 ft., Aug. 23, 1894 (*Nuttall*, 1678).

TILLETIA Tul.

T. TRITICI (Bjerk.) Wint.
  Ustilago tritici, C. Bauhin. On living leaves of wheat, Monongalia Co., near Morgantown (*Millspaugh*).

UROCYSTIS Rabenh.

U. ANEMONES (Pers.) Schrœt.
  On living leaves and under stem cuticle of *Actæa alba*, Monongalia Co., near Morgantown (*Millspaugh*).

UREDINACEÆ.

UROMYCES Link.

U. Polygoni (Pers.) Fckl.
  Uredospores on *Polygonum erectum*, Aug. 2, 1894 (*Nuttall*, 1642).

U. TRIFOLII (Hedw.) Lev.
  On living leaves, *Trifolium pratense*, Mason Co., near Point Pleasant (*Millspaugh*). On *Trifolium*, July 13, 1894 (*Nuttall*, 1604).

U. APPENDICULATUS (Pers.) Link.
  On living leaves of pole beans, Monongalia Co., near Morgantown (*Millspaugh*).

U. Caladii (Schwein) Farl.
  On *Arisæma triphyllum* (uredospores), May 28, 1894 (*Nuttall*, 1511).

U. Hyperici (Schwein) Curt.
  Æcidiospores on *Hypericum mutilum*, at Rupert's, July 25, 1894 (*Nuttall*, 1625).

U. Terebinthi (DC.)
  On living leaves *Rhus radicans*, Oct. 17, 1895 (*Nuttall*, 1876).

U. LESPEDEZÆ (Schwein) Peck.
  On living leaves *Lespedeza violacea*, Monongalia Co., near Morgantown (*Millspaugh*).

U. HEDYSARI-PANICULATI (Schwein) Farl.
  On living leaves *Meibomia canescens*, Mason Co., near Point Pleasant (*Millspaugh*). On leaves *M. paniculata*, July 17, 1894 (*Nuttall*, 1610).

U. Howei Pk.
  On *Asclepias Syriaca*, Oct. 13, 1895 (*Nuttall*, 1869).

MELAMPSORA Cast.

M. farinosa (Pers.) Schrœt.
  On *Salix nigra*, Oct. 17, 1893. Spores at first hyaline (22 x 13 μ) but the granules finally turn yellow (22 μ), and perfectly fill the spore (25 x 18 μ) (*Nuttall*, 1107).

PUCCINIA Pers.

P. Helianthi Sz.
   On *Helianthus decapetalus*, Sept. 19, 1895 (*Nuttall*, 1851).

P. Violæ (Schum.) DC.
   On *Viola hastata*, æcidial stage; æcidia 18 x 25 µ. A species of small reddish caterpillar found feeding on the spores, April 30, 1893. Uredo stage on *Viola rotundifolia* or *V. blanda*, April 30, 1893 (*Nuttall*, 906).

P. Convolvuli (Pers.) Cast.
   On *Convolvulus repens*. Æcidium May 3, Uredo June 14, Teleuto. Oct. 4, 1894; all on same vine (*Nuttall*, 1516).

P. Convolvuli ——————— var.
   On dead stems of *Convolvulus repens*, Feb. 19, 1895 (*Nuttall*, 1793).

P. PIMPINELLÆ (Strauss) Link.
   On living leaves *Osmorrhiza Claytonii*, Monongalia Co. near Morgantown (*Millspaugh*).

P. Menthæ Pers.
   On *Cunila origanoides*, Nov. 27, 1894. Teleutospores 28 x 20 µ, not yet verruculose (*Nuttall*, 1753).

P. coronata Corda.
   On *Holcus lanatus*, Uredo. June 30, 1893; teleuto. Nov. 1, 1893, on same specimen. Length of pedicel 5 to 7.5 µ very thick, corona + 38 µ broad, teeth 12.5 µ, teleutospores 50 x 15 µ (*Nuttall*, 1265).

P. RUBIGO-VERA (DC.) Wint.
   On leaves *Triticum vulgare*, Wood Co., near Kanawha Station (*Millspaugh*).

P. Caricis (Schum.) Reb.
   On *Carex* sp. July 10, 1894, uredospores and teleutospores (*Nuttall*, 1590).

P. HIERACII (Schum.) Mart.
   P. flosculosorum Roehl. On living leaves *Carduus lanceolatus*, Mason Co., near Point Pleasant (*Millspaugh*). On *Taraxacum Taraxacum*, Oct. 20, 1894 (*Nuttall*, 1721).

P. SUAVEOLENS (Pers.) Rostr.
   On living leaves *Carduus lanceolatus*, Wood Co., near Kanawha Station (*Millspaugh*).

P. Sorghi Schwein.
   Uredo. and teleutospores on *Zea Mays*, Sept. 7, 1894 (*Nuttall*, 1676).

P. Conoclinii Seymour.
   On *Eupatorium cœlestinum*, Sept. 18, 1895 (*Nuttall*, 1849).

P. Anemones-Virginiana Sz.
   On *Anemone Virginiana*, Sept. 18, 1895 (*Nuttall*, 1850).

P. Heuchera Sz.
  P. Spreta Pk., *P. Tiarella* B. & C.   On *Tiarella cordifolia*.   Oct. 21, 1895 (*Nuttall*, 1886).

P. Smilacis Schwein.
  Uredospores on *Smilax glauca*, Oct. 14, 1894 (*Nuttall*, 1708).

P. Podophylli Schwein.
  On *Podophyllum peltatum*, May 31, 1894 (*Nuttall*, 1515).

P. tenuis Burrill.
  On *Eupatorium ageratoides*, June 1, 1894 (*Nuttall*, 1519).

P. Asteris Duby.
  On *Aster cordifolius*, Nov. 24, 1894 (*Nuttall*, 1758, 645).

GYMNOSPORANGIUM, Hedw.

G. clavariiforme (Jacq.) Rees.
  Æcidiospores on *Cratægus* sp., Aug. 2, 1894 (*Nuttall*, 1637).

G. juniperinum (Linn.) Fr.
  Teleutospores on *Juniperus Virginiana*, April 27, 1894 (*Nuttall*, 1473).

G. MACROPUS Link.
  On *Juniperus Virginiana*, Mercer Co., near Princeton (*Millspaugh*). Æcidia on *Pyrus coronaria*, Aug. 2, 1893 (*Nuttall*, 1157).

PHRAGMIDIUM Link.

P. POTENTILLÆ (Pers.) Karst.
  On *Potentilla Canadensis*, uredospores, Monongalia Co., near Morgantown (*Millspaugh*). On *P. Canadensis*, uredo. March 15, 1894, teleutospores, Oct. 5, 1894 (*Nuttall*, 1400?).

P. subcorticium (Schrank.) Wint.
  On *Rosa humilis*, June 18, 1893 (*Nuttall*, 1008).

COLEOSPORIUM Lev.

C. SENECIONIS (Pers.) Fr.
  On living leaves of *Pinus echinata* (æcidia), Wood Co., near Lockhart's Run (*Millspaugh*).

C. SONCHI (Pers.) Lev.
  On living leaves *Vernonia Noveboracense*, Mason Co., near Point Pleasant (*Millspaugh*). On *Aster cordifolius*, Dec. 3, 1894 (*Nuttall*, 1760).

C. Ipomœæ (Schwein) Burrill.
  On *Ipomœa pandurata*, Oct. 15, 1894.   Spores 85 × 23 µ (*Nuttall*, 1720, 608).

C. Vernoniæ B. & C.
  On *Vernonia Noveboracense* at Rupert's, Sept. 25, 1894. Spores 100 × 30 µ (*Nuttall*, 1702, 595).

C. Solidaginis (Schwein.) Thum.
On *Solidago Canadensis*, June 19, 1894 (*Nuttall*, 1550).

ÆCIDIUM Pers.

Æ. Impatientis Schwein.
On *Impatiens biflora*, June 21, 1894 (*Nuttall*, 1558).

Æ. HOUSTONIANUM Schwein.
On *Houstonia cærulea* (spermogonia), Monongalia Co., near Morgantown (*Millspaugh*). On leaves of *H. longifolia*, June 1, 1894 (*Nuttall*, 1518).

PERIDERMIUM Lev.

P. PECKII Thum.
On living leaves *Tsuga Canadensis*, Pocahontas Co., near Traveler's Repose (*Millspaugh*).

P. BALSAMEUM Peck.
Under surface living leaves *Abies Balsamea*, Randolph Co., Shades-of-Death (*Millspaugh*).

UREDO Pers.

U. Agrimoniæ (DC.) Schroet.
On *Agrimonia striata*, July 10, 1894 (*Nuttall*, 1591).

U. CÆOMA NITENS Schwein.
Cæoma nitens. On living leaves *Rubus hispidus*, Monongalia Co., near Morgantown (*Millspaugh*). On *Rubus villosus*, May 2, 1893 (*Nuttall*, 907).

PERISPORIACEÆ.

PODOSPHÆRA Kunze.

P. OXYACANTHÆ (DC.) De By.
On living leaves of *Prunus* cult., *Cratægus oxyacantha* and *Diospyros Virginiana*, Monongalia Co., near Morgantown (*Millspaugh*).

P. TRIDACTYLA (Wallr.) DeBy.
On living leaves of *Prunus* cult., Cabell Co., near Huntington (*Millspaugh*).

SPHÆROTHECA Lev.

S. HUMULI (DC.) Burrill.
On living leaves *Agrimonia striata*, Preston Co., near Terra Alta (*Millspaugh*).

S. Castagnei Lev.
On living leaves *Erechtites hieracifolia*, Nov. 11, 1894. Asci 78 x 58 μ, spores+20 x 12 μ (*Nuttall*, 1740).

PHYLLACTINIA Lev.

P. suffulta (Reb.) Sacc.
On living leaves *Castanea dentata*, Oct. 1893 (*Nuttall*, 1315), and on *Magnolia Fraseri*.

UNCINULA Lev.

U. Ampelopsidis, Peck.
   On cultivated grapes, Monongalia Co., near Morgantown (*Millspaugh*). On leaves *Parthenocissus quinquefolia*, Sept. 20, 1894 (*Nuttall*, 1683).

U. Americana How.
   On leaves *Vitis cordifolia*, Sept. 20, 1894 (*Nuttall*, 1684).

MICROSPHÆRA Lev.

M. Alni (DC.)
   On leaves *Castanea dentata*, alt. 1,800 ft., Oct. 20, 1893 (*Nuttall*, 1218, 169).

M. erineophila Peck.
   On leaves *Fagus atropunicea*, Dec. 20, 1894 (*Nuttall*, 1773).

M. Grossulariæ Lev.
   On leaves *Sambucus Canadensis*, Oct. 5, 1894 (*Nuttall*, 1693).

M. elevata Burr. and Bess.
   On leaves of *Catalpa Catalpa*, alt. 2,200 ft. Oct. 2, 1894 (*Nuttall*, 1690).

M. Russellii Clint.
   On *Oxalis stricta*, Aug. 9, 1694 (*Nuttall*, 1650).

M. Vaccinii Schw.
   On *Epigœa repens*, Oct. 1893. Threads slender, sharply pointed, somewhat rough, asci 5-spored, 50 to 65 x 30 to 40 μ, spores 18 to 20 x 10 to 11 μ (*Nuttall*, 1255).

M. quercina Schw.
   On *Quercus palustris*, at Rupert's, Aug. 26, 1894 (*Nuttall*, 1686, 591).

ERYSIPHE (Hedw.) DC.

E. Cichoracearum DC.
   On *Xanthium Canadense*, Nov. 1, 1893 (*Nuttall*, 1223), and on *Eupatorium purpureum*.

E. communis (Wall.) Fr.
   On *Eupatorium ageratoides*, Oct. 14, 1894 (*Nuttall*, 1707).

E. Graminis DC.
   On living leaves *Poa pratensis*, Preston Co., near Terra Alta (*Millspaugh*).

E. Liriodendri Schw.
   On *Liriodendron Tulipifera* in deep shade, Short Creek, alt. 1,150 ft., Oct. 9, 1894 (*Nuttall*, 1697).

EUROTIUM Link.

E. herbariorum (Wigg) Link.
   On damp leaves *Liriodendron Tulipifera* neglected in plant press, Sept. 1, 1894 (*Nuttall*, 1681).

ASTERINA Lev.
A. Leemingii E. & E.
On *Galax aphylla*, May 4, 1894 (*Nuttall*, 1493, 475).

DIMEROSPORIUM Fckl.
D. Galactis E. & E.
On leaves of *Galax aphylla* in conjunction with the last species above, May 4, 1894 (*Nuttall*, 1576, 475).

D. Collinsii (Schw.) Thum.
On leaves *Amalanchier Canadensis*, Glade Creek, May 4, 1894 (*Nuttall*, 1490, 472).

SCORIAS Fries.
S. spongiosa (Schw.) Fr.
On living *Fagus atropunicea*, at Rupert's July 26, 1894. Spores 16 to 18 x 5 μ (*Nuttall*, 1634).

SPHÆRIACEÆ.
VALSA Fries.
V. ceratophora Tul.
On fire killed *Hicoria minima*, Oct. 17, 1894. On *Acer saccharinum*, L. Asci 38 x 5 μ, spores 7.5 to 10 x 1.5 to 1.75 μ (*Nuttall*, 1711).

V. Diospyri E. & E. Proc. Phil., Acad., 340 (1894).
TYPE HABITAT: On dead limbs *Diospyros Virginiana*, Dec. 10, 1893 (*Nuttall*, discov. 1308, 253).
Stroma consisting of the slightly blackened substance of the bark, convex, about 2 mm. diameter, not circumscribed. Perithecia 4 to 10 in a stroma, subglobose, .25 to .33 mm. diameter, necks converging and united above in a small, black disk which perforates the pustuliform-elevated epidermis, but does not rise above it. Ostiola short, conic-cylindrical, with a smooth, round opening crowded and finally obliterating the disk. Asci clavate-lanceolate, p. sp. 25 x 5 μ, 8-spored, paraphysate. Sporidia allantoid, hyaline, 8 to 10 x 1.5 to 2 μ. Spermogonia (Cytispora), stroma multilocular gray inside, opening by a single, central pore. Spermatia allantoid, hyalins, moderately curved, 4 to 5 x 1.25 μ.

V. etherialis E. & E. Proc. Phila. Acad., 341 (1894).
TYPE HABITAT: On dead limbs of *Acer rubrum*, Feb. 1894 (*Nuttall*, discov. 1304, 373).
Stromata cortical, thickly scattered, convex 1 to 1.5 mm. diameter. Perithecia 6 to 12 together, circinate, buried in the unaltered substance of the bark, small, 150 to 250 μ diameter their short necks terminating in an erumpent, compact fascicle of obtuse, black, slightly umbilicate ostiola closely embraced by the epidermis and scarcely rising above it. Asci (p. sp.) fusoid, 15 to 22 x 4 to 4.5 μ, stipitate, 8-spored. Sporidia biseriate, allantoid, hyaline, curved, slender, 5 to 6 x about 1 μ. When well developed, the epider-

mis is raised into subdiscoid pustules in which the slight protuberances indicate the position of the subjacent perithecia.

V. delicatula C. & E. has fewer, larger perithecia and broader sporidia. *V. miscrospora* Cke. & Plowr. has also larger perithecia and yellowish sporidia, and the ostiola are more or less distinctly sulcate, indicating its close relationship to *Eutypella*. In *V. etherialis* the sporidia both in and out of the asci are perfectly hyaline.

V. coronata (Hoffm.) Fr.

On young, fire-killed *Castanea dentata*, Nov. 14, 1893 (*Nuttall*, 1263, 209).

V. albopuncta E. & E., sp. nov.

TYPE HABITAT: On dead limbs *Liriodendron Tulipifera*, Oct., 1894 (*Nuttall*, discov. 1712, 600).

Stromata minute (.5 to 7.5 mm.), subseriate, included in the thick epidermis and not penetrating the inner bark, white throughout, and without any distinct circumscribing line. Perithecia 3 to 6 in a stroma, pale slate-color, 110 to 130 μ diameter; necks very slender, terminating in minute, subglobose, slate-colored ostiola tardily erumpent around the margin of the minute, snow-white, pulverulent disk. Asci clavate-cylindrical, 50 x 6 μ, short-stipitate, obtuse above, paraphysate? Sporidia biseriate, allantoid, hyaline, moderately curved, 6 to 9 x 1.5 to 2 μ.

A beautiful species. The lines of snow-white disks, which barely perforate the ruptured epidermis and are closely surrounded by its torn and slightly raised margin, present a very neat appearance.

V. Abietis Fr.

On *Tsuga Canadensis* Short Creek, alt. 1,100 ft., Feb. 2, 1893 (*Nuttall*, 1349).

V. Vitis (Schw.) Fckl.

On *Vitis* sp., March 26, 1894 (*Nuttall*, 1432).

V. præstans B. & C.

On dead twigs *Nyssa aquatica*, Nov. 14, 1893 (*Nuttall*, 1247). Spores 10 to 12 x 3 to 4 μ.

V. Nyssæ Cooke.

On fire killed *Nyssa aquatica*, Nov. 14, 1893 (*Nuttall*, 1689).

V. subclypeata C. & Peck.

On young fire killed *Sassafras Sassafras*, Nov. 14, 1893 (*Nuttall*, 1262, 209).

V. ambiens (Pers.) Fr.

On *Asimina triloba, Cornus florida* and *Aralia spinosa*, Feb. 18, 1894 (*Nuttall*, 1383).

V. Chionanthi E. & E., Proc., Phila. Acad., 340 (1894).

TYPE HABITAT: On dead limbs of *Chionanthus Virginica*, March, 1894 (*Nuttall*, discov. 1456, 228).

Perithecia 4 to 10, globose, .25 to .33 mm. diameter, buried in the unchanged substance of the bark, with convergent necks, terminating in short-cylindrical, obtuse, perforated ostiola erumpent in a close fascicle perforating and slightly raising the bark. Asci clavate, p. sp. 40 to 45 x 8 to 10 μ, 8-spored, paraphysate? Sporidia allantoid, hyaline, 12 to 15 x 3.5 to 4.5 μ, biseriate above.

Spermogonia (*Cytispora Chionanthi* E. & E.) buried in the bark flask-shaped, .5 to .75 μ diameter, multilocular, the cells soon confluent, the apex erumpent and perforated by a single pore. Sporules allantoid, 4 to 6 x 1 to 1.25 μ, borne on basidia branched above, the branches erect, straight, nucleate, 7 to 10 μ long.

V. pauperata C. & E.
On *Acer rubrum*, March 26, 1894 (*Nuttall*, 1444, 423).

V. leucostoma (Pers.) Fr.
On peach tree, Dec. 2, 1894 (*Nuttall*, 1768).

V. Linderæ Peck.
On *Benzoin Benzoin*, April 11, 1895 (*Nuttall*, 1796).

EUTYPELLA Nits.

E. densissima E. & E., Proc. Phila. Acad., 341 (1894).
TYPE HABITAT: On dead limbs *Aralia spinosa*, Feb., 1894 (*Nuttall*, 363).

Stromata scattered, cortical, depressed-conical, 2 to 3 mm. diameter, not circumscribed, but staining the bark olive-gray. Perithecia numerous, often 50 to 70 in a stroma, 100 to 120 μ diameter, closely packed, their slender necks terminating in obtusely conical, 4 cleft, black, densely crowded ostiola erumpent in a brown disk surrounded by the ruptured epidermis. The disk is soon obliterated, so that only the crowded, black, subshining ostiola are seen. Asci clavate-fusoid, p. sp. 25 to 30 x 4 μ. Sporidia biseriate, allantoid, hyaline, moderately curved, 8 to 10 x 1.5 to 2 μ.

E. rugiella (C. & E.) Sacc.
On *Acer rubrum*, May 4, 1893 (*Nuttall*, 921).

E. stellulata (Fr.) Sacc.
On *Robinia Pseudacacia*, March 29, 1893 (*Nuttall*, 33).

E. Platani Sz.
On *Platanus occidentalis* in drift. Spores 7.5 to 8 x 1.5 to 2 μ. Oct. 21, 1895 (*Nuttall*, 1885).

EUTYPA Tul.

E. spinosa (Pers.) Tul.
On dry dead logs, June 29, 1893 (*Nuttall*, 1105).

E. milliaria (Fr.) Sacc.
On river drift wood, April 20, 1894. Asci 150 x 6 μ spores 10 x 2 μ (*Nuttall*, 1477).

DIATRYPE Fr.

D. Stigma (Hoffm.) Fr.
On *Castanea dentata*, April 15, 1895 (*Nuttall*, 1799).

D. platystoma (Schw.) Berk.
On *Magnolia Fraseri*, Feb. 8, 1894 (*Nuttall*, 1380, 342).

DIATRYPELLA C. & DeNot.

D. verruciformis (Ehrh.) Nits.
On *Alnus rugosa*, Nov. 20, 1893 (*Nuttall*, 1258).

ROSELLINIA DeNot.

R. aquila (Fr.) De Not.
On dead limbs, March 21, 1893 (*Nuttall*, 919, 19).

R. corticium (Schw.) Sacc.
On dead oak, alt. 1,800 ft., Short Creek. Spores 25 to 30 x 10 to 12.5 μ. Dec. 16, 1893 (*Nuttall*, 1310).

R. subiculata (Schw.) Sacc.
On dead dry *Robinia Pseudacacia*, July 15, 1893. Perithecia clustered or connate, each 3 to 5 μ, black, ostiola papillate. Spores 9 to 12.5 x 5 to 6 μ somewhat inequilateral, elliptical, colored. (*Nuttall*, 1129).

R. pulveracea (Ehrh.) Fckl.
On dead wood, Nov. 1893. Spores 10 to 15 x 7 to 9 μ (*Nuttall*, 1338).

R. millegrana (Schw.) Sacc.
On dead *Platanus occidentalis*, Aug. 2, 1893 (*Nuttall*, 1161).

R. abietina trichota C. & Ell.
On *Pinus Virginiana*, Jan. 7, 1895 (*Nuttall*, 1784, 675).

BOMBARDIA Fr.

B. fasciculata Fr.
On wet dead limb, *Magnolia Fraseri*, on ground, Sep. 16, 1895 *Nuttall*, 1830).

ANTHOSTOMA Nits.

A. micrœcium E. & E., Proc. Phila. Acad., 344 (1894).
TYPE HABITAT: On dead limbs *Asimina triloba*, Feb. 12, 1894 (*Nuttall*, discov. 1377).
Stroma cortical, faintly circumscribed, 1 to 1.5 mm. diameter, orbicular, convex. Perithecia 4 to 8 in a stroma, globose, minute (200 to 250 μ), circinate, necks slender, short, converging, with the minute papilliform ostiola erumpent in a small, black, hemispherical disk, which barely pierces the pustuliform-elevated epidermis, and is closely embraced by it. Asci cylindrical, 80 to 110 x 8 to 10 μ, paraphysate 8-spored. Sporidia uniseriate, elliptical, brown, continuous, 2-nucleate, 12 to 14 x 6 to 7 μ.
Distinguished by its very small stroma and perithecia.

A. microplacum (B. & C.) Sacc.
   On *Sassafras Sassafras*, alt. 1,800 ft., March 21, 1893 (*Nuttall*, 915).

XYLARIA Hill.

X. polymorpha (Pers.) Grev.
   On dead logs, April 7, 1893 (*Nuttall*, 890).

X. corniformis Fr.
   On rotten limb, Sept. 9, 1893. On *Magnolia Fraseri*, Nov. 1895 (*Nuttall*, 1194).

X. Hypoxylon (Linn.) Grev.
   On dead log, March 10, 1893 (*Nuttall*, 807).

X. flabelliformis (Schw.) B. & C.
   On *Carpinus Caroliniana*, May 13, 1893 (*Nuttall*, 957).

X. Cornu-Damæ (Schw.) Berk.
   On wet rotten log, alt. 2,000 ft., Aug. 24, 1893. Spores 20 to 21 x 4.5 μ (*Nuttall*, 1179).

USTULINA Tul.

U. vulgaris Tul.
   On dead and rotting stumps, March 8, 1893 (*Nuttall*, 954).

HYPOXYLON Bull.

H. atroviride E. & E., Proc. Phila. Acad., 346 (1894).
   TYPE HABITAT: On bark of dead tree, *Betula* or *Quercus*, Dec., 1893 (*Nuttall*, discov. 1320, 275).
   Stroma pulvinate, 1 to 1.5 cm. across, and about 4 mm. thick, orbicular, covered above with a thin (.5 mm.) carbonaceous crust, which is soon covered by a dark green layer of the ejected spores, laterally and internally dirty-umber color. Perithecia (which constitute the entire inner substance of the stroma) ovate compressed, and including the long, stout neck, about 3 mm. long and 1 mm. broad below. Ostiola papilliform, soon covered and obscured by the ejected sporidia. Asci cylindrical 100 x 3.5 to 4 μ (p. sp. 40 to 45 long), paraphysate, 8-spored. Sporidia uniseriate, oblong-elliptical, pale brown under the microscope, 2-nucleate, 4.5 to 5.5 x 2 μ.
   This is a well-marked species. The substance of the stroma, except the superficial carbonaceous layer, is friable, and in this respect as well as the color resembles *H. Petersii* B. & C., from which, however, in other respects it is very distinct.

H. coccineum Bull.
   On *Aralia spinosa*, alt. 1,300 ft., Aug. 18, 1893 (*Nuttall*, 1173, 140).

H. Nuttallii E. & E., Proc. Phila. Acad., 346 (1894).
   TYPE HABITAT: On bark of dead *Magnolia Fraseri* at Glade Creek, May 1894 (*Nuttall*, discov. 1494, 477).

Stromata gregarious, subconfluent, depressed-hemispherical or strongly convex, 3 to 6 mm. diameter, purplish-black, mammillose. Perithecia small (about .25 mm.) scattered irregularly through the stroma, which is rather soft and brownish within. Ostiola crowning the mammillose projections on the surface of the stroma, papilliform, soon deciduous, leaving a round perforation. The asci in the spec. examined had disappeared. Sporidia brown, oblong-elliptical, sub-inequilateral, 7 to 8 x 3 to 4 μ (exceptionally 9 x 5 μ).

H. Howeianum Peck..
On decorticated *Magnolia Fraseri*, alt. 1,800 ft., Sept. 12, 1893 (*Nuttall*, 1203, 158).

H. FUSCUM (Pers.) Fr.
On dead and decorticated *Acer saccharum*, Grant Co., near Bayard (*Millspaugh*). On dead *Alnus rugosa*, Oct. 31, 1893. Spores 12 x 6 to 7 μ (*Nuttall*, 1221).

H. multiforme Fr.
On dead *Betula* sp., alt. 1,800 ft., Short Creek, Aug. 11, 1893 (*Nuttall*, 1147).

H. perforatum (Schw.) Fr.
On dead twig, Feb. 3, 1894. On *Ilex opaca*, Dec. 28, 1894 (*Nuttall*, 1351). Spores 10 x 5 μ. On *Magnolia Fraseri*, Nov. 1895.

H. rubiginosum (Pers.) Fr.
On dead hard wood of *Robinia Pseudacacia*, Feb. 25, 1893 (*Nuttall*, 949, 39).

H. Sassafras (Schw.) Berk.
On *Sassafras Sassafras*, March 21, 1893. Spores 8 to 12 x 3 to 4 μ (*Nuttall*, 917).

H. stigmateum Cooke
On living *Quercus* sp., originating under the outer bark which it pushes off, or at times remains attached at one edge and stands away like a lid. Asci, total length, 150 x 10 μ, fertile portion 120 x 10 μ, spores black, elliptical, 16 to 20 x 6 to 10 μ. Feb. 2, 1894 (*Nuttall*, 1350).

H. colliculosum (Schw.) Nits.
On *Rhododendron maximum*, alt. 1,800 ft., Short Creek, Dec. 16, 1893 (*Nuttall*, 1330, 289).

DALDINIA DeNot.

D. concentrica (Bolt.) C. & DeN.
On bark of dying *Acer* sp., April 15, 1893 (*Nuttall*, 905).

D. vernicosa (Schw.) C. & DeN.
On dead trees, March, 1895 (*Nuttall*, 1790).

NUMMULARIA Tul.

N. punctulata (B. & Rav.) Sacc.
On dead branch of *Quercus* sp., Aug. 16, 1893 (*Nuttall*, 1151).

GNOMONIELLA Sacc.

G. Coryli (Batsch.) Sacc.
On *Corylus Americana* at Rupert's, Aug. 5, 1894 (*Nuttall*, 1647).

PHYSALOSPORA Niessl.

P. Ilicis (Schl.) Sacc.
On dead leaves of *Ilex opaca*, July 21, 1894. Asci 7.5 to 10 µ (*Nuttall*, 1616).

TRICHOSPHÆRIA Fckl.

T. pulchriseta Peck.
On dry firm splinters of dead log, alt. 1,800 ft., Short Creek, March 6, 1894 (*Nuttall*, 1412, 382).

BOTRYOSPHÆRIA Ces. & DeNot.

B. Quercuum (Schw.) Sacc.
On *Quercus* sp., *Vitis* sp., *Pinus Virginiana*, *Opulaster opulifolius*, and *Parthenocissus quinquefolia*. Perithecia 2 to 10 (*Nuttall*, 925, 14).

B. Quercuum ———————var.
On cultivated *Rubus*, Feb. 25, 1895 (*Nuttall*, 1794, 685).

B. Araliæ Curtis.
On *Aralia spinosa*, Feb. 24, 1894. Spores 20 to 30 x 8 to 10 µ (*Nuttall*, 1395).

B. pyriospora (Ellis) Sacc.
On *Chionanthus Virginica*, March 28, 1894. Asci, fertile portion, 75 x 15 µ (*Nuttall*, 1438).

B. Hibisci ———————forma.
On *Celastrus scandens*, April 27, 1895 (*Nuttall*, 1819, 707). Spores 26 to 35 x 6 to 7.5 µ.

CRYPTOSPORELLA Sacc.

C. compta (Tul.) Sacc.
On dead limbs of *Fagus atropunicea*, Nov. 17, 1893. Asci, fertile portion, 100 x 12.5 to 15 µ, spores granular 22 x 10 µ (*Nuttall*, 1256).

SPHÆRELLA Ces. & DeNot.

S. maculiformis (Pers.) Awd.
On leaves of *Castanea dentata* on ground, Dec. 13, 1893 (*Nuttall*, 1314).

S. conicola Sacc.
    On dead cones of *Tsuga Canadensis*, Dec. 16, 1893. Spores 10 x 3 μ (*Nuttall*, 1311).

S. Gaultheriæ C. & P.
    On *Gaultheria procumbens*, June 8, 1894 (*Nuttall*, 1534).

S. nyssæcola Cooke?
    On *Nysa aquatica*, Oct. 10, 1894 (immature) (*Nuttall*, 1719, 607).

DIDYMELLA Sacc.

D. Physocarpi E & E., Proc. Phila. Acad., 1894, 335.
    TYPE HABITAT: On *Opulaster opulifolius*, May 12, 1894 (*Nuttall*, 1507, 488).
    Perithecia gregarious, covered by the pustuliform epidermis, about .25 mm. diameter, white inside, depressed-globose, the papilliform ostiolum barely penetrating the epidermis. Asci clavate-cylindrical, short-stipitate, 85 to 90 x 10 to 12 μ, paraphysate, 8-spored. Sporidia biseriate, fusoid, 4-nucleate, uniseptate, constricted at the septum, hyaline, 19 to 22 x 4 to 5 μ, mostly a little curved.

MELANCONIS Tul.

M. modonia Tul.
    On *Castanea dentata*, Nov. 14, 1893 (*Nuttall*, 1274, 221).

HERCOSPORA Tul.

H. Tiliæ (Fr.) Tul.
    On *Tilia heterophylla*, Feb. 16, 1894. Spores 18 x 7.5 μ (*Nuttall*, 1834, 346).

DIAPORTHE Nits.

D. Gladioli E. & E. ?
    On *Caulophyllum thalictroides*, July 8, 1894. Asci 38 x 5 to 7 μ, spores septate, 4-nucleate, about 10 x 3 μ (*Nuttall*, 1603, 553).

D. Araliæ E. & E., Proc. Phila. Acad., 339 (1894).
    TYPE HABITAT: On *Aralia spinosa*, Feb. 2, 1894 (*Nuttall*, discov. 1356, 312).
    Stroma buried in the wood and circumscribed by a penetrating, black line, elliptical, about 5 x 4 mm. Perithecia buried in the stroma, few (6 to 10) globose, .5 to .75 mm. diameter, their short-cylindrical ostiola projecting from a black, tubercular disk seated on the surface of the wood and perforating the pustuliform-elevated epidermis, but scarcely rising above it. Asci clavate-cylindical, 40 to 45 x 5 to 6 μ, paraphysate, 8-spored. Sporidia biseriate, oblong, 4-nucleate, becoming uniseptate and slightly constricted, hyaline, obtuse, 12 to 13 x 2.5 to 3 μ.
    Allied to and resembling *D. ocularia* C. & E.

D. CHOROSTATE **Halesiæ** E. & E., Proc. Phila. Acad., 339 (1894).
    TYPE HABITAT: On dead limbs of *Mohrodendron Carolinum*, May, 1894 (*Nuttall*, discov. 1541).

Perithecia 4 to 8, loosely circinate. .75 mm. horn-color inside, becoming nearly black, sunk in the wood, necks converging with their obtuse, smooth, hemispherical ostiola erumpent in a close fascicle, closely surrounded by the ruptured epidermis. Asci slender, 55 to 60 x 6 to 7 μ, short-stipitate. Sporidia subbiseriate, fusoid-oblong, hyaline, 2 to 4-nucleate, becoming uniseptate and slightly constricted, straight, 12 to 15 x 2.5 to 3 μ.

There is no distinct circumscribing line around the stroma, but the inner surface of the bark is uniformly blackened.

D. Chorostate Tetrapteræ E. & E., Proc. Phila. Acad., 339 (1894).

TYPE HABITAT: On dead limbs *Mohrodendron Carolinum*, May, 1894 (*Nuttall*, discov. 1542).

Stroma cortical, 1.5 to 2 mm. diameter, surrounded by a black line which does not penetrate the wood. Perithecia 4 to 12, circinate, 5 mm. diameter, sunk to the wood and leaving their impress on its surface but not penetrating it. Ostiola obtusely rounded and perforated, erumpent in a compact fascicle and closely surrounded by the ruptured epidermis. Asci clavate-cylindrical, 75 to 80 x 12 μ. Sporidia biseriate, oblong-fusoid, slightly curved, subobtuse, hyaline, uniseptate and constricted at the septum, each cell with a large nucleus, 9 to 22 x 5 to 7 μ.

Differs from *D. Halesiæ* E. & E., in its smaller perithecia, not sunk in the wood, and its much larger sporidia.

D. Chorostate Aceris Fckl.

On *Acer saccharinum*, L., Jan. 26, 1894 (*Nuttall*, 1739).

D. Hydrangeæ E. & E., sp. nov.

TYPE HABITAT: On dead stems *Hydrangea arborescens*, Nov. 1894 (*Nuttall*, discov. 1756, 641).

Perithecia scattered, ovate-globose, 350 to 380 μ diameter, sunk in the wood, which is not at all discolored. Ostiola stout, erumpent, short-cylindrical, or conic-cylindrical, the apex papilliform. Asci (p. sp.) oblong-cylindrical, 50 to 60 x 8 μ, 8-spored, obscurely paraphysate. Sporidia biseriate, oblong elliptical, hyaline, uniseptate, slightly constricted, 12 to 15 x 3 to 4 μ, ends subacute.

This may be the *Sphæria* spoken of by Schweinitz as found by him on limbs of *Hydrangea*, in company with his *Sphæria* (*Teichospora*) *Hydrangeæ*.

D. Chorostate cercophora (Ellis.) Sacc.

On *Ilex opaca* Dec. 23, 1893, March 15, 1894 (*Nuttall*, 1333).

D. Chorostate oncostoma (Du B.) Fckl.

On *Robinia Pseudacacia*, April 7, 1894. Spores 17 to 19 x 4 to 5 μ (*Nuttall*, 1446).

D. Chorostate sociata (C. & E.) Sacc.

On *Benzoin Benzoin*, April 13, 1895. Helminthospores 75 to 100 x 15 μ. 7-septate (*Nuttall*, 1798).

D. Chorostate obscura (Peck) Sacc.

On *Rubus villosus*, Feb. 13, 1893 (*Nuttall*, 1313, 260).

D. Euporthe aculeata (Schw.) Sacc.
On *Phytolacca decandra*, Nov. 14, 1894. Asci 40 to 55 x 6 to 7.5 µ. Spores 12.5 to 18 x 3 to 3.5 µ (*Nuttall*, 1754, 639).

D. Tetrastaga rostellata (Fr.) Nits.
On *Rubus odoratus*, May 31, 1894 (*Nuttall*, 1528, 560).

AMPHISPHÆRIA Ces. & DeNot.

A. pinicola Rehm.
On *Pinus rigida* at Glade Creek, and on *Pinus Virginiana*, May 4, 1894. Spores very variable + 35 x 12 µ (*Nuttall*, 1499, 480).

VALSARIA Ces. & DeNot.

V. exasperans (Ger.) Sacc.
On *Juglans cinerea*, Nov. 3, 1893 (*Nuttall*, 1260, 202).

MASSARIA DeNot.

M. Magnoliæ E. & E., sp. nov.
TYPE HABITAT: On bark of dead limbs *Magnolia acuminata*, April 25, 1895 (*Nuttall*, discov. 1818, 700, 705).
Perithecia scattered, buried in the bark, depressed-globose, .75 to 1.25 mm. diameter, the subconical ostiolum piercing but not perceptibly raising the bark. Asci broad oblong, p. sp. 150 to 200 x 55 to 65 µ with a very short, nodular stipe, 8-spored, paraphysate. Sporidia crowded-biseriate, oblong or clavate-oblong, 3 to 5-septate, mostly 3-septate, when young, hyaline at first, finally deep brown and then with only one distinct septum, though often 1 to 4 other faint septa can be seen. There is a distinct constriction at the main septum, which is a little below the middle of the spore, but none at the other faint septa which are often wanting. The sporidia measure 65 to 80 x 20 to 25 µ, larger than in *M. fœdans* (Tode), which has sporidia about 50 x 20 µ, 3-septate and constricted at all the septa, besides being more distinctly narrowed below.

LEPTOSPHÆRIA (Pers.) DeNot.

L. Doliolum (Pers.) DeNot.
On *Polymnia Uvedalia* and *Helianthus decapetalus*, Nov. 16, 1894. Perithecia covered by outer bark. Asci, fertile part 110 x 6 µ, stipitate, spores overlapping at ends. Spores 22 x 4 µ, 23 x 4.5 µ, 25 x 5 µ, 27 x 5 µ, 30 x 5 µ; 3-septate, nucleate, constricted at septum when mature; straight, one-sided, or curved (*Nuttall*, 1744).

L. vagabunda Sacc.
On dead stems *Hydrangea arborescens*, Nov. 21, 1894. Asci 125 to 150 x 7.5 µ total length (*Nuttall*, 1745).

L. ogilviensis (B. & Br.) Ces. & DeNot.
On *Cimicifuga racemosa*, July 4, 1894 (*Nuttall*, 1586).

L. clavigera (C. & E.) Sacc.
On old stems *Phytolacca decandra*, Nov. 14, 1894 (*Nuttall*, 1741).
Spores + 43 x 6 µ.

L. orthogramma (B. & C.)
On *Zea Mays*, Aug. 10, 1895 (*Nuttall*, 1832, 722).

MELANOMMA Nits & Fckl.

M. Pulvis-pyrius (Pers.) Fckl.
On decorticated *Magnolia Fraseri*, alt. 1,800 ft., Short Creek, Sept. 10, 1893. Spores 15 x 3.5 µ (*Nuttall*, 1200).

TREMATOSPHÆRIA Fckl.

T. vitigena E. & E., sp. nov.
TYPE HABITAT: On old, decaying wood of *Vitis rupestris*, April, 1894 (*Nuttall*, discov. 454).
Perithecia gregarious, sunk in the wood all except the obtuse, convex apex, .5 to .75 mm. diameter, depressed-globose, the buried part rather thin-walled, the erumpent, convex apex thick, solid, like the stromatic shield of *Clypeosphæria*. Ostiolum papilliform, soon perforated. Asci clavate-cylindrical, paraphysate, 8 spored, 86 to 100 x 10 to 12 µ. Sporidia sub-biseriate, fusoid-oblong, 3-septate, and constricted, subacute, pale-brown, 20 to 25 x 6 to 7 µ.

PSEUDOVALSA Ces. & DeNot.

P. sigmoidea (C. & E.)
On dead limbs *Quercus Prinus*. Spores 50 to 88 x 5 to 7 µ (*Nuttall*, 1828, 717).

LASIOSPHÆRIA Ces. & DeNot.

L. ovina (Pers.) Ces. & DeNot.
On *Juglans cinerea*, and parasitic on *Hypoxylon*, Short Creek, alt. 1,800 ft., Dec. 16, 1893. Spores 50 to 60 x 6 to 7.5 µ. Asci 135 x 12.5 µ (*Nuttall*, 1322).

ACANTHOSTIGMA DeNot.

A. decastylum (Cooke) Sacc.
On dead log, June 18, 1893 (*Nuttall*, 1018).

HERPOTRICHIA Fckl.

H. diffusa (Schw.)
On dead twig, Sept. 10, 1893 (*Nuttall*, 1197).

CALOSPORA Sacc.

C. aculeans (Schw.) Sacc.
On *Rhus hirta* and *copallina*, March 29, 1894. Spores 15 to 17 x 3 µ, aculeate (*Nuttall*, 1440).

C. Rhoina (C. & Ell.) Sacc.
  On *Rhus hirta*, Dec. 9, 1893. Spores 15 to 18 x 5? µ hyaline, 4-nucleate, uniseptate constricted at septum. (*Nuttall*, 1348, 306).

PYRENOPHORA Fr.

P. calvescens (Fr.) Sacc.?
  On *Chenopodium anthelminticum*, Aug. 10, 1895 (*Nuttall* 1845, 736).

TEICHOSPORA Fckl.

T. nitida E. & E.
  On *Rubus villosus*, Apr. 25, 1895. Asci 75 x 12? µ. Spores 20 to 23 x 9 to 10 µ (*Nuttall*, 1817, 706).

PLEOSPHÆRIA Speg.

P. corticola E. & E., Proc. Phila. Acad., 1894, 332.
  TYPE HABITAT: On bark of *Pinus rigida*, Glade Creek, June 24, 1894 (*Nuttall*, discov. 1582).
  Perithecia scattered, superficial, ovate, 300 to 400 µ diameter, carbonaceo-membranaceous, pilose-strigose, hairs 100 to 200 x 5 to 6 µ, soon opaque, very faintly and sparingly septate, here and there collected into closely compacted fascicles resembling stout bristles. Ostiolum papilliform, obtuse. Asci oblong-cylindrical, abruptly short-stipitate, 80 to 100 x 20 to 25 µ. Paraphysate? Sporidia crowded, acutely elliptical, nearly hyaline at first, becoming olive-brown and 5 to 7 septate and muriform, but not constricted.
  Comes near *P. strigosa* Sacc., but perithecia rather smaller, not depressed, and hairs fasciculate.

P. ———— sp.
  On *Tecoma radicans*, Feb. 20, 1894 (*Nuttall*, 1414, 385).

CUCURBITARIA Gray.

C. Fraxini E. & E.
  On *Fraxinus Americana*, Apr. 27, 1894 (*Nuttall*, 1523).

C. elongata (Fr.) Grev.
  On *Robinia Pseudacacia*, Jan. 15, 1894 (*Nuttall*, 1783).

OPHIOBOLUS Riess.

O. porphyrogonus (Tode) Sacc.
  On *Vernonia Noveboracensis*, Apr. 24, 1895 (*Nuttall*, 1820, 702).

O. acuminatus (Sow.)
  On *Zea Mays*, Aug. 10, 1895 (*Nuttall*, 1839, 728).

O. fulgidus (C. & P.) Sacc.
  On *Vernonia Noveboracensis*, Apr. 24, 1895 (*Nuttall*, 1821, 703).

CRYPTOSPORA Tul.

C. femoralis (Peck) Sacc.
On *Alnus rugosa*, Feb. 25, 1894. Asci 60 to 75 x 12.5 to 15 μ. Spores 50 to 65 x 3.5 μ in middle and enlarging to 5 μ at each end (*Nuttall*, 1318).

C. cinctula (C & P) Sacc?
On *Castanea dentata*, Dec. 8, 1893. Asci about 75 x 7.5 μ. Spores 60 to 75 x 4 μ, hyaline, nucleate, curved, often slightly thickened toward one end (*Nuttall*, 1296, 245).

C. trichospora (C. & P.) Sacc?
On *Quercus sp.*, Feb. 1894. Spores+50? μ (*Nuttall*, 1450).

HYPOCREACEÆ.

HYPOMYCES Fr.

H. rosellus (Alb. & Schw.) Tul?
On *Hymenocetum* on *Magnolia Fraseri*, March 6, 1894 (*Nuttall*, 1417, 387).

H. aurantius (Pers.) Fckl.
On *Stereum* sp. Sept. 3, 1893 (*Nuttall*, 1198). Short Creek, alt. 1,800 ft.

NECTRIA Fr.

N. cinnabarina (Tode) Fr.
On *Aralia spinosa*, March 5, 1894. Asci 75 x 7.5 μ. Spores 20 to 23 x 4 to 5 μ (*Nuttall*, 1405, 374).

N. coccinea (Pers.) Fr?
On bark of dead *Magnolia Fraseri*, March 1894. Asci 65 x 7.5 μ. Spores 10 to 15 x 3.5 to 6 μ (*Nuttall*, 1472, 451).

N. ditissima Tul.
On dead and fallen *Robinia Pseudacacia*, on *Magnolia Fraseri*, Oct. 17, 1893 (*Nuttall*, 1115, 162).

N. vulpina, Cke.
On bark of dead *Ulmus pubescens*? Oct. 17, 1894. Spores 10 x 5 μ, 1-septate, 2-guttulate (*Nuttall*, 1216, 164).

N. episphæria (Tod.) Fr.
On dead fallen twigs, Aug. 15, 1893 (*Nuttall* 1175, 143).

APONECTRIA Sacc.

A. inaurata (B. & Br.) Sacc.
On *Rhus copallina*, Mar. 24, 1894 (*Nuttall*, 1431). Microspores 3 x 1 μ. Spores 10 to 12.5 x 3 μ.

HYPOCREA Fr.

H. Virginiensis E. & E. Proc. Phila. Acad., 442 (1893).
TYPE HABITAT: On leaves of *Rhododendron maximum*, Aug. 12, 1893 (*Nuttall*, discov. 1163).

Epiphyllous, stroma carnose, scattered, sub-hemispherical or depressed-turbinate, 1 to 2 mm. diameter, of a yellowish gray color, subtruncate above and obscurely margined (when mature). Perithecia buried in the stroma, ovate, membranaceous, 110 to 150 μ diameter. Ostiola hemispherical, prominent, black, broadly perforated and sometimes collapsed. Asci clavate-cylindrical, p. sp. 40 to 45 x 7 to 8 μ, short-stipitate, filiform-paraphysate, 8-spored. Sporidia biseriate, oblong-fusoid, yellowish-hyaline, uniseptate, slightly constricted at the septum, obtusely pointed at the ends, 10 to 12 x 3 to 3.5 μ.

H. viridans B. & C. seems to differ in its hidden ostiola (ostiolis latitantibus).

H. tenerrima E. & E., Proc. Phila. Acad., 442 (1893).

TYPE HABITAT: Incrusting moss, leaves, twigs, living *Gaultheria procumbens*, etc. July 1893 (*Nuttall*, discov. 1138, 123).

Perithecia gregarious, minute (.16 mm.), clothed (except the black apex) with a thin white tomentum, seated on a thin snow-white, tomentose-arachnoid subiculum. Asci cylindrical, 40 x 3 μ, without paraphyses, 8-spored. Sporidia uniseriate, oblong, obtuse, hyaline, 5 to 6 x 2 μ, with a single nucleus in the centre (becoming uniseptate)?

This is closely allied to *H. subcarnea* E. & E., but differs in the color of the subiculum, the black apex of the perithecia, the narrower asci, and rather longer sporidia.

HYPOCREOPSIS Karst.

H. riccoidea (Bolt.) Karst.
On *Kalmia latifolia*, alt. 2,000 ft., Aug. 24, 1893. Spores apparently moniliform (*Nuttall*, 1178).

GIBBERELLA Sacc.

G. Saubinetii (Mont.) Sacc.
On *Asparagus officinalis*, Nov. 1, 1893 (*Nuttall*, 1243, 190).

BROOMELLA Sacc.

B. Ravenelii (Berk.) Sacc.
On *Acer rubrum*, April 4, 1894 (*Nuttall*, 1461, 439).

PLEONECTRIA Sacc.

P. Missouriensis (E. & E.)
On dead stick, March 10, 1893 (*Nuttall*, 871).

CORDYCEPS Fries.

C. militaris (Linn.) Link.
In laurel thicket on ground, Aug. 12, 1893, Keeney's Creek (*Nuttall*, 1205, 161).

C. ophioglossoides (Ehrh.) Link.
   On ground in wet woods, Aug. 24, 1893 (*Nuttall*, 1172).

DOTHIDEACEÆ.
PHYLLACHORA Nits.

P. GRAMINIS (Pers) Fckl.
   On living leaves of *Hysterix Hysterix*, Fayette Co., near Nuttallburg (*Millspaugh*). On *Elymus Canadensis*, Oct. 28, 1893 (*Nuttall*, 1250, 192).

P. Caricis (Fr.) Sacc?
   On *Korycarpus diandrus*, March 1, 1894 (immature) (*Nuttall*, 1402, 238).

DOTHIDELLA Speg.

D. Ulmæ (Sz.) E. & E.
   On *Ulmus pubescens*, Nov. 5, 1894 (*Nuttall*, 1749, 629).

PLOWRIGHTIA Sacc.

P. MORBOSA (Schw.) Sacc.
   On limbs of cultivated Plum and Cherry, Monongalia Co., near Morgantown (*Millspaugh*).

MICROTHYRIACEÆ.
MYIOCOPORON Speg.

M. Smilacis (De Not) Sacc.
   On *Smilax* sp. April 12, 1895 (*Nuttall*, 1807).

LOPHIOSTOMACEÆ.
LOPHIOTREMA Sacc.

L. Nucula (Fr.) Sacc.
   On dead heartwood of *Liquidambar Styraciflua*, April 20, 1894 (*Nuttall*, 1479, 459).

LOPHIDIUM Sacc.

L. nitidum E. & E., Proc. Phila. Acad., 333 (1894).
   TYPE HABITAT: On *Vitis* cult. Feb. 2, 1894 (*Nuttall*, discov. 1336, 295).
   Perithecia scattered, semi-erumpent, small (200 to 250 μ diameter) black and shining, subhemispherical, the flattened base immersed in the bark. Ostiolum compressed, thin, narrow, sometimes obsolete. Asci cylindrical, short (8 to 10 μ), stipitate, about 100 x 10 to 12 μ, paraphysate, 8-spored. Sporidia uniseriate, oblong-elliptical, yellow-brown, 5 to 7-septate with a longitudinal septum running through two or more cells, 19 to 22 x 8 to 10 μ, ends mostly rounded and obtuse, not at all or only slightly constricted in the middle.

L. compressum (Pers.) Sacc.
   On *Salix nigra falcata*, April 23, 1894.   Asci 70 to 100 x 15 μ, Spores 25 to 30 x 8 to 10 μ (*Nuttall*, 1481, 461).

HELVELLACEÆ.
MORCHELLA Dill.

M. esculenta (Linn.) Pers.
   Along an old road among grasses and leaves under an oak, April 18, 1893 (*Nuttall*, 897).

M. angusticeps Peck.
   On ground, Short Creek, April 18, 1893. Spores 25 to 28 x 15 μ (*Nuttall*, 895).

M. _____ sp.
   On ground, Short Creek, 5 cm. high, with smooth spores 28 x 17 μ, April 18, 1893 (*Nuttall*, 896).

GYROMITRA Fr.

G. curtipes Fr.
   On ground below cliffs, Short Creek. Asci, fertile part 50 x 16 to 18 μ. Total length 350 μ. Spores 22 to 30 x 10 μ, 2-nucleate (*Nuttall*, 1813).

HELVELLA Linn.

H. macropus (Pers.) Karst?
   On ground in woods at base of cliffs, July 15, 1893 (*Nuttall*, 1097).

MITRULA Fr.

M. phalloides (Bull.) Chev.
   In water on leaves of *Quercus Prinus*, etc., spores to 20 x 3 μ. Masterson's Glade, June 11, 1893 (*Nuttall*, 935).

M. lutescens B & C.
   On ground and on dead logs in deep woods, alt. 2,000 ft. (*Nuttall*, 1024).

SPATHULARIA Pers.

S. clavata (Schæf.) Sacc?
   In woods among dead leaves, stipe dark brown, spores *short* 25 μ, July 10, 1893 (*Nuttall*, 1087).

VIBRISSEA Fr.

V. truncorum (A. & S.) Fr.
   On wet dead sticks, alt. 1,800 ft., June 15, 1893 (*Nuttall*, 991).

PEZIZACEÆ.
RHIZINA Fr.

R. inflata (Schæf.) Quél.
On sandstone rock in sandy loam. Blackish-brown, spreading, 2 to 9 cm. x 1 to 3 cm., convex, loosely attached to the soil by strong rootlets from all parts of the underside, margin strongly rolled inward. Asci 375? to 415 x 12.5 μ, spores hyaline, apiculate, large 40 x 10 μ. Keeney's Creek, Nov. 3, 1893 (*Nuttall*, 1224).

GEOPYXIS Pers.

G. nebulosa Cooke.
On dead wet wood at low and high altitudes, Aug. 10, 1893 (*Nuttall*, 1177).

G. carbonaria A. & S.
On ground upon which logs had been burned the previous autumn, April 18, 1893 (*Nuttall*, 908).

PEZIZA Dill.

P. aurantia Pers.
On wet and freshly crushed sandstone ballast, and on filling of sandstone cut on railroad. Spores curiously rough and apiculate at both ends. Nov. 3, 1893 (*Nuttall*, 1225).

P. badia Pers.
On ground, Short Creek, April 18, 1893 (*Nuttall*, 922).

OTIDEA Pers.

O. onotica ochracea Fr.
On ground and on rotten *Tsuga Canadensis*, July 14, 1893. Asci 175 x 10 μ total length, spores 11 to 13 x 7.5 μ, nuclei 2 (*Nuttall*, 1098).

HUMARIA Fr.

H. echinosperma Peck.
In soil of ditch, July 20, 1894 (*Nuttall*, 1630).

SARCOSCYPHA Fr.

S. coccinea Jacq.
On sticks, on ground in damp shady place, March 20, 1893 (*Nuttall*, 852).

S. floccosa Schw.
On a stick in a laurel thicket, alt. 2,000 ft., July 12, 1893 (*Nuttall*, 1112).

LACHNEA Fr.

L. SCUTELLATA, Linn.
On rotting log *Fagus atropunicea* and under bark of wet log *Quercus alba*, Monongalia Co., near Morgantown (*Millspaugh*). On rotten wood in old drift of mine, and on bare sandy ground among pebbles, Short Creek, May 11-17, 1893 (*Nuttall*, 936).

L. umbrarum Fr.
On open bare sandy soil, Short Creek, May, 1893 (*Nuttall*, 1107).

L. hirta Schum.
On floor of cave, July 25, 1893 (*Nuttall*, 1127).

L. vitellina Pers.
On dead log. Asci 235 x 15 μ, Short Creek, July 2, 1893 (*Nuttall*, 1114).

L. erinaceus, Schw.
On underside of log *Quercus alba*, Monongalia Co., near Morgantown (*Millspaugh*).

SCLEROTINIA Fuckel.

S. trifoliorum Eriks.
On ground in open woods, May 18, 1893 (*Nuttall*, 960).

HELOTIUM Fr.

H. lacteum E. & E., Proc. Phila. Acad., 145 (1893).
On bare log, Dec. 16, 1893. Pure white, stipitate, plane .4 to .6 mm. asci clavate 95 to 110 x 7.5 μ. Spores curved 16 to 25 x 3 to 4 μ, nuclei 4, paraphyses slender, Short Creek near the falls (*Nuttall*, 1318).

H. herbarum (Pers.) Fr.
On *Polymnia Uvedalia*, Nov. 15, 1894. Cups 6 to 12 mm. diameter, stipes 1 to 2 mm. long. Asci 55 to 75 x 7.5 to 10 μ. Spores 12 to 15 x 2.5 μ (*Nuttall*, 1755).

H. confluens Schw.
On dead logs, alt. 1,800 ft. Oct. 20, 1893 (*Nuttall*, 1213).

H. citrinum (Hedw.) Fr.
On wet dead log. Short Creek, alt. 1,800 ft. Sept. 12, 1893. (*Nuttall*, 1201).

H. castaneum Sacc.
On leaves of *Rhododendron maximum*. Short Creek, alt. 1,800 ft. Sept. 12, 1893 (*Nuttall*, 1206).

PHIALEA Fr.

P. virgultorum (Vahl.) Sacc.
On old grape twigs on wet ground. Asci 105 x 7.5 μ. Spores 18 x 4 μ. Nov. 1, 1894 (*Nuttall*, 1735).

PSEUDOHELOTIUM Fckl.

P. fibrisedum (B. & C.) Sacc.
On wet dead wood of *Juglans cinerea*, Dec. 5, 1894. More than 2 mm diameter, margin ciliate, red-maculate; asci oblong short-stipitate, total length 65 x 7.5 μ (*approx.*), paraphyses filiform. Spores hyaline 1-septate (?) oblong, straight or slightly curved, 12 to 18 x 3 μ (*Nuttall*, 1764).

CYATHICULA De Not.

C. quisquiliaris E. & E., Proc. Phila. Acad., 451 (1893).

TYPE HABITAT: On dead racemes of Quercus Prinus, on dead leaves, on rock in woods, April 2, 1893 (*Nuttall*, discov. 941).

Gregarious, sessile, 1 to 1.5 mm. diameter, cup-shaped, disk pale with a tinge of brick color when dry, dull, dirty-white and purpuraceo-squammulose outside, margin distinctly cleft-toothed and incurved when dry. Asci cylindrical, subsessile, 55 to 65 x 6 to 7 μ, with filiform paraphyses scarcely thickened above. Sporidia uniseriate, or sub-biseriate above, elliptical, hyaline, continuous, 6 to 8 x 3 to 4 μ.

CHLOROSPLENIUM Fr.

C. æruginosum (Œder) De N.

On loose core inside dead tree, Nov. 6, 1893. Disk more brilliant than margin in light and when young, in shadow varying to pure white. Asci over 105 x 7.5 μ total length, spores guttate 12.5 x 3 μ (Nuttall, 1235).

C. versiforme (Pers.) Karst.

On rotten mossy log, Short Creek, Oct. 28, 1893 (*Nuttall*, 1238).

C. Schweinitzii Fr.

Top of oak log, Dec. 10, 1893. Yellow in spring, green in autumn and winter (*Nuttall*, 1276).

MOLLISIA Fr.

M. Dehnii (Rabenh) Karst.

On *Potentilla Monspeliensis*, July 21, 1894 (*Nuttall*, 1618).

M. pinastri (C. & P.) Sacc.

On *Pinus Virginiana*, Dec. 3, 1894 (*Nuttall*, 1763).

M. CINEREA (Batsch.) Karst.

Peziza cinerea Batsch. On decayed log, Monongalia Co., near Morgantown (*Millspaugh*).

PYRENOPEZIZA Fuckel.

P. lacerata (C. & P.) Sacc.

On *Rubus odoratus*, May 31, 1894. Asci 45 to 50 x 5 to 6 μ. Spores 8 to 12.5 x 2 to 2.5 μ (*Nuttall*, 1529).

TAPESIA Pers.

T. sanguinea (Pers.) Fckl.

On dead log, and on *Magnolia Fraseri* and *Juglans cinerea*, June 10, 1894 (*Nuttall*, 1546).

T. fusca (Pers.) Fckl.

On rotten burned log *Tsuga Canadensis;* on dead rotting log *Juglans cinerea*, alt. 1,300 ft. Asci 45 to 92 x 495 μ. Spores 8 to 10 x 2 μ. Short Creek, Feb. 2, 1894 (*Nuttall*, 1365).

T. subiculata (Schw.) Sacc.
On wet sticks, June 15 and Oct. 25, 1893. Spores large, 10 x 3 μ (*Nuttall*, 992).

LACHNELLA Fr.

L. Virginica E. & E., Proc. Phila. Acad. 349 (1894).
TYPE HABITAT: On decaying wood of *Magnolia Fraseri*, Feb., 1894 (*Nuttall*, discov. 1410, 380).
Gregarious, sessile, .75 to 1.2 mm. diameter. Disk pallid, concave, nearly closed when dry, margin fringed with brown septate hairs, 100 to 125 x 3 μ, outside clothed with shorter reddish-brown hairs. Asci about 50 x 5 μ, clavate-cylindrical, short stipitate, paraphysate, 8-spored. Sporidia sub-biseriate, oblong, 6 to 8 x 1.5 to 2.5 μ.

TRICHOPEZIZA Fuckel.

T. ——————— sp.
Torn end of firm dead tree, Short Creek, alt. 1,800 ft. Dec. 16, 1893 (*Nuttall*, 1326).

T. albo-lutea (Pers.) Sacc.?
On rotten log, Short Creek, June 18, 1893, stipitate (*Nuttall*, 1013).

T. capitata (Peck) Sacc.
On leaves *Quercus palustris* on ground in woods, alt. 2,000 ft., June 18, 1893. At Rupert's, July 26, 1894 (*Nuttall*, 1011).

DASYSCYPHA Fr.

D. virginea (Batsch) Fckl.
On dead sticks on wet cliff, and on wet dead wood of *Juglans cinerea*, June 12, 1893 (*Nuttall*, 841).

D. Ellisiana (Rehm.) Sacc.
On *Pinus rigida*, top of Cavendish cliff, April 8, 1894 (*Nuttall*, 1447).

HELOTIELLA Sacc.

H. Nuttallii E. & E., Proc. Phila. Acad., 351 (1894).
TYPE HABITAT: On wet shady side of rotten log, March 15, 1894 (*Nuttall*, discov. 1425, 397).
Ascomata gregarious, sessile, flat-hemispherical, .5 to 1 mm. diameter, cup-shaped when fresh, contracted and sub-spherical when dry with only a small round apical opening, orange color throughout, disk watery-orange, outside and fringed margin paler. Substance fibrous, the fibers prolonged above so as to make a marginal fringe of pale yellow, roughish straight hairs. Asci clavate-cylindrical, sessile, curved, 50 to 60 x 5 to 6 μ. Paraphyses filiform, hardly thickened above, with a series of orange-colored, globose nuclei. Sporidia biseriate, oblong, hya-

line, obtuse, uniseptate, but not constricted, 8 to 10 x 2.5 to 3 μ. The outside of the ascomata is slightly hairy so that the species might be referred to *Solenopeziza* if that is really worthy of generic distinction.

DERMATELLA Karst.

D. viticola E. & E., Proc. Phil. Acad., 352 (1894).

TYPE HABITAT: On dead shoots of *Vitis* (cult.) Nov. 1893 (*Nuttall*, discov. 1337, 295).

Sessile, convex-discoid and pale when moist, concave and flesh-color when dry, and then scarcely projecting above the surface of the bark. .50 to .75 mm. diameter. Asci clavate-cylindrical, about 70 x 12 μ, with filiform paraphyses, 8-spored, sub-sessile. Sporidia subbiseriate, oblong elliptical, hyaline, 1 to 3-septate (3 to 4-nucleate at first), 15 to 18 x 6 to 6.5 μ.

BELONIDIUM Mont.

B. aurelia (Pers.) DeNot.

Peziza aurelia, Pers. On a dead leaf in rotten log, Monongalia Co., at Little Falls (*Millspaugh*).

ERINELLA Sacc.

E. miniopsis (Ell.) Sacc.

On wet rotten wood, May 1893 (*Nuttall*, 934).

ASCOBOLACEÆ.

ASCOBOLUS, Pers.

A. furfuraceus Pers.

On old dung of cow, June 8, 1893 (*Nuttall*, 974).

A. carbonarius Karst.

On bare spots where logs were burned by forest fire the previous winter, associated with *Geopyxis carbonaria*. It appears that only the prolonged burning of large logs makes proper habitat for this species, as it does not grow where the fire was light. May 20, 1893 (*Nuttall*, 926).

ASCOPHANUS Boud.

A. granuliformis (Cr.) Boud. ?

On dung of cow, Dec. 1893 (*Nuttall*, 1340, 298).

A. carneus (Pers.) Boud.

On dung of cow Oct. 10, 1893 (*Nuttall*, 1249, 182).

DERMATEACEÆ

URNULA Fr.

U. Craterium (Schw.) Fr.

On dead twigs on ground, Short Creek, April 15, 1893 (*Nuttall*, 898).

DERMATEA Fr.

D. Chionanthi E. & E?
Macrostylospores of this species? on *Chionanthus Virginica*, March, 25, 1894 (*Nuttall*, 1454, 426).

D. lobata Ellis.
On the maculæ of *Pestalozzia Guepinii* on leaves of *Rhododendron maximum*. Asci 130 x 12.5 μ spores 15 x 8 μ. Aug. 15, 1895 (*Nuttall* 1162, 132).

TYMPANIS Tode.

T. Oxydendri E. & E., Proc. Phila. Acad., 352 (1894).
TYPE HABITAT: On dead limbs of *Oxydendron arboreum*, Dec. 12, 1893 (*Nuttall* discov., 1296, 258).

Cespitose, 3 to 5 together, erumpent, at length deciduous, black .5 to .75 mm. diameter, contracted below into a short thick stipe, margin subundulate. Asci cylindrical 110 to 130 x 15 to 18 μ including the short stipe. Paraphyses slender, abundant, Sporidia numerous, minute, oblong, hyaline or yellowish 2.5 to 3 x 1 μ, Allied to *T. fasciculata*, but asci larger and sporidia smaller.

CENANGELLA Sacc.

C. Aceris (Hazsl.) Sacc.
On bark of dying *Acer rubrum*, June 10, 1894. Sporidia 15 x 6 μ (*Nuttall*, 1554).

SCLERODERRIS Fr.

S. rhabarbarina (Berk) E. & E.
On *Rubus Baileyanus*, Dec. 8, 1893, Short Creek. Asci total length 63 to 75 x 17 to 21 μ, 8-spored, clavate, very short stipitate. Spores 20 to 27 x 6 to 7.5 μ, nucleate, becoming clearly 3-septate and rather one-sided (*Nuttall*, 1294, 242).

S. pallidula (Cooke) Sacc.
On dead branches and bark of *Acer saccharinum*, L., Feb. 26, 1894. On *Oxydendron arboreum*. Sporidia 20 to 22 x 7 μ (*Nuttall*, 1408, 665).

BULGARIACEÆ.

LEOTIA Hill.

L. lubrica (Scop.) Pers.
On ground, alt. 1,800 ft., Short Creek, Aug. 14, 1893 (*Nuttall*, 1150).

ORBILIA Fr.

O. rubella (Pers.)
On decorticated log, *Liriodendron Tulipifera*, Sept. 19, 1895 (*Nuttall*, 1858, 748).

O. vinosa (A. & S.) Karst.
On *Poria spissa*, Nov. 6, 1893 (*Nuttall*, 1261).

O. occulta (Rehm) Sacc.
On dead log, Aug. 20, 1893 (*Nuttall*, 1202).

O. coccinella (Somm.) Karst.
On dead log *Juglans cinerea*, Short Creek, July 25, 1893 (*Nuttall*, 1134, 663).

O. Xanthostigma Fr.
On decorticated limbs *Magnolia Fraseri*, Sept. 1895 (*Nuttall*, 1855, 742, 743).

BULGARIA Fr.

B. inquinans (Pers.) Fr.
In clefts of bark of trees and railroad ties, Oct. 10, 1893 (*Nuttall*, 1210).

CORYNE Tul.

C. URNALIS (Nyl.) Sacc.
On rotting log *Fagus atropunicea*; under bark of *Quercus alba* log, Monongalia Co., near Morgantown (*Millspaugh*). On wet mossy logs, alt. 1,800 ft. and over, Oct. 10, 1893 (*Nuttall*, 1212, 167).

HOLWAYA Sacc.

H. ophiobolus (Ellis) Sacc.
On bark of dead *Magnolia Fraseri*, alt. 1,800 ft., Dec. 16, 1893, Short Creek (*Nuttall*, 1323, 279).

STICTACEÆ.
PROPOLIS Fr.

P. faginea (Schrad.) Karst.
On *Juglans cinerea* and on old board of *Liriodendron Tulipifera*, Dec. 5, 1894 (*Nuttall*, 1765, 660). On *Liquidambar styraciflua*.

P. Leonis (Tul.) Rehm.
On bark of *Pinus rigida* and *Virginiana*, June 31, 1894 (*Nuttall*, 1581).

STICTIS Pers.

S. fimbriata Schw.
On strobiles of *Pinus Virginiana*, alt. 2,000 ft., March, 1894 (*Nuttall*, 1468, 443). Sporidia 5 to 7 x 1.5 μ.

PHACIDIACEÆ.
RHYTISMA (Pers.) Fr.

R. punctatum (Pers.) Fr.
On leaves of *Acer Pennsylvanicum*, alt., 2,000 ft., Oct. 22, 1893 (*Nuttall*, 1217, 168).

R. decolorans Fr.
On *Xolisma ligustrina*, at Rupert's, July 26, 1894 (*Nuttall*, 1638, 569).

R. Prini Schwein.
On leaves of *Ilex verticillata*, at Rupert's, Sept. 7, 1894 (*Nuttall*, 1677).

PATELLARIACEÆ.
DURELLA Tul.
D. commutata Fckl.
On dead log, Short Creek, Dec. 16, 1893 (*Nuttall*, 1328).

LECANIDION Rabenh.
L. atratum (Hedw.) Rabenh.
On *Aralia spinosa*, Feb. 17, 1894. Sporidia 50 x 12.5 μ (*Nuttall*, 1390, 359).

L. Hamamelidis (Peck) Sacc.
On bark of *Hamamelis Virginica*. Sporidia 1 to 3 septate when mature. Dec, 18, 1894 (*Nuttall*, 1772).

CALICIACEÆ.
CALICIUM Pers.
C. tigillare (B. & Br.) Sacc.
On *Polyporus pergamenus*, Aug. 23, 1893 (*Nuttall*, 1159).

GYMNOASCACEÆ.
EXOASCUS Fckl.
E. DEFORMANS (Berk.) Fckl.
Taphrina deformans Tul. On leaves of *Amygdalus Persica*, Jefferson Co., near Charlestown (*Millspaugh*).

E. PRUNI Fckl.
Taphrina Pruni Tul. On fruits of *Prunus domestica*, Monongalia Co., at Morgantown (*Millspaugh*).

HYSTERIACEÆ.
GLONIUM Mühl.
G. stellatum Mühl.
On rotten oak plank, and on *Sassafras Sassafras*, July 28, 1893 (*Nuttall*, 1128).

G. parvulum (Ger.) Sacc.
On fence rails *Castanea dentata*, April 20, 1894 (*Nuttall*, 1496).

G. simulans Ger.
On old fence rails, alt. 2,000 ft., March 16, 1894. Asci 75 x 7.5 to 10 μ. Spores 13 to 18 x 5 μ. On *Juglans cinerea*, asci 65 x 10 μ. Spores 12 to 15 x 4 to 5 μ (*Nuttall*, 1415).

HYSTERIUM Tod.
H. Kalmiæ Schw.?
On dead *Kalmia latifolia*, Nov., 1893 (*Nuttall*, 1287, 232).

HYSTEROGRAPHIUM Corda.

H. insidens (Schw.) Sacc.
On old fence rails, April 6, 1894. Largest spores 43 x 7.5 μ, 11-septate (*Nuttall*, 1452).

H. subrugosum (C. & E.) Sacc.
On old fence rails, May 26, 1894. Spores 33 to 35 x 12.5 μ (*Nuttall*, 1522).

H. Mori (Schw.) Rehm.
On old fence rails, April 6, 1894 (*Nuttall*, 1451).

HYPODERMA DC.

H. Desmazieri DuBy.
On living leaves or *Pinus echinata*. Wood Co., near Lockhart's Run (*Millspaugh*).

H. virgultorum DC.
On *Rubus Baileyanus*, Dec. 5, 1893 (*Nuttall*, 1293).

H. commune (Fr.) Duby.
On *Hydrangea arborescens*, Nov. 3, 1893 (*Nuttall*, 1259). On old petioles *Aralia spinosa* (*Nuttall*, 1830, 719).

LOPHODERMIUM Chev.

L. Rhododendri (Schw.)
On *Rhododendron maximum*, Sept. 4, 1893 (*Nuttall*, 1192).

L. Pinastri (Schrad.) Chev.
On leaves of *Pinus rigida*, Short Creek, Aug. 2, 1893 (*Nuttall*, 1158).

L. culmigenum (Fr.) Karst.
On straw brought in from Ohio, May 24, 1894. Measurements of asci and spores prove to be the same as those of *L. arundinaceum* (Schrad.) Chev. (*Nuttall*, 1496).

OSTROPA Fr.

O. cinerea (Pers.) Fr.?
Issuing from cracks in a decorticated log, May 31, 1894 (*Nuttall*, 1526).

AGARICACEÆ.

AMANITA Pers.

A. verna Fr.
On ground in open woods, July 11, 1893. Spores round 7.5 μ (*Nuttall*, 964).

A. muscaria Linn.
Rooted on buried limb of *Betula lenta*, Grant Co., near Bayard (*Millspaugh*).
An ecarunculate form, apparently of this species, on leaf mold in deep woods, same locality.

A. muscaria alba Peck.
On ground in laurel thicket, Short Creek, alt. 2,000 ft. Has the odor of buttermilk. Spores 9 x 6 µ (*Nuttall*, 1131).

A. flavo-rubens Berk.
On ground in woods, Short Creek, July 6, 1893 (*Nuttall*, 1078).

A. polypyramis B. & C.
Among bushes, alt. 2,400 ft., July 6, 1893. Largest stipes 15 cm. long, thick, heavy and deep in ground. Pileus 15 cm. broad. Spores 10 x 6 µ (*Nuttall*, 1101).

AMANITOPSIS Roze.

A. nivalis (Grev.) Sacc.
In loam on rocks in laurel tangle, June 26, 1893 (*Nuttall*, 1004).

TRICHOLOMA Fr.

T. fumoso-luteum Peck?
On unknown substance, June 15, 1893, Short Creek (*Nuttall* 990).

CLITOCYBE Fr.

C. illudens Schwein.
On old stumps in clusters of about eight, dark and deep rich orange color throughout, +20 cm. x +12 cm. broad, stipe + 25 mm. thick. Spores +6 µ diameter, uneven. July 14, 1893 (*Nuttall*, 1093).

C. laccata Scop.
Common in wet sand, bank of Short Creek, alt. 2,000 ft., July 28, 1893. Spores 10 µ diameter, echinate (*Nuttall*, 1124).

COLLYBIA Fr.

C. radicata Relh.
On leaf mold in rich woods, Monongalia Co., near Morgantown (*Millspaugh*). May 17, 1893 (*Nuttall*, 980).

C. platyphylla Fr.
On mold and moss on trunk of tree, Short Creek, June 15, 1893 (*Nuttall*, 981).

C. velutipes Curt.
About roots of rotting stumps, Jan. 31, 1895 (*Nuttall*, 830).

C. conigenoides Ellis.
On last year's cones *Magnolia Fraseri*, Sept. 18, 1895 (*Nuttall*, 1848).

C. dryophila Bull.
In moss on log in deep woods, Grant Co., near Bayard (*Millspaugh*).

MYCENA Fr.

M. ———— sp.
White. On mossy stump, July 4, 1893 (*Nuttall*, 1019).

M. galericulata Scop.
 In rich woods under oak twig, and oak bark on log, Monongalia Co., near Morgantown (*Millspaugh*). On damp dead logs, May 7, 1893 (*Nuttall*, 930).

M. epipterygia Scop.
 On moss-covered log and in clefts of bark, Feb. 28, 1893 (*Nuttall*, 948).

OMPHALIA Fr.

O. campanella Batsch.
 On leaf mold at base of *Castanea dentata*, Preston Co., near Terra Alta (*Millspaugh*). On rotten log in thicket, June 18, 1893 (*Nuttall*, 1009).

PLEUROTUS Fr.

P. corticatus Fr.?
 On fallen *Acer* sp. Gills not anastomosing, July 28, 1893 (*Nuttall*, 1123).

P. sapidus Kalchbr.
 On dead log, Feb. 2, 1893 (*Nuttall*, 850).

P. serotinus Schrad.
 On dead trunks, Nov. 20, 1893 (*Nuttall*, 1267).

P. cyphelliformis Berk.
 On dead stems of *Polymnia Uvedalia*, Nov. 15, 1894 (*Nuttall*, 1742).

P. niger Fr.
 On bark of dead tree, May 13, 1893 (*Nuttall*, 953).

HYGROPHORUS Fr.

H. nitidus B. & C.
 On decayed log, May 14, 1893 (*Nuttall*, 968).

LACTARIUS Fr.

L. cilicioides Fr.
 On border of woods and swamp, July 4, 1893 (*Nuttall*, 1020).

RUSSULA Pers.

R. emetica Fr.?
 In woods, July 4, 1893 (*Nuttall*, 1021).

CANTHARELLUS Adans.

C. minor Peck?
 On ground in woods, alt. 2,000 ft., July 4, 1893 (*Nuttall*, 1023).

C. Wrightii Berk?
 Wet sand of river bank in shade, July 18, 1893. Whole plant light red except gills, which are little deeper red than salmon-color, gills decurrent, veined between, pileus more convex than

plane, and depressed edge wavy, rather tough. Largest 4 cm. broad, stem 5 cm. high, 5 mm. thick. Spores 7.5 to 8.5 x 3.5 to 5 μ, apparently rough and guttulate inward (*Nuttall*, 1104).

C. tubæformis Fr.?
On rotten wood in woods, alt. 2,000 ft., July 4, 1893 (*Nuttall*, 1022).

C. floccosus Schw.
On open bank of stream in laurel thicket, alt. 2,000 ft., June 20, 1893. Largest squamules .75 cm. long, thick and triangular, forming a cone which closes the funnel below the top an inch or more. Spores 15 x 7.5 μ (*Nuttall*, 992).

NYCTALIS Fr.

N. asterophora Fr.
On dead Agaric in deep damp woods, July 14, 1893. Stars 20 μ diameter (*Nuttall*, 1096).

MARASMIUS Fr.

M. semihirtipes Peck.
On dead leaves, sticks, etc., Short Creek, May 14, 1893 (*Nuttall*, 967).

M. ramealis (Bull.) Fr.
Very common on twigs and leaves in laurel thickets, June 15, 1893 (*Nuttall*, 994).

M. OPACUS B. & C.
Common on dead branches *Rhododendron maximum*, Grant Co., near Bayard (*Millspaugh*).

M. campanulatus Peck.
On dead leaves and sticks in damp woods, Short Creek, alt. 1,300 ft., Aug. 16, 1893 (*Nuttall*, 1153).

M. ROTULA (Scop.) Fr.
On dead limb of *Betula lenta*, Grant Co., near Bayard (*Millspaugh*). On stick in open woods, June 8, 1893 (*Nuttall*, 972).

LENTINUS Fr.

L. STRIGOSUS Fr.
On dead log *Betula lutea*, Grant Co., near Bayard (*Millspaugh*). On dead logs, common, May 6, 1893 (*Nuttall*, 904).

PANUS Fr.

P. stipticus (Bull.) Fr.
On fallen dead limb, Jan. 29, 1893 (*Nuttall*, 950).

P. dorsalis Bosc.
On *Tsuga Canadensis*, Sept., 1893 (*Nuttall* 1253, 196).

TROGIA Fr.

T. crispa (Pers.) Fr.
On various dead dry logs and limbs, March 21, 1893 (*Nuttall*, 875).

LENZITES.

L. betulina (Linn.) Fr.
On logs, Sept. 6, 1893 (*Nuttall*, 837).

L. SEPIARIA Fr.
On decorticated stumps *Picea Mariana,* Tucker Co., near Falls of Blackwater (*Millspaugh*).
A resupinate form on dead logs *Tsuga Canadensis* Grant Co.

L. abietina (Bull.) Fr.
On dead branches *Tsuga Canadensis*, alt. 1,600 ft., Dec. 15, 1893 (*Nuttall*, 1301).

L. corrugata Klot.
On *Castanea dentata*, alt. 1,800 ft., Dec. 19, 1893 (*Nuttall*, 1302).

SCHIZOPHYLLUM Fr.

S. COMMUNE Fr.
On bark log *Quercus alba*, Grant Co., near Bayard. On dead twig *Pyrus Malus*, Monongalia Co., near Morgantown (*Millspaugh*) On dead logs, Jan. 30, 1893 (*Nuttall*, 827).

VOLVARIA Fr.

V. BOMBYCINA (Pers.) Fr.
On dead insect sp? Monongalia Co., near Morgantown (*Millspaugh*).

CLITOPILUS Fr.

C. abortivus Fr.
Wet woods, alt. 1,800 ft, aborted specimens in quantity, Sept. 4, 1893 (*Nuttall*, 1190).

AGARICUS Linn.

A. Rodmani Peck.
On ground, June 28, 1893 (*Nuttall*, 1005).

A. campester Linn.
On lawn, June 24, 1893 (*Nuttall*, 1002).

A. silvicola Vitt.
In woods, Short Creek, alt. 1,150 ft. (*Nuttall*, 1699). Spores 5 to 7 x 3 to 4 μ.

A. silvaticus Schæff.
In woods, Short Creek, July 2, 1893 (*Nuttall*, 1117).

STROPHARIA Fr.

S. STERCORARIA Fr.
On decaying vegetable matter, Preston Co., near Terra Alta (*Millspaugh*).

HYPHOLOMA Fr.

H. SUBLATERITIUM Schæff.
Under bark log *Fraxinus Americana*, Monongalia Co., near Morgantown (*Millspaugh*).

H. elæodes Fr?
On sticks on ground, May 18, 1893 (*Nuttall*, 858).

COPRINUS Pers.

C. variegatus Peck?
On stick in shady place, Aug. 11, 1893 (*Nuttall*, 1143).

C. micaceus (Bull) Fr.
On bases of stumps in woods, July 8, 1893 (*Nuttall*, 1081).

C. domesticus (Pers.) Fr.
In woods on mixture of manure and leaf mold. June 29, 1893 (*Nuttall*, 1007).

C. semilanatus Peck?
In heavily manured asparagus bed in garden, Apr. 29, 1893 (*Nuttall*, 903).

C. ephemerus Fr.
On horse dung, July 2, 1893 (*Nuttall*, 1113).

C. angulatus Peck.
On baked soil where log had been burned, with *Peziza carbonaria*, May 8, 1893 (*Nuttall*, 932).

PANÆOLUS Fr.

P. CAMPANULATUS Linn.
On cow dung in deep coniferous woods, Grant Co., near Bayard (*Millspaugh*). Plentiful on manured lawn, May 8, 1893, (*Nuttall*, 933).

PSATHYRELLA Karst.

P. disseminata Pers.?
In rotten mold about the base of a stump, a mass about 1 meter containing perhaps thousands of specimens. Specimens 3 to 5 cm. high, thin, fleshless. Pileus 1 cm. broad, 8 mm. high, slightly umbonate, sulcate striate, mealy, gray. Stems white, smooth 1 mm thick, at first slightly furfuraceous. Largest stems 6 cm., broadest pileus 18 mm. Spores 6 to 10 x 3 to 5 μ (*Nuttall*, 1189). Sept. 3. 1893.

POLYPORACEÆ.

BOLETUS Dill.

B. speciosus Frost.
On ground in woods, alt. 2,000 ft. July 16, 1893 (*Nuttall*, 1099).

B. chrysenteron Fr.
In deep woods, June 18, 1893 (*Nuttall*, 987).

B. parasiticus Bull.
On *Scleroderma vulgare* wet woods, alt. 1,800 ft., Sept. 4, 1893. (*Nuttall*, 1191).

B. edulis Bull.
Old field under *Rhus copallina*, June 20, 1893. Pileus 15 x 10 cm. stipe 4.5 cm. Spores 10 to 14 x 3 to 4 μ (*Nuttall*, 990).

STROBILOMYCES Berk.

S. strobilaceus (Scop.) Berk.
Shady fence row, alt. 2,300 ft., Sept. 16, 1893 (*Nuttall*, 1100). Spores about 10 μ, round.

FISTULINA Bull.

F. hepatica Fr.
On dead stumps, alt. 2,000 ft., July 16, 1893 (*Nuttall*, 1102).

POLYPORUS Mich.

P. brumalis (Pers.) Fr.
On dead logs, Mar. 6, 1893 (*Nuttall*, 1835).

P. pocula (Schw.) B. & C.
On dead *Rhus copallina*, Glade Creek, May 4, 1894 (*Nuttall*, 1495, 478).

P. arcularius (Batsch) Fr.
On rotten logs, Short Creek, May 6, 1893. Largest 4 cm. broad, stipe 2.3 cm. (*Nuttall*, 929).

P. varius Fr.
On dead logs, Aug. 18, 1893. Thin, tough, 20 cm. broad (*Nuttall*, 840).

P. UMBELLATUS Fr.
In dry exposed hollow of oak stump, Monongalia Co., near Morgantown (*Millspaugh*).

P. lactifluus Peck.
On ground in open woods, June, 1893; Aug. 24, 1893. Height 30 cm., greatest breadth 60 cm. (*Nuttall*, 1171).

P. BERKELEYI Fr.
In dry exposed hollow of oak stump, Monongalia Co., near Morgantown (*Millspaugh*).

P. SULPHUREUS (Bull.) Fr.
On decaying oak stump, Monongalia Co., near Morgantown (*Millspaugh*).

P. nidulans Fr.
P. niveus, Fr. On dead trunk *Prunus serotina*, Short Creek, alt. 1,000 ft., July 8, 1894 (*Nuttall*, 1599, 548).

P. ADUSTUS (Willd.) Fr.
On dead branch *Rhus hirta*, and in decayed stump *Hicoria ovata*, Monongalia Co., near Morgantown (*Millspaugh*). On sides of dead logs, Feb. 2, 1893 (*Nuttall*, 851).

P. hypococcineus Berk?
A resupinate form of this species, or new (E. & E.). Underside of dead log, Oct. 15, 1893 (*Nuttall*, 1214, 166).

P. pubescens (Schum.) Fr.
On dead *Betula* sp. July 27, 1894 (*Nuttall*, 1673).

P. resinosus (Schrad.) Fr.
On dead log, March 24, 1893 (*Nuttall*, 879).

P. Pilotæ Schw.
On dead rotten log, Sewell Valley, Aug. 23, 1894 (*Nuttall*, 1661).

FOMES Fr.

F. LUCIDUS (Leys.) Fr.
On dead logs *Tsuga Canadensis*, Preston Co., near Terra Alta (*Millspaugh*). On old stumps in deep woods, April 10, 1893, full grown in June (*Nuttall*, 892).

F. volvatus Peck.
On west side *Pinus Virginiana*, March 8, 1893 (*Nuttall*, 870).

F. pinicola Fr.
On fallen trunks *Tsuga Canadensis*, Short Creek, May 1, 1893 (*Nuttall*, 924).

F. APPLANATUS (Pers.) Wallr.
On dead *Acer saccharum* and *Quercus palustris*, *alba* and *rubra* Wood Co., near Kanawha Station, and McDowell Co., near Elkhorn. On dead *Fraxinus Americana*, Grant Co., near Bayard, and Monongalia Co., near Morgantown (*Millspaugh*). On dead logs, Jan., 1893 (*Nuttall*, 828).

F. FOMENTARIUS (Linn.) Fr.
On dead *Betula lutea*, Grant Co., near Bayard (*Millspaugh*). On dead log, at Rupert's, July 26, 1894 (*Nuttall*, 1635).

F. RIMOSUS Berk.
On dead *Robinia Pseudacacia*, Monongalia Co., near Morgantown (*Millspaugh*). On same sp. and on oak? alt. 2,000 ft., March 21, 1893 (*Nuttall*, 914).

F. CARNEUS Nees.
On dead decorticated *Picea Mariana*, Tucker Co., near Falls of Blackwater (*Millspaugh*). On *Pinus Virginiana*, March, 1893 (*Nuttall*, 865).

POLYSTICTUS Fr.

P. PERGAMENUS Fr.
On dry exposed oak railroad tie, Monongalia Co., near Morgantown (*Millspaugh*). On various dead trees, Feb. 17, 1893 (*Nuttall*, 847).

P. CINNABARINUS (Jacq.) Fr.
On dead limbs of cultivated *Prunus*, Monongalia Co., near Morgantown (*Millspaugh*). On various dead deciduous trees, Jan. 31. 1893 (*Nuttall*, 829).

P. versicolor (Linn.) Fr.
   On decorticated stump *Picea Mariana*, Tucker Co., near Falls of Blackwater. Under bark of log *Quercus alba*, Monongalia Co., near Morgantown (*Millspaugh*). On various dead trees, Feb., 1893 (*Nuttall*, 834).

P. hirsutus Fr.
   On dead twig cultivated *Pyrus Malus*, Monongalia Co., near Morgantown. On dead *Betula lutea*, and on log *Liriodendron Tulipifera*. A form with white spores, on roots fallen *Betula lenta*, Grant Co., near Bayard (*Millspaugh*). On *Fagus atropunicea*, Keeney's Creek, Oct. 20, 1893 (*Nuttall*, 1211).

P. abietinus Fr.
   On fallen *Tsuga Canadensis*, Grant Co., near Bayard (*Millspaugh*). On *Pinus Virginiana*, March 4, 1894 (*Nuttall*, 1420, 390).

MUCRONOPORUS E. & E.

M. Everhartii E. & Gall.
   On *Ulmus pubescens*, Nov. 6, 1893 (*Nuttall*, 1598).

M. Gilvus (Sz) E. & E.
   On *Castanea dentata*, July 20, 1894 (*Nuttall*, 1169, 558).

M. ferruginosus (Schrad.) E. & E.
   On *Juglans cinerea*, Aug. 29, 1893 (*Nuttall*, 1183).

PORIA Pers.

P. vulgaris Fr.
   On various dead limbs, Feb. 2 and Nov. 20, 1893 (*Nuttall*, 833). A nodular form on oak ties, Nov. 5, 1894 (*Nuttall*).

P. obducens Pers.
   On underside of dead log, Feb. 8, 1893 (*Nuttall*, 1297, 246).

P. nigra Berk.
   On side and beneath dead *Hicoria?* log. Effused, long and narrow, perennial (*Nuttall*, 1268).

P. tomento-cincta B. & R.
   Effused on bark underside of log *Betula lenta*, 60 x 30 cm. One layer taken off on Sept. 16, the same surface of the bark was found to be again covered with the species on Oct. 5, 1895. (*Nuttall*, 1865, 752). On *Magnolia Fraseri*, Nov. 1895.

P. vaporaria Fr.
   On *Prunus serotina*, Dec. 8, 1893 (*Nuttall*, 1295, 244).

P. Tulipiferæ Schw.
   On *Liriodendron Tulipifera*, April 13, 1893 (*Nuttall*, 893).

P. xantha Fr.
   On *Pinus Virginiana*, March 21, 1893 (*Nuttall*, 913).

P. micans (Ehrenb.) Fr.
On burned log, Short Creek, alt. 1,300 ft., Nov. 24, 1893 (*Nuttall*, 1277, 223).

P. corticola Fr.
Underside of young dead *Liriodendron Tulipifera*, diffused through clefts of bark, incrusting other polypori, etc. Alt. 925 ft., Nov. 20, 1893 (*Nuttall*, 1280).

P. sinuosa Fr.?
Appears to be between this and *Irpex obliquus*, preferably this (E. & E.). On *Kalmia latifolia*. Short Creek, alt. 1,800 ft., Aug. 12, 1893 (*Nuttall*, 1166, 138).

P. farinella Fr.
On dead log, Short Creek, alt. 1,800 ft., Sept. 12, 1893 (*Nuttall*, 1204, 160).

TRAMETES Fr.

T. Ohioensis Berk.
On dead standing sapling, Short Creek, alt. 1,800 ft., April 10, 1894 (*Nuttall*, 1467).

T. sepium Berk.
On dry railroad ties, Monongalia Co., near Morgantown (*Millspaugh*). Resupinate form on dead oak beams over a boiler, Dec. 15, 1893 (*Nuttall*, 1300).

T. mollis Fr.?
On drift wood, March 1893 (undeveloped) (*Nuttall*, 1597, 550).

T. odorata Wulf.
On dead limbs in a drain, July 20, 1894 (*Nuttall*, 1628, 557). *Ozonium auricomum*, Link., a curious tawny mycelium, supposed to be intimately connected with this species was found here with this specimen.

D. ambigua Berk.
Trametes ambigua (Berk.) Fr. On dead *Acer* sp., Feb. 2, 1893 (*Nuttall*, 846).

DÆDALIA Pers.

D. confragosa Pers.
On dead *Cornus florida*, Feb. 20, 1894 (*Nuttall*, 1774).

D. unicolor (Bull.) Fr.
On dead *Hicoria ovata*, Dec. 8, 1893 (*Nuttall*, 1298, 247).

MYRIADOPORUS Peck.

M. induratus Peck.
Top of decayed oak stump, Monongalia Co., near Morgantown (*Millspaugh*). Professor Peck remarks, in a letter, on receipt of the specimens: "This is probably only an imperfect condition of *Poria abducens*."

FAVOLUS Fr.
F. Europæus Fr.
   On dead branch, Feb. 12, 1894 (*Nuttall*, 1360). Spores 12.5 x 3 µ somewhat curved, obliquely apiculate. Feb. 17, 1895 (*Nuttall*, 1788).

GLŒOPORUS Mont.
G. CONCHOIDES Mont.
   On oak chips, Monongalia Co., near Morgantown (*Millspaugh*).

MERULIUS Hall.
M. TREMELLOSUS Schrad.
   Under bark *Quercus alba* log, Monongalia Co., near Morgantown (*Millspaugh*). On *Alnus rugosa*, Oct. 31, 1893 (*Nuttall*, 1220).

M. rubellus Peck.
   On dead *Quercus alba*, Short Creek, Nov. 9, 1893 (*Nuttall*, 1244).
   Also found parasitic on *Stereum versicolor*. In some cases the hymenium simply covers the under surface of the Stereum. In nearly all specimens observed it grows at the base of the host to which it is at least partly adherent. Largest pileus 5 x 5 cm., sometimes laterally connected for 15 cm.

M. Corium Fr.
   On branches, April 27, 1895 (*Nuttall*, 1822, 699).

M. molluscus Fr.
   On dead limb *Tsuga Canadensis*, Short Creek, alt. 1,800 ft., Feb. 8, 1894 (*Nuttall*, 1399).

M. ambiguus Berk.
   On dead *Prunus serotina*, Short Creek, alt. 975 ft., Jan. 1894 (*Nuttall*, 1602).

M. lachrymans (Jacq.) Fr.
   On bottom of box in cellar, Feb. 14, 1894 (*Nuttall*, 1379, 341).

M. pulverulentus Fr.
   Underside of old logs, Oct. 19, 1893. Spores orange colored, nucleate, 10 x 6 µ (*Nuttall*, 1208).

POROTHELIUM Fr.
P. lacerum Fr.
   On dead trunk, Feb. 11, 1894 (*Nuttall*, 1381, 343).

SOLENIA Hoffm.
S. ochracea Hoffm.
   On dry dead log, Short Creek, alt. 1,800 ft., Dec. 16, 1893 (*Nuttall*, 1327, 285).

S. villosa Pers.
   On fallen dead limb of *Quercus* sp., Sept. 1895 (*Nuttall*, 1854, 741).

HYDNACEÆ.
HYDNUM Linn.
H. imbricatum Linn.
: In oak woods, June 18, 1893 (*Nuttall*, 988).

H. adustum Schwein.
: On dead limbs on ground, Aug. 11, 1893. Nuclei at first cream-colored gradually changing from perifery to center through reddish purple to dark brown (*Nuttall*, 863).

H. coralloides Scop.
: In decayed cleft on living *Fagus atropunicea*, Feb. 13, 1893 (*Nuttall*, 845).

H. erinaceus Bull.
: On top dead log and in hollow of living *Fagus atropunicea*, alt. 1,800 ft., Nov. 27, 1894 (*Nuttall*, 1752).

H. ochraceum Pers.
: Underside of dead log, April 7, 1893. *Stegonotis fusca* found growing upon this species (*Nuttall*, 891).

H. croceum (Schw.) Fr.
: Effused in crevices of dead log, Short Creek, alt. 1,800 ft., March 6, 1894 (*Nuttall*, 1426, 398).

H. cinnabarinum (Schw.) Fr.
: Effused under bark of dry dead limb, June 20, 1893 (*Nuttall*, 997).

H. ———— sp.
: Underside old decayed log, Feb. 13, 1893. Effused 36 x 12 cm. or more (*Nuttall*, 844).

TREMELLODON Pers.
T. gelatinosum (Scop.) Pers.
: On dead *Tsuga Canadensis* Aug. 13, 1893 (*Nuttall*, 1148).

IRPEX Fr.
I. lacteus Fr.
: On dead *Rhus hirta*, Monongalia Co., near Morgantown (*Millspaugh*).

I. sinuosus Fr.
: On dead sticks, Dec. 10, 1893 (*Nuttall*, 1309, 255).

I. obliquus (Schrad.) Fr.?
: On *Magnolia Fraseri*, Feb. 8, 1894 (*Nuttall*, 1385, 347).

RADULUM Fr.
R. orbiculare Fr.
: On *Carpinus Caroliniana?* Nov. 27, 1893 (*Nuttall*, 1270).

R. Magnoliæ B. & C.
> On *Magnolia Fraseri*, Feb. 9, 1894, Short Creek, alt. 1,800 ft. (*Nuttall*, 1352).

PHLEBIA Fr.

P. merismoides Fr.
> On mossy bark of dead log, Dec. 1, 1893 (*Nuttall*, 1289). On *Magnolia Fraseri*, Nov. 1895.

P. radiata Fr.
> On *Alnus rugosa*, Oct. 31, 1893 (*Nuttall*, 1219).

GRANDINIA Fr.

G. granulosa Fr.
> On underside dead log, May 20, 1893 (*Nuttall*, 1304).

G. crustosa (Pers.) Fr.
> On *Rhododendron maximum*, May 20, 1893. On *Liquidambar Styraciflua*, Oct. 2, 1894 (*Nuttall*, 909 ident. Massee).

ODONTIA Pers.

O. farinacea Fr.
> Underside dead *Tsuga Canadensis*, Nov. 9, 1893, Short Creek, alt. 1,300 ft. (*Nuttall*, 1245).

KNEIFFIA Fr.*

K. setigera Fr.
> In interstices dead log, Dec., 1893 (*Nuttall*, 1290, 231).

THELEPHORACEÆ.

THELEPHORA Ehrh.

T. sebacea Pers.
> On stem of *Aster* sp., damp shady woods, July 25, 1893 (*Nuttall*, 1120).

T. pedicellata Schwein.
> On *Ostrya Virginiana*, Feb. 8, 1894 (*Nuttall*, 1370, 328).

STEREUM Pers.

S. versicolor (Sw.) Fr.
> On *Quercus* sp. and *Betula lenta*, March 7, 1893 (*Nuttall*, 856).

S. fasciatum Sz.
> In dead stumps, alt. 2,000 ft., March 8, 1893 (*Nuttall*, 860).

S. versicolor *var.* (Peck).
> On dry oak railroad ties, Monongalia Co., near Morgantown (*Millspaugh*).

---

* A section of the genus Œnothera has been elevated to generic rank by Raimann, in Engler & Prantl's *Natur. Pflanzenf.*, and Spach's *Kneiffia* (1835) re-instated to designate it. Fries' genus Kneiffia (1836) has, however, been so long established in mycologic literature, that we are loth to make any change at this time, feeling that the re-instating of Spach's Kneiffia is hardly proper, with Fries' genus well established.

FIELD COLUMBIAN MUSEUM.

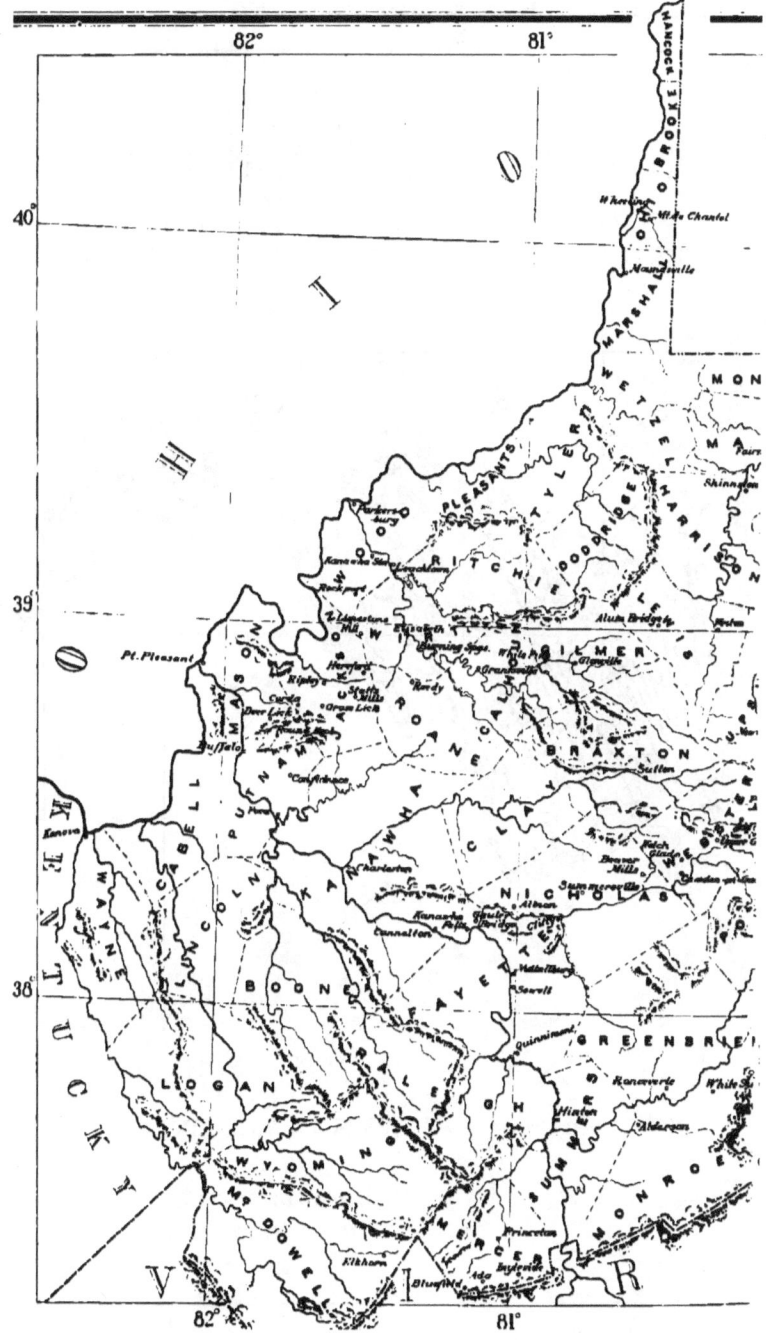

COUNTY MAP OF WEST VIRGINIA FOR MILLSPAUGH & NUTTALL'S FLORA OF WEST VIRGINIA. 1896.

S. purpureum Pers.
> On stump in pine woods (*Liriodendron?*) Dec. 9, 1893 (*Nuttall*, 1281, 391).

S. hirsutum (W.) Fr.
> On log, Nov. 24, 1893. Short Creek, alt. 1,300 ft. (*Nuttall*, 1277, 224).

S. sanguinolentum (A. & S.) Fr.
> On *Tsuga Canadensis*, Feb. 8, 1894 (*Nuttall*, 1386, 251).

S. SULPHURATUM B. & Rav.
> On log *Quercus alba*, Monongalia Co., near Morgantown (*Millspaugh*).

S. FRUSTULOSUM (Pers.) Fr.
> On log *Quercus* sp., Monongalia Co., near Morgantown (*Millspaugh*). On dead wood, March 7, 1893 (*Nuttall*, 857).

S. Pini Fr.
> On *Pinus Virginiana*, April 6, 1894 (*Nuttall*, 1469, 445).

S. ochraceo-flavum Schw.
> On small dead twigs, March 21, 1894 (*Nuttall*, 1416).

S. albo-badium Schwein.
> On dead sticks and twigs of various trees, April 27, 1893 (*Nuttall*, 1269).

S. SERICEUM Schw.
> On dead twig *Betula lenta*, Grant Co., near Bayard (*Millspaugh*). On *Rhus copallina*, March 6, 1894 (*Nuttall*, 1419, 389).

S. COMPLICATUM Fr.
> On roots of overturned *Betula lenta*, Grant Co., near Bayard; on dry oak railroad ties, Monongalia Co., near Morgantown (*Millspaugh*). On dead trees and on *Quercus Prinus*, Dec. 8, 1893 (*Nuttall*, 867, 235).

S. versiforme B. & C.?
> On *Castanea dentata*, Jan. 18, 1893 (*Nuttall*, 1347, 305).

S. triste B. & C.
> On *Rhododendron maximum* in thicket, alt. 1,800 ft. Feb. 8, 1894 (*Nuttall*, 966, 350).

S. acerinum Pers.
> On living tree trunks, March 7, 1893 (*Nuttall*, 858).

HYMENOCHÆTE Lev.

H. rubiginosa (Schr.) Lev.
> On dead log, March, 1893 (*Nuttall*, 911).

H. tabacina (Sow.) Lev.
> On dead twigs, March 1893 (*Nuttall*, 910).

H. corrugata (Fr.) Lev.
 On decorticated limb *Betula lenta*, Grant Co., near Bayard (*Millspaugh*). On *Magnolia Fraseri*, Feb. 8, 1894. Setæ 38 x 7.5 μ (*Nuttall*, 1364).

H. unicolor B. & C.?
 On *Betula lenta*, on dead *Kalmia latifolia?* July 1, 1893 (*Nuttall*, 1111, 96).

CORTICIUM Fr.

C. salicinum Fr.
 On dead *Salix nigra*, March 15, 1894 (*Nuttall*, 1401).

C. Oakesii B. & C.
 On living *Ostrya Virginica*, March 21, 1893 (*Nuttall*, 877).

C. globiferum E. & E.
 Underside of dead log in deep laurel thicket, Short Creek, March 25, 1893 (*Nuttall*, 940).

C. arachnoideum Berk.
 On dead damp twigs in dense pile, Jan. 18, 1894. Diffused for 30 x 8 cm. Spores 4 to 5 x 2 to 3 μ. The species when fresh has a wrinkled or crusted appearance looking very like a *Merulius*, but soon becomes flat and plane (*Nuttall*, 1344, 303).

C. radiosum Fr.
 On dead trunk, partly beneath loose bark, Short Creek, May 18, 1893 (*Nuttall*, 965).

C. leve Pers.
 On *Hamamelis Virginica*, Dec. 20, 1894 (*Nuttall*, 1500).

C. albo-flavescens E. & E., sp. nov.
 TYPE HABITAT: On bark of dead *Tsuga Canadensis*, Feb. 24, 1894 (*Nuttall*, discov. 1394).
 At first orbicular, subpezizoid, 1 to 2 mm. diameter, becoming more irregular in shape and 1 cm. or more diameter, lower stratum milk-white, consisting of loosely interwoven, branching threads, and extending out beyond the pale-olivaceous or yellowish, membranaceous hymenium so as to form a thin subfimbriate, white margin. Spores abundant, globose, with a single large nucleus, 4 to 6 μ diameter, slightly colored.
 The hymenium has only a slight tinge of olive and is perhaps better described as light-drab color.

C. leptaleum E. & E., sp. nov.
 TYPE HABITAT: On under side dead sapling *Magnolia Fraseri*, alt. 1,800 ft. April 11, 1895 (*Nuttall*, discov. 1803, 690).
 Thin, closely adnate, grayish-white, pulverulent, soon cracking into areas 2 to 3 mm across, with margins incurved so as to resemble the shallow cups of some *Peziza*. Spores oblong, hyaline, continuous, 10 to 12 x 4 μ, borne on cylindrical basidia 30 to 40 x 6 μ, with two stout sporophores. There are also other smaller

(immature)? sporidia, globose (4 to 6 μ) or elliptical, 5 to 7 x 3 to 3.5 μ. The membrane on which the hymenium stands where exposed on the incurved margin of the pezizoid areas is pale brown.

C. Petersii B. & C.
: On *Betula* sp. and *Vitis* sp., March 21, 1893 (*Nuttall*, 912).

C. colliculosum B. & C.
: On dead logs in laurel thicket, Short Creek, May 1893 (*Nuttall*, 1088).

C. prasinum B. & C.
: On dead burned log, Feb. 2, 1894 (*Nuttall*, 1382, 344).

C. lilacino-fuscum B. & C.
: On dead limb *Hicoria* sp., Short Creek, alt. 1,800 ft., March 5, 1894 (*Nuttall*, 1403).

C. ochraceum Fr.
: On underside dead log *Tsuga Canadensis*, May 8, 1893 (*Nuttall*, 931).

C. incarnatum (Pers.) Fr.
: On underside dead log and on *Ulmus pubescens*, April 18, 1893 (*Nuttall*, 923).

C. lilacinum Schroet.
: On firm wood of dead log, March 6, 1894, Short Creek, alt. 1,800 ft. (*Nuttall*, 1427, 399).

C. subgiganteum Berk.
: On *Hicoria ovata*, Dec. 14, 1893. Spores 16 x 5 μ (*Nuttall*, 1312, 262).

C. martianum B. & C.
: On underside of wet log, Dec. 16, 1893. When fresh this species is the color of fresh blood. Short Creek, alt. 1,800 ft. (*Nuttall*, 1324, 281).

C. scutellare B. & C.
: On *Magnolia Fraseri*, *Sambucus Canadensis* and *Pinus Virginiana*, Aug. 18, 1893 (*Nuttall*, 1176, 144).

ASTEROSTOMA Massee.

A. corticolum Massee.
: On wild vine *Vitis* sp., in pine woods, alt. 2,000 ft., Feb. 1893 (*Nuttall*, 1000).

A. cervicolor (B. & C.) Massee.
: On bark of living *Quercus* sp., Short Creek, alt. 1,800 ft. (*Nuttall*, 1325, 282).

PENIOPHORA Cooke.

P. quercina (Fr.) Cooke.
: On *Castanea dentata*, Jan. 18, 1893 (*Nuttall*, 1346, 305).

P. cinerea (Fr.) Cooke.
   On dead limb, March 1893 (*Nuttall*, 945, 170).

CONIOPHORA DC.

C. ———— sp.
   Near *C. submembranacea* (B. & Br.). On *Zea Mays*, Aug. 10, 1895 (*Nuttall*, 1846, 737).

C. olivacea (Fr.) Karst.
   In dark place underside old railroad ties, Nov. 5, 1894 (*Nuttall*, 1750, 631).

EXOBASIDIUM Woron.

E. RHODODENDRI Cram.
   Forming "cups" near the tips or margins of living leaves of *Rhododendron maximum*. Common in Grant and Tucker Counties. I understand from Prof. Peck that this is his first knowledge of the occurring of this species in North America (*Millspaugh*).

CLAVARIACEÆ.

CLAVARIA Vaill.

C. amethistina Bull.
   On ground, June 20, 1893 (*Nuttall*, 993).

C. pyxidata Pers.
   On rotten log, June 10, 1893 (*Nuttall*, 975).

C. formosa Pers.
   On ground in laurel thicket, and deep woods, alt. 2,000 ft., July 9, 1893. Spores 12.5 x 5 µ (*Nuttall*, 1085).

C. FLACCIDA Fr.
   On leaf mold, in deep woods, Grant Co., near Bayard (*Millspaugh*).

C. fusiformis Sowerb.
   On low ground in open woods, alt. 2,000 ft., July 9, 1893 (*Nuttall*, 1086).

C. juncea Fr.
   On leaf mold in bottom of dead hollow stump. Oct. 28, 1893 (*Nuttall*, 1232, 179).

C. mucida Pers.
   On upper side dead wet logs, Oct. 20, 1893 (*Nuttall*, 1231, 178).

CALOCERA Fr.

C. viscosa (Pers.) Fr.
   On bark of *Magnolia Fraseri*. Short Creek, alt. 1,800 ft., Feb. 8, 1894. Spores 12.5 x 4 µ (*Nuttall*, 1387, 354).

LACHNOCLADIUM Lev.

L. semivestitum B. & C.
 On dead wet limbs, alt. 1,800 ft., Sept. 18, 1895. Three to five inches high (*Nuttall*, 1867, 753).

TREMELLINACEÆ.

HIRNEOLA Fr.

H. Auricula-Judæ (Linn.) Berk.
 On damp sticks, June 15, 1893, Short Creek (*Nuttall*, 993).

EXIDIA Fr.

E. glandulosa (Bull) Fr.
 On bark *Juglans cinerea*, alt. 2,000 ft., Feb. 20, 1893 (*Nuttall*, 946).

E. alba (Huds.) Bref.
 On dead log, June 23, 1893 (*Nuttall*, 999).

ULOCOLLA Bref.

U. foliacea (Pers.) Bref.
 On dead twig, Nov. 10, 1893. Spores $+ 12.5 \times 6$ to 7μ (*Nuttall*, 1281).

TREMELLA Dill.

T. frondosa Fr.
 On *Rhododendron maximum*, Dec. 16, 1893 (*Nuttall*, 1321).

T. aurantia Fr.
 On bark *Pinus Virginiana*, alt. 2,000 ft., March 20, 1893 (*Nuttall*, 947).

T. intumescens Sm.?
 On dead limbs *Hicoria* sp., Short Creek, Dec. 16, 1893. Spores 10 to 13 × 3 to 4 μ, curved (*Nuttall*, 1332).

T. virens Schwein.
 On dead branch *Cornus florida*, Aug. 17, 1893 (*Nuttall*, 1155). Spores mostly 7 × 5 μ or round 7 μ diameter.

NÆMATELIA Fr.

N. nucleata (Schw.) Fr.
 On *Aralia spinosa*, alt. 1,300 ft., Aug. 18, 1893 (*Nuttall*, 1174, 142). On *Magnolia Fraseri*.

DACRYOMYCES Nees.

D. ——————— sp.
 Of this form Mr. J. B. Ellis says: "It seems to be a Dacryomyces. I find the same thing here at Newfield, N. J., but have never been able to decide upon it, and though I have sent it to

various European mycologists, I have never received a definite opinion from them." The form occurs on oak limbs on ground, Dec. 1893; is of a bright orange-red color, with curved spores 7.5 to 10 x 4 μ (*Nuttall*, 1271, 217).

D. deliquescens (Bull.) Dub.
On underside dead rotten limb *Pinus Strobus*, Dec. 13, 1894 (*Nuttall*, 1770).

D. Syringæ (Schum.)?
On dead limbs of *Platanus occidentalis*, Nov. 10, 1895 (*Nuttall*, 1889).

D. stellatus Nees.
On clean dead wood *Tsuga Canadensis*, Dec. 20, 1893 (*Nuttall*, 1331).

D. corticioides Ell.
On decayed *Tsuga Canadensis*, Short Creek, alt. 1,750 ft., Dec. 16, 1893. Lemon yellow .25 cm. to 3.5 x 1.5 cm. Spores hyaline, nucleate 9 to 12.5 x 5 to 7 μ obliquely apiculate at one end (*Nuttall*, 1316, 271).

D. minor Peck?
On *Kalmia latifolia*, Short Creek, alt 1,800 ft., March, 1894. Spores 10 to 12 x 4 μ (*Nuttall*, 1532).

GUEPINIA Fr.

G. spathularia (Schw.) Fr.
On *Quercus* sp., Jan. 1, 1894. Spores uniseptate 10 x 4 μ (*Nuttall*, 1782).

HORMOMYCES Bon.

H. fragiformis Cooke.
On bark dead *Fagus atropunicea*, Grant Co., near Bayard (*Millspaugh*). On dead wood, May 18, 1893 (*Nuttall*, 963). *Hypsilophora fragiformis* (Fr.) Lev.

Lichenes.

USNACEÆ.

RAMALINA Ach.

R. rigida (Pers.) Tuck.
On trees, alt. 2,000 ft. (*Nuttall*, 1060).

R. calcicaris fastigiata Fr.
On trees, alt. 2,000 ft. (*Nuttall*, 869).

R. miniuscula Nyl.
On *Acer saccharinum*, alt. 2,000 ft. (*Nuttall*, 1696).

CETRARIA Ach.

C. ciliaris (Ach.) Tuck.
On *Pinus Virginiana*, alt. 1,800 ft. (*Nuttall*, 861).

C. lacunosa Ach.
On *Pinus Virginiana*, alt. 1,800 ft. (*Nuttall*, 1053).

C. aurescens Tuck.
On *Rhododendron maximum*, alt. 1,850 ft. (*Nuttall*, 1050).

USNEA Ach.

U. BARBATA (L.) Fr.
Wirt Co., on old trees, common, Burning Springs. Randolph Co., on *Rhododendron maximum*, common, Cheat Bridge. Mercer Co., on oak twigs, Bluefield; and elsewhere about State, common on trees, rocks and old fence rails (*Millspaugh*). On trees, alt. 2,000 ft. (*Nuttall*, 819).

U. BARBATA FLORIDA Fr.
Mercer Co., on oak chips and twigs among dead leaves at Bluefield (*Millspaugh*). On trees, alt. 2,000 ft. (*Nuttall*, 859).

THELOSCHISTES Norm.

T. parietinus (Linn.) Norm.
On *Robinia Pseudacacia*, alt. 2,000 ft. (*Nuttall*, 1145).

T. concolor (Dicks.) Tuck
On *Robinia Pseudacacia*, alt. 2,000 ft. (*Nuttall*, 1144).

PARMELIEÆ.
PARMELIA Ach.

P. perlata (Linn.) Ach.
   On *Acer rubrum*, and on sandstone boulders (*Nuttall*, 848).

P. Borreri Turn.
   On oak, alt. 1,850 ft. (*Nuttall*, 1032).

P. BORRERI RUDECTA Tuck.
   On *Robinia Pseudacacia*, Monongalia Co., along Falling Run (*Millspaugh*, 1531).

P. colpodes (Ach.) Nyl.
   On oak, alt. 1,850 ft. (*Nuttall*, 1141).

P. OLIVACEA (L.) Ach.
   On *Liriodendron* log newly felled, Monongalia Co., Falling Run (*Millspaugh*, 1343).

P. CAPERATA (L.) Ach.
   Monongalia Co., on sandstone rocks, and base of beech, Falling Run (*Millspaugh*, 1283).

PHYSCIA DC.

P. LUCOMELA (L.) Michx.
   Mercer Co., with moss on wet limestone ledge, Beaver Spring (*Millspaugh*, 1539).

P. ciliaris (Linn.) DC.
   On mossy sandstone rocks (*Nuttall*, 1063).

P. ciliaris crinalis Schær.
   On moss, alt. 1,850 ft. (*Nuttall*, 1042).

P. aquila (Ach.) Nyl.
   On rocks and on moss (*Nuttall*, 1035).

P. stellaris (Linn.) Tuck.
   On sandstone rock (*Nuttall*, 872).

P. stellaris aipolia Nyl.
   On sandstone rock (*Nuttall*, 1778).

UMBILICARIÆ.
UMBILICARIA, Hoffm.

U. Dillenii Tuck.
   On sandstone rocks (*Nuttall*, 823).

U. Pennsylvanica Hoffm.
   On sandstone rocks (*Nuttall*, 849).

U. pustulata (Linn.) Hoffm.
   On faces of sandstone cliffs (*Nuttall*, 855).

PELTIGERIEÆ.
STICTA Schreb.

S. HERBACEA (Huds.) Ach.
  McDowell Co., on oaks, Elkorn (*Millspaugh*).

S. erosa (Eschw.) Tuck.
  On trees, alt. 1,850 ft. (*Nuttall*, 982).

S. PULMONARIA (L.) Ach.
  Wirt Co., on trunks of oaks, near Burning Springs (*Millspaugh*, 327). On trees, alt. 1,875 ft. (*Nuttall*, 824).

S. quercizans (Michx.) Ach.
  On trees and rocks (*Nuttall*, 1057).

PELTIGERA Willd.

P. APHTHOSA (K.) Hoffm.
  Monongalia Co., on rock ledge, near Cassville (*Millspaugh*). On rocks among mosses, alt. 1,800 ft. (*Nuttall*, 1090).

P. ———— sp. *non fruct.*
  On *Rhododendron maximum* (*Nuttall*, 938).

P. horizontalis (Linn.) Hoffm.
  On rocks among mosses, alt. 1,875 ft. (*Nuttall*, 1091).

P. canina (Linn.) Hoffm.
  On earth, rocks and trees (*Nuttall*, 1061).

PANNARIEÆ.
PANNARIA Delis.

P. rubiginosa (Thunb.) Delis.
  On mossy logs (*Nuttall*, 1055).

P. leucosticta Tuck.
  On mossy logs and rocks (*Nuttall*, 1064).

P. nigra (Huds.) Nyl.
  On sandstone rocks (*Nuttall*, 1077).

COLLEMEÆ.
COLLEMA Hoffm.

C. myochroum Nyl.
  On *Rhododendron maximum*, alt. 1,875 ft. (*Nuttall*, 1058).

LEPTOGIUM Fr.

L. pulchellum (Ach.) Nyl.
  On oak (*Nuttall*, 1067).

L. tremelloides (Linn. f.) Fr.
On sandstone rock (*Nuttall*, 1093).

L. chloromelum stellans Tuck.
On *Quercus coccinea*, alt. 2,400 ft. (*Nuttall*, 1146).

LECANOREÆ.
PLACODIUM DC.

P. elegans (Link.) DC.
On sandstone boulders at base of cliffs, alt. 1,800 ft. (*Nuttall*, 862).

P. CERINUM (Hedw.) Naeg. & Hepp.
Monongalia Co., on bark of beech, Falling Run (*Millspaugh*, 1357). On *Robinia Pseudacacia*, alt. 2,000 ft. (*Nuttall*, 1030).

P. ferrugineum (Huds.) Hepp.
On top of wet sandstone rock (*Nuttall*, 1092).

P. camptidium, Tuck.
On trees (*Nuttall*, 1786).

LECANORA, Ach.

L. coarctata Ach.
On pieces of sandstone under drip of wet cliff, alt. 1,800 ft. (*Nuttall*, 1780).

L. subfusca (Linn.) Ach.
On trees and rocks (*Nuttall*, 1038).

L. ATRA (Huds.) Ach.
Monongalia Co., on bark *Liriodendron* log, newly felled, Falling Run (*Millspaugh*, 1342). On flat exposed surface sandstone rock, same locality (1287).

L. deplanans Nyl.
On rocks in bed of creek, alt. 1,300 ft., Fayette Co. in Short Creek (*Nuttall*, 1126).

L. varia (Ehrh.) Nyl.
On trees (*Nuttall*, 1036).

L. pallescens (Linn.) Schær.
On trees and rails (*Nuttall*, 937).

L. tartarea (Linn.) Ach.
On sandstone rocks (*Nuttall*, 886).

L. cervina (Pers.) Nyl.
The light colored form on wet rocks; the dark form on dry rocks (*Nuttall*, 854).

L. privigna (Ach.) Nyl.
On sandstone rocks (*Nuttall*, 1028).

Lecanora deplanans Nyl., sp. nov.—Thallus glauco-cinerascens tenuis areolato-rimosus determinatus; apothecia badio-rufescens (satis diluta) innata subconcaviuscula, latit. 0.5–0.7mm; spora ellipsoidea, long. 0.015–16, crass. 0.009–1.010mm; epithecium inspersum. In toto gelatina hymenialis fulvo-rubescens.

Videtur species e stirpe *Lecanora cervina*, spermatiis ellipsoideis.

On rocks in bed of creek. West Virginia, Short Creek, alt. 1300 feet, L. W. Nuttall coll. no. 1126.

(INSERT OPPOSITE PAGE 178).

RINODINA Mass.

R. oreina (Ach.) Mass.
  On sandstone rocks at base of cliff, alt. 1,800 ft. (*Nuttall*, 952).

R. sophodes (Ach.) Nyl.
  On small sandstone rocks (*Nuttall*, 1072).

PERTUSARIA DC.

P. velata (Turn.) Nyl.
  On *Magnolia Fraseri* and other trees (*Nuttall*, 1044).

P. multipuncta (Turn.) Nyl.
  On sandstone rocks in bed of creek (*Nuttall*, 1043).

P. leioplaca (Ach.) Schær.
  On oak (*Nuttall*, 1041).

P. pustulata (Ach.) Nyl.
  On trees (*Nuttall*, 853).

THELOTREMA Ach.

T. subtile Tuck.
  On trees (*Nuttall*, 1056).

MYRIANGIUM Mont. & Berk.

M. Duriæi (Mont. & Berk.) Tuck.
  On dead bush (*Nuttall*, 1062).

CLADONIEÆ.

CLADONIA Hoffm.

C. MITRULA Tuck.
  Monongalia Co., on an old beech log, Falling Run (*Millspaugh*, 1346).

C. cariosa (Ach.) Spreng.
  On earth, Fayette Co. (*Nuttall*, 1066).

C. PYXIDATA (L.) Fr.
  Monongalia Co., along Falling Run, on bare sandstone rocks (*Millspaugh*, 1281); on moss in clay soil (*Millspaugh*, 1285); on decayed log (*Millspaugh*, 1338); base of beech in soil (*Millspaugh*, 1282); on earth (*Nuttall*, 1031).

C. fimbriata (Linn.) Fr.
  On an old log, Fayette Co. (*Nuttall*, 1059).

C. fimbriata tubæformis Fr.
  On an old log (*Nuttall*, 1059).

C. GRACILIS (L.) Nyl.
  Monongalia Co., along Falling Run, on decayed log (*Millspaugh*, 1337); among mosses on clay soil (*Millspaugh*, 1286).

C. gracilis verticillata Fr.
   On earth (*Nuttall*, 885).

C. sobolescens Nyl.
   On earth (*Nuttall*, 839).

C. papillaria (Ehrh.) Hoffm.
   On earth (*Nuttall*, 1068).

C. delicata (Ehrh.) Fl.
   On top of stump (*Nuttall*, 1065).

C. cæspiticia (Pers.) Fl.
   On sandstone rocks (*Nuttall*, 1075).

C. FURCATA RACEMOSA Floerk.
   Monongalia Co., large patches on ground under chestnuts, at Dille's; Mercer Co., same growth under oaks, near Beaver Spring (*Millspaugh*) on earth (*Nuttall*, 1045).

C. RANGIFERINA (L.) Hoffm.
   Monongalia Co., on moss, Falling Run (*Millspaugh*, 1361); on earth, rocks and rails (*Nuttall*, 825).

C. macillenta (Ehrh.) Hoffm.
   On rotten logs (*Nuttall*, 1070).

C. pulchella Schwein.
   On dead wood (*Nuttall*, 838).

C. CRISTATELLA Tuck.
   Monongalia Co., on an old decayed log, Falling Run (*Millspaugh*, 1336).

LECIDEÆ.

BÆOMYCES Pers.

B. roseus Pers.
   On ground (*Nuttall*, 873).

BIATORA Fr.

B. russula (Ach.) Mont.
   On bark of tree (*Nuttall*, 1046).

B. varians (Ach.) Tuck.
   On bark of tree (*Nuttall*, 978).

B. ulignosa (Schrad.) Fr.
   On rotten stumps (*Nuttall*, 1054).

B. fuliginosa Ach.
   On ground (*Nuttall*, 1089).

B. Schweinitzii Tuck.
   On *Rhododendron maximum* (*Nuttall*, 1052).

B. rubella (Ehrh.) Rab.
   On mossy trunk of tree (*Nuttall*, 1029).

Lecidea Nuttallii Calk. & Nyl., sp. nov.—Apothecia nigra parva; epithecium impressum; spora fusca oviformis 1-septata, long 0.014–16, crass. 0.005–6mm; hypothecium fuscum. In toto gelatina hymenialis vinose rubescens.

Super thallum *Ricasolia sublævis* Nyl. West Virginia, near Nuttalburg, L. W. Nuttall coll. no. 1781.

Lecidea Virginiensis Calk. & Nyl., sp. nov.—Thallus glaucescens tenuis laevigatus rimulosus citrino-flavus; apothecia fusca aut nigra convexiuscula immarginata latit. circ. 0.5mm, intus medio sordida; spora oblonga incoloris, long. 0.009–0.012, crass. 0.004–6mm; epithecium et pars media hypothecii dilute fuscescens. In toto gelatina hymenialis coerulescens, dein theca vinose rubescens.

E stirpe videtur *Lecidea sanguineo-atra*, prope *Lecideam delineatam* Nyl.

On sandstone rock under the drip of a wet cliff. West Virginia, near Nuttalburg, L. W. Nuttall coll. no. 1779.

(INSERT OPPOSITE PAGE 181).

B. inundata Fr.
  On sandstone rock (*Nuttall*, 1074).

B. suffusa Fr.
  On bark of tree (*Nuttall*, 1095).

LECIDEA Ach.

L. Tennesseensis Nyl.
  On sandstone rock (*Nuttall*, 1073).

L. fuliginea Ach.
  On upper side of dead log (*Nuttall*, 1787).

L. Nuttallii Calkins. mss.
  Parasitic on *Sticta erosa* (*Nuttall*, 1781).

L. Virginiensis Calkins. mss.
  On sandstone rock under drip of wet cliff (*Nuttall*, 1779).

L. ericina Nyl.
  Bark of trees (*Nuttall*, 1047).

BUELLIA DeNot.

B. myriocarpa (DC.) Mudd.
  On bark of trees (*Nuttall*, 1185).

B. petræa (Fl.) Tuck.
  On sandstone rocks (*Nuttall*, 1071).

GRAPHIDACEÆ.

OPEGRAPHA Humb.

O. varia (Pers.) Fr.
  Bark of trees (*Nuttall*, 1034).

O. atra Pers.
  Bark of trees (*Nuttall*, 1033).

GRAPHIS Ach.

G. scripta (Linn.) Ach.
  On bark of trees (*Nuttall*, 1051).

G. scripta recta Schær.
  On bark of *Betula lutea* and of *B. lenta* (*Nuttall*, 1026).

G. elegans (Sm.) Ach.
  On bark of trees, Fayette Co. (*Nuttall*, 1039).

G. dendritica Ach.
  On bark of *Betula lenta*, etc. (*Nuttall*, 1037).

ARTHONIA Ach.

A. cinnabarina Wallr.
  Bark of tree (*Nuttall*, 939).

A. aleuromela Nyl. mss.
  On bark of oak, alt. 2,000 ft. (*Nuttall*, discov. 1182).

A. dispersa (Schrad.) Nyl.
  On bark of young *Tsuga Canadensis*, etc. (*Nuttall*, 1142).

A. astroidea Ach.
  On bark of *Liriodendron Tulipifera* (*Nuttall*, 1816).

A. punctiformis Ach.
  On bark (*Nuttall*, 1076).

A. tædiosa (Nyl.) Fr.
  On bark (*Nuttall*, 1069).

A. spectabilis Fl.
  On bark (*Nuttall*, 1025).

AGYRIUM Fr.
A. rufum (Pers.) Fr.
  On smooth dead wood (*Nuttall*, 1814).

CALICIACEÆ.
CALICIUM Pers.
C. subtile Fr.
  On sticks, dead leaves, etc., under cliff (*Nuttall*, 1226).

VERRUCARIACEÆ.
ENDOCARPON Hedw.
E. miniatum (Linn.) Schær.
  On wet cliffs (*Nuttall*, 1049).

E. miniatum complicatum Schær.
  On wet cliffs (*Nuttall*, 1823).

TRYPETHELIUM Spreng.
T. virens Tuck.
  On *Ilex opaca* (*Nuttall*, 1040).

T. exocanthum Tuck.
  On *Fagus atropunicea* (*Nuttall*, 1181).

PYRENULA Ach.
P. rhyponta Ach.
  On bark of *Hamamelis Virginica* (*Nuttall*, 1184).

P. nitida Ach.
  On *Betula lenta* bark (*Nuttall*, 1027).

P. pachycheila Tuck.
  On bark of *Fagus atropunicea* (*Nuttall*, 1048).

Arthonia aleuromela Nyl., sp. nov.—Thallus albus subfarinaceus chrysogonidicus tenuissimus; apothecia subrotundata vel oblonga, prominula, latit. 0.4–0.5mm; spora oblongo-oviformis parte inferiore attenuata, 1-septata, long. 0.010–11, crass. 0.003mm. In toto gelatina hymenialis cœrulescens, dein obscurata.

Thallus detritus subaureus, CaCl vix reagens. Gonidia chroolepoidea fulvescentia.

On bark of *Quercus sp.* West Virginia, near Nuttallburg, alt. 2000 feet, L..W. Nuttall coll. no. 1182.

Hepaticae.

JUNGERMANNIACEÆ.

Frullania Asa-Grayana Mont.
Frullania plana Sull.
(*Nuttall*).
Jubula Hutchinsiæ Sullivantii Spruce.

ARCHILEJUNEA Spruce.

A. calypeata (Schw.) Spruce.
    Lejunea calypeata Schw. (*Nuttall*).
Radula Xalapensis Mont.
Radula tenax Lindb.

BELLINCINIA Raddi.

B. platyphylla (L.) O. K.
    Porella platyphylla Lindb.
B. Porella (Dicks.) O. K.
    Porella pinnata Schw.
Trichocolea tomentella (Ehrh.) Dumort.
Herbertia adunca (Dicks.) S. F. Gray.
Bazzania trilobata (L.) S. F. Gray.
Bazzania deflexa (Mart.) Underw.
Cephalozia media Lindb.
    Cephalozia multiflora Spruce (*Nuttall*).
Cephalozia curvifolia (Dicks.) Dumort.
(*Nuttall*).
Odontochisma Sphagni (Dicks.) Dumort.
(*Nuttall*).
Blepharostoma trichophyllum (L.) Dumort.
Kantia trichomanis (L.) S. F. Gray.
Geocalyx graveolens (Schrad.) Nees.
Scapania undulata (L.) Dumort.
    Randolph Co., at Pickens, on clay at the banks of a spring (*Millspaugh*).
Scapania nemorosa (L.) Dumort.
Diplophyllum taxifolium (Wahlenb.) Dumort.

PLAGIOCHILA VIRGINICA, A. W. Evans, Fl. W. Va., 497 (1892) Plate.

Growing in wide, depressed, and intricate tufts; stems ascending from a prostrate caudex, simple or sparingly branched, sometimes geniculate and rooting at the joints, otherwise eradiculose; leaves contiguous or somewhat imbricated, widely patent, ovate or rhomboid-ovate, the dorsal margin decurrent, slightly reflexed, entire, the ventral margin plane or reflexed at base, mostly entire, the apex broad, rounded or truncate, sharply and irregularly spinulose; amphigastria none.

Stems 1 to 3 cm. long, with the leaves 1 to 2 mm. wide; leaves 1.2 mm. long, 0.7 mm. wide; spines short, acute, separated by rounded sinuses, varying in number from 2 to 8 on each leaf, usually 4 or 5; leaf-cells averaging 0.023 mm. in diameter in middle of leaf, thin-walled and scarcely thickened at the angles.

Mercer: on walls of dry limestone cave, Beaver Spring (1550).

PLAGIOCHILA PORELLOIDES Lindenb.

HARPANTHUS SCUTATUS (Web. & Mohr.) Spruce.

JUNGERMANNIA EXSECTA Schmid.

MARSUPELLA Dumort.

M. emarginata (Ehrh.) Dumort.
Randolph Co., at Pickens, on clay bank of a small spring. (*Millspaugh*)

PELLIA EPIPHYLLA (L.) Dumort.

METZGERIA CONJUGATA Lindb.
(*Nuttall*).

ANEURA MULTIFIDA (L.) Dumort.

Aneura sessilis Spreng.
(*Nuttall*).

MARCHANTIACEÆ.

MARCHANTIA POLYMORPHA Linn (*Nuttall*).

CONOCYPHALUM CONICUM (L.) Dumort.

Musci.

POLYTRICHACEÆ.
Polytrichum commune Linn.
Polytrichum Ohiœnse Ren. & Card.
Polytrichum piliferum Schreb.
Polytrichum tenue (Menz.) E. G. Britton.

DIPHYSCIUM, Mohr.
D. foliosum Mohr (*Nuttall*).

BUXBAUMIA Haller
B. aphylla Linn (*Nuttall*).
Catharinea angustata Brid.
Catharinea undulata Web. & Mohr.

GEORGIACÆ.
Georgia pellucida (L.) Rabenh.

FISSIDENTACEÆ.
Fissidens adiantoides (L.) Hedw.
Fissidens decipiens De Not.

MNIACEÆ.
Astrophyllum sylvaticum Lindb.
Astrophyllum rostratum Schrad.
Astrophyllum punctatum (L.) Lindb.
Astrophyllum hornum (L.) Lindb.
Sphærocephalus heterostichus (Brid.) E. G. Britton.

BARTRAMIACEÆ.
Bartramia pomiformis (L.) Hedw.
  On ground, Greenbrier Co., Kate's Mountain, alt. 3,300 ft. (*Small & Vail*).
Bartramia pomiformis crispa (Sw.) Schimp.
Bartramia fontana (L.) Brid.

BRYACEÆ.

BRYUM BIMUM Schreb.
BRYUM ARGENTEUM Linn.
BRYUM PROLIFERUM (L.) Sibth.
LEPTOBRYUM PYRIFORME (L.) Wils.

FUNARIACEÆ.

FUNARIA HYGROMETICA (L.) Sibth.
FUNARIA HYGROMETICA PATULA Br. & Sch.
FUNARIA FLAVICANS Michx.
PHYSCOMITRIUM PYRIFORME (L.) Brid.

TORTULACEÆ.

LEERSIA STREPTOCARPA (Hedw.) Lindb.
TORTULA MURALIS (L.) Hedw.
BARBULA HUMILIS Hedw.
BARBULA TORTUOSA (L.) Web. & Mohr.
MOLLIA VIRIDULA (L.) Lindb.

DICRANACEÆ.

LEUCOBRYUM GLAUCUM (L.) Br. & Sch.
DICRANODONTIUM VIRGINICUS, E. G. Britton, Fl. W. Va., 488 (1892) Plate.

Monongalia: On sandstone boulder along a woodland path, Tibb's Run (*Millspaugh*, 1635).

Plants bright glossy green, stems matted below by a red tomentum, leafy nearly to apex, denudate roughened above, with a few leaves at summit; leaves erect or secund, straight or curled and twisted, often 5 mm. long, narrowly subulate, from a short, thick base, caducous ones with a long, slender, smooth point; persistent ones serrate, blade inflexed, cells densely chlorophyllose, filled with oil globules, those of the basal angles clear. Diœcious, the antheridia terminal in conspicuous heads, bracts brown at base, apex subulate, serrate; perichætial bracts 3-4 mm. long, from a short base, suddenly subulate, dentate at apex; pedicels lateral by the growth of innovations, 1½-2 cm. long, pale, glossy yellow, twisted in two directions, very slender, arcuate when young, becoming erect before capsules mature. Capsule cylindric, ribbed only at the mouth, 1½-2 mm. long, beak straight or curved, shorter than the capsule, peristome bright red, *not deep set*, teeth split unequally to middle, striolate at base, pale and granulose above, annulus none, spores small, calyptra cucullate, 2 mm. long, beaked, entire. Maturing in summer.

Differs from European specimens of *D. longirostre* collected by Seringe; in the longer, paler, more slender, scarcely arcuate pedicels, longer capsules, peristome not deep set, and teeth split only to the middle, more united than figured in the Bryologia

Europea, Table 88. It may be distinguished from *Campylopus Virginicus*, also remarkable for its caducous leaves, by the longer, more slender subulate point, which is entire or minutely serrate and smooth on the back, by the thick base, with inflexed blades, and by the shape of the basal cells at the angles.

DICRANODONTIUM MILLSPAUGHI, E. G. Britton, Fl. W. Va., 488 (1892) Plate.

Monongalia: on sandstone boulder, deep woods, Tibb's Run (*Millspaugh*, 1596).

Plant slight yellowish green, silky, cæspitose; stems matted with rufous tomentum at base, 1–3 cm. long, a few denudate, roughened by the fragments of the slightly caducous leaves. Leaves secund or erect-spreading, 4–5 mm. long, narrowly subulate from a broad base 1–1½ mm. long, becoming tubular above with inrolled margins, basal angles not auricled, filled by large hyaline cells to the base of the broad, brown vein, those of the blade oblong or square next the vein, becoming spindle-shaped and prosenchymatous toward the margin, vein thick, excurrent into a dentate slender tip, rough on back. Diœcious, perichætium 5–7 mm. long, bracts sheathing half their length, tapering to a long, slender, obscurely serrate tip, outer shorter, abruptly subulate, more sharply serrate; pedicels recurved, burying the capsules among the leaves, becoming erect when old, 5-8 mm. long, stout and twisted in two directions; capsules pyriform-cylindric with a distinct neck, length about 1 mm. without the lid, which is as long as the rest of the capsule, with a straight beak; calyptra cucullate, entire; peristome red, connivent, teeth deep set, slender, split to middle, or perforate to base, striolate below, granulose above; annulus none, mouth bordered by a dense, dark rim. Maturing in summer, old capsules persistent, not sulcate.

Differs from European specimens of *D. longirostre* in the structure of the base of the leaf, lacking the suddenly inflated basal auricles; differing also in the cells above the base, teeth not split to base, occasionally only perforate. From *D. Virginicus* it may be distinguished by the less caducous leaves, shorter, stouter, more arcuate pedicels, smaller capsules, and longer sheathing perichætium.

Through the kindness of Dr. Robinson I have been able to compare these specimens with those collected by Sullivant on Grandfather Mt. in 1843. His also are fruiting, and an excellent drawing is preserved, hence I am able to assert that the specimens are almost identical. Sullivant's showing no naked stems, but many of the leaves are caducous. Dr. Braithwaite kindly compared the West Virginia specimens with *Campylopus pyriformis*, sending me specimens of this and the variety *Mulleri*, and sketches of the bases of the leaves. It is evident that Sullivant was mistaken in referring his specimens to *C. flexuosus*, as they are more closely allied to *Dicranodontium longirostre*, var. *alpinus*.

DICRANUM FLAGILLARE Hedw.

DICRANUM SCOPARIUM (L.) Hedw.

Dicranum longifolium Hedw. (*Nuttall*).
DICRANUM FULVUM Hook.
DICRANELLA HETEROMALLA (L.) Schimp.
DITRICHUM PALLIDUM Schreb.
CERATODON PURPUREUS (L.) Brid.

GRIMMIACEÆ.

WEISSIA AMERICANA (P. Beauv.) Lindb.
Weissia ulophylla Ehrh. (*Nuttall*).
ORTHOTRICHUM BRAUNII Br. & Sch.
Orthotrichum Ohioense S. and L. (*Nuttall*).

HYPNACEÆ.

THUIDIUM RECOGNITUM (Hedw.) Lindb.
ANOMODON ROSTRATUS (Hedw.) Schimp.
ANOMODON ATTENUATUS (Schreb.) Hedw.
AMBLYSTEGIUM ADNATUM Hedw.
AMBLYSTEGIUM SERPENS (L.) Br. & Sch.
AMBLYSTEGIUM ORTHOCLADON (Beauv.) Aust. *Amblystegium serpens orthocladon* (Beauv.) Aust.
AMBLYSTEGIUM VARIUM (Hedw.) Lindb.
AMBLYSTEGIUM IRRIGUUM (Hook. & Wils.) Br. & Sch.
AMBLYSTEGIUM RIPARIUM (L.) Br. & Sch.
AMBLYSTEGIUM CHRYSOPHYLLUM (Brid.) De Not.
HYPNUM DENTICULATUM Linn.
HYPNUM PALUSTRE ?
HYPNUM MOLLE Dicks.
HYPNUM PROLIFERUM Linn.
HYPNUM RUTABULUM Linn.
HYPNUM RECURVANS Schwaeger.
HYPNUM MICROCARPUM C. Muell.
HYPNUM HIANS Hedw.
HYPNUM DEMISSUM Wils.
HYPNUM PLUMOSUM Huds. *Brachythecium salebrosum*, Br. & Sch.

STEREODONTACEÆ.

THELIA HIRTELLA (Hedw.) Sull.
THELIA ASPRELLA (Schim.) Sull.
HYLOCOMIUM PARIETINUM (L.) Lindb.
Hylocomium rugosum (L.) De Not.
  Greenbrier Co., Kate's Mountain, alt. 3,300 ft., on ground (*Small & Vail*).

Hylocomium triquetrum (L.) Br. & Sch.
Campylium hispidulum (Brid.) Mitt.
Campylium chrysophyllum (Brid.) E. G. Britton.
    Greenbrier Co., Kate's Mountain, alt. 3,300 ft., on ground (*Small & Vail*).
Campylium chrysophyllum tenellum L. & J.
Ptilium crista-castrense (L.) De Not.
Stereodon imponens (Hedw.) Brid.
Stereodon cupressiforme (L.) Brid.
Stereodon curvifolius (Hedw.) Brid.
Pylaisia velutina Br. & Sch.
Plagiothecium denticulatum Br. & Sch.
Plagiothecium denticulatum densum Br. & Sch.
Plagiothecium Sullivantiæ Schimp.
Cylindrothecium seductrix (Hedw.) Sull.
Cylindrothecium cladorhizans (Hedw.) Schimp.
Entodon palatinus (Neck.) Lindb.

NECKERACEÆ.

Neckera pennata (L.) Hedw. (*Nuttall*).
Climacium Americanum Brid.
Leucodon julaceus (Hedw.) Sull.
Leucodon brachypus Brid.
Hedwegia ciliata Ehrh. (*Nuttall*)

Sphagna.

SPHAGNACEÆ.

Sphagnum cymbifolium Ehrh.

Petridophyta.

OPHIOGLOSSACEÆ.

OPHIOGLOSSUM VULGATUM Linn.
BOTRYCHIUM TERNATUM (Thunb.) Sw.
BOTRYCHIUM TERNATUM AUSTRALE (R. Br.) Eaton.
BOTRYCHIUM TERNATUM RUTÆFOLIUM Man.
BOTRYCHIUM TERNATUM OBLIQUUM (Muhl.) Milde.
BOTRYCHIUM TERNATUM DISSECTUM (Spreng.) Milde.
BOTRYCHIUM VIRGINIANUM (Linn.) Sw.

FILICES.

POLYPODIUM VULGARE Linn.
POLYPODIUM VULGARE *forma* BISSERATA Millsp. Fl. W. Va., 479 (1892).
"A form with regularly doubly-serrate thinnish fronds. On mossy boulders along the Blackwater fork of Cheat river."
POLYPODIUM POLYPODIOIDES (Linn.) Hitch. *Polypodium incanum* Sw.
CHEILANTHES LANOSA (Michx.) Watt. *C. vestita* (Spreng.) Sw.
CHEILANTHES GRACILIS (Fee.) Met. *C. lanuginosa*, Nutt.
PELLÆA ATROPURPUREA (Linn.) Link.
PTERIS AQUILINA Linn.
ADIANTUM PEDATUM Linn.
ASPLENIUM PINNATIFIDUM Nutt.
ASPLENIUM TRICHOMANES Linn.
ASPLENIUM PLATYNEURON (Linn.) Oakes.
ASPLENIUM MONTANUM Willd.
ASPLENIUM ANGUSTIFOLIUM Michx.
ASPLENIUM ACROSTICHIOIDES Sw.
ASPLENIUM FILIX-FŒMINA (Linn.) Bernh.
CAMPTOSORUS RHIZOPHYLLUS (Linn.) Link.
PHEGOPTERIS PHEGOPTERIS (Linn.) Underw.
PHEGOPTERIS HEXAGONOPTERA (Michx.) Fee.
PHEGOPTERIS DRYOPTERIS (Linn.) Fee.
DRYOPTERIS THELYPTERIS (Linn.) A. Gray. *Aspidium Thelypteris* (L.) Sw.
DRYOPTERIS NOVEBORACENSE (Linn.) A. Gray. *Aspidium Noveboracense* (L.) Sw.
DRYOPTERIS FRAGRANS (Linn.) Schott. *Aspidium fragrans* (L.) Sw.

DRYOPTERIS SPINULOSA (Retz.) O. K. *Aspidium spinulosum* (Retz.) Sw.
DRYOPTERIS SPINULOSA INTERMEDIA (Muhl.) Underw. *Aspidium spinulosum* var. *intermedium* Eaton.
DRYOPTERIS SPINULOSA DILATATA (Hoffm.) Underw. *Aspidium spinulosum* var. *dilatatum* Hook.
DRYOPTERIS SIMULATA Davenport, Bot. Gaz. 29, 495 (1894).
 Aspidium spinulosum var. Comparing my specimens from the deep, wet woods of Randolph Co. with specimens of *D. simulata* recently sent me by Professor Davenport, I find them identical. In publishing the species Professor Davenport includes it under Dryopteris as well as Aspidium, Nephrodium and Lastrea.
DRYOPTERIS CRISTATA (Linn.) A. Gray. *Aspidium cristatum* (L.) Sw.
DRYOPTERIS GOLDIEANA (Hook) A. Gray. *Aspidium Goldieanum* Hook.
DRYOPTERIS FILIX-MAS (Linn.) Schott. *Aspidium Filix-mas* Sw.
DRYOPTERIS MARGINALIS (Linn.) A. Gray. *Aspidium marginale* Sw.
DRYOPTERIS ACROSTICHIOIDES (Michx.) O. K. *Aspidium achrostichioides* Sw.
DRYOPTERIS ACROSTICHIOIDES SCHWEINITZII (Beck). *Aspidium achrostichioides Schweinitzii* (Beck.) B. S. P.
CYSTOPTERIS BULBIFERA (Linn.) Bernh.
CYSTOPTERIS FRAGILIS (Linn.) Bernh.
ONOCLEA SENSIBILIS Linn.
WOODSIA OBTUSA (Spreng.) Torr.
DICKSONIA PUNCTILOBULA (Michx.) A. Gray.
OSMUNDA REGALIS Linn.
OSMUNDA CLAYTONIANA Linn.
OSMUNDA CINNAMOMEA Linn.

EQUISETACEÆ.

EQUISETUM ARVENSE Linn.
EQUISETUM SYLVATICUM Linn.
EQUISETUM HYEMALE Linn.
EQUISETUM LÆVIGATUM A. Br.

LYCOPODIACEÆ.

LYCOPODIUM LUCIDULUM Michx.
LYCOPODIUM ANNOTINUM Linn.
LYCOPODIUM OBSCURUM Linn (*Nuttall*).
LYCOPODIUM CLAVATUM Linn.
LYCOPODIUM COMPLANATUM Linn.

SELAGINELLACEÆ.

SELAGINELLA RUPESTRIS (Linn.) Spring.

Anthophyta.

CONIFERACEÆ.

THUJA OCCIDENTALIS Linn.
JUNIPERUS COMMUNIS Linn.
JUNIPERUS VIRGINIANA Linn.
    Jefferson Co., plentiful near Harper's Ferry, trunks 7 to 9 inches in diameter.
TAXUS MINOR (Michx.) Britton. *Taxus baccata* var. *Canadensis* A. Gray.
PINUS STROBUS Linn.
PINUS TÆDA Linn.
PINUS RIGIDA Mill.
PINUS PUNGENS Michx. f.
PINUS VIRGINIANA Mill.
    Greenbrier Co., slopes of Kate's Mountain, alt. 3,300 ft. (*Small & Vail*).
PINUS ECHINATA Mill.
PICEA MARIANA (Mill.) B. S. P.
TSUGA CANADENSIS (Linn.) Carr.
ABIES BALSAMEA (Linn.) Miller.

TYPHACEÆ.

TYPHA LATIFOLIA Linn.

SPARGANIACEÆ.

SPARGANIUM EURYCARPUM Engelm.

NAIDACEÆ.

POTAMOGETON LONCHITES Tuck. *P. fluitans* Roth.

ALISMACEÆ.

ALISMA PLANTAGO-AQUATICA Linn.
SAGITTARIA LATIFOLIA Willd. *S. sagittæfolia* Linn. forma *hastata* et *angustifolia*.
SAGITTARIA GRAMINEA Michx.

HYDROCHARITACEÆ.

UDORA CANADENSIS (Michx.) Nutt. *Elodea Canadensis* Michx.

GRAMINACEÆ.

SPARTINA CYNOSUROIDES (Linn.) Willd.
PASPALUM SETACEUM Michx.   *P. setaceum ciliatifolium* (Michx.) is included.
PASPALUM LÆVE Michx.
PANICUM SANGUINALE Linn.
PANICUM SANGUINALE *forma* DEPAUPERATA, Vasey.
    This form from dry sterile fields along Falling Run, Monongalia Co., was given the prominence of a form name by Dr. Vasey (1892).
PANICUM PROLIFERUM Lam.   *P. proliferum geniculatum* (Eu.) Vasey, included.
PANICUM CAPILLARE Linn.
PANICUM CAPILLARE AGRESTRE Gatt.
PANICUM ANCEPS Michx.
PANICUM AGROSTIDIFORME Lam.   *P. agrostioides* Trin.
PANICUM VIRGATUM Linn.
PANICUM WALTERI Poir.   *P. latifolium Linn.*
PANICUM CLANDESTINUM Linn.
PANICUM DEPAUPERATUM Muhl.
PANICUM DICHOTOMUM Linn.
    forma COMMUNE Man.
    forma FASCICULATUM Man.
    forma GRACILE Man.
PANICUM DICHOTOMUM ELATUM.
PANICUM PUBESCENS Lam.
PANICUM CRUS-GALLI Linn.
PANICUM CRUS-GALLI HISPIDUM (Muhl.) Torr.
CHAMÆRAPHIS GLAUCA (Linn.) O. K.
CHAMÆRAPHIS VIRIDIS (Linn.) Millsp. Fl. W. Va. (1892).
CHAMÆRAPHIS ITALICA (Linn.) O. K.
CENCHRUS TRIBULOIDES Linn.
HOMALOCENCHRUS VIRGINICUS (Willd.) Britton.
HOMALOCENCHRUS ORYZOIDES (Linn.) Poll.
TRIPSACUM DACTYLOIDES Linn.
ANDROPOGON PROVINCIALIS Lam.
ANDROPOGON SCOPARIUS Michx.
ANDROPOGON VIRGINICUS Linn.
ANDROPOGON NUTANS LINNÆNUS Hack.
PHALARIS ARUNDINACEA Linn.
ARISTIDA DICHOTOMA Linn.
ARISTIDA OLIGANTHA Michx.
ARISTIDA LANATA Poir.

MUHLENBERGIA SOBOLIFERA (Muhl.) Trin.
MUHLENBERGIA MEXICANA (Linn.) Trin.
MUHLENBERGIA SYLVATICA (Torr.) A. Gray.
MUHLENBERGIA DIFFUSA Schreb.
BRACHYELYTRUM ERECTUM (Schreb.) Beauv.   *Brachyelytrum aristosum* (Michx.) B. S. P.
BRACHYELYTRUM ERECTUM GLABRATUM (Vasey.)
Brachyelytrum aristosum glabratum Vasey, mss. In Millsp. Flora W. Va., 469 (1892).

A new variety discovered by Mr. L. W. Nuttall. It agrees with the species except that it is perfectly smooth, and has an awn pointed second glume which is about one-half the length of the flowering glume. Its most striking peculiarity is that it has invariably two culms from each rootstock.

High, rocky woods, rare.

PHLEUM PRATENSE Linn.
AGROSTIS ALBA Linn.
AGROSTIS ALBA VULGARIS (With.) Thurb.
Forma ARISTATA Millsp. in Fl. W. Va , 469 (1892).
AGROSTIS PERENNANS (Walt.) Tuck.
AGROSTIS HIEMALIS (Walt.) B. S. P.
Calamagrostis cinnoides (Muhl.) Scribn. (*Nuttall*).
CINNA ARUNDINACEA Linn.
ARRHENATHERUM ELATIUS (Linn.) Beauv.
HOLCUS LANATUS Linn.
DANTHONIA SPICATA (Linn.) Beauv.
DANTHONIA COMPRESSA Austin.
ELEUSINE INDICA (Linn.) Gærtn.
DACTYLOCTENIUM ÆGYPTICUM (Linn.) Willd.   *Eleusine Ægyptica* Pers.
SIEGLINGIA SESLERIOIDES (Michx.) Scribn.   *Sieglingia cuprea* (Michx.)
EATONIA OBTUSATA (Michx.) A. Gray.
EATONIA PENNSYLVANICA (DC.) A. Gray.
ERAGROSTIS HYPNOIDES (Lam.) B. S. P.
ERAGROSTIS ERAGROSTIS (Linn.) Karst.   *Eragrostis minor* Host,
ERAGROSTIS MAJOR Host.
ERAGROSTIS PILOSA (Linn.) Beauv.
ERAGROSTIS CAROLINIANA (Spreng.) Scribn.   *Eragrostis Purshii* Schrad.
ERAGROSTIS CAPILLARIS (Linn.) Nees.
ERAGROSTIS FRANKII Meyer.
MELICA MUTICA Walt.
KORYCARPUS DIANDRUS (Michx.) O. K.   *Corycarpus Americanus* (Beauv.)
UNIOLA LATIFOLIA Michx.
DACTYLIS GLOMERATA Linn.
POA ANNUA Linn.

Poa compressa Linn.
    Forma depauperata Fl. W. Va., 472 (1892).
Poa pratensis Linn.
Poa trivalis Linn.
Poa sylvestris A. Gray.
Poa alsodes A. Gray.
Poa autumnalis Muhl.   *Poa flexuosa* Muhl. not Wahl.
Poa brevifolia Muhl.
Panicularia Canadensis (Michx.) O. K.
Panicularia elongata (Torr.) O. K.
Panicularia nervata (Willd.) O. K.
    Forma major Fl. W. Va., 473 (1892).
Festuca octoflora Walt.
Festuca elatior Linn.
Festuca elatior pratensis (Huds.) Hack.   *Festuca pratensis* Huds.
Festuca nutans Willd.
Bromus hordeaceus Linn.   *Bromus mollis* Linn.
Bromus secalinus Linn.
Bromus racemosus Linn.
Bromus ciliatus Linn.
Lolium perenne Linn.
Elymus Virginicus Linn.
Elymus Canadensis glaucifolius (Willd.) Torr.
Elymus striatus Willd.
Elymus striatus villosus (Muhl.) A. Gray.
Hystrix Hystrix (Linn.) Millsp. Fl. W. Va., 474 (1892).

CYPERACEÆ.

Cyperus flavescens Linn.
Cyperus diandrus Torr.
Cyperus esculentus Linn.
Cyperus strigosus Linn.
Cyperus refractus Engelm.
Cyperus Lancastriensis Porter.
Kyllinga pumila Michx.
Dulichium arundinaceum (Linn.) Britton.   *Dulichium spathaceum* Pers.
Eleocharis tuberculosa (Michx.) R. & S.
Eleocharis ovata (Roth.) R. & S.
Eleocharis palustris (Linn.) R. & S.
Eleocharis palustris glaucescens (Willd.) A. Gray.
Eleocharis tenuis (Willd.) Schult.
Eleocharis acicularis (Linn.) R. & S.
Fimbristylis autumnalis (Linn.) R. & S.

SCIRPUS AMERICANUS Pers.   *Scirpus pungens* Vahl.
SCIRPUS LACUSTRIS Linn.
SCIRPUS SYLVATICUS Linn.
SCIRPUS ATROVIRENS Muhl.
SCIRPUS POLYPHYLLUS Vahl.
SCIRPUS LINEATUS Michx.   *Eriophorum lineatum* (Michx.) Benth & Hook.
SCIRPUS CYPERINUS (Linn.) Kunth.   *Eriophorum cyperinum* Linn.
ERIOPHORUM VIRGINICUM Linn.
RYNCHOSPORA GLOMERATA (Linn.) Vahl.
CAREX FOLLICULATA Linn.
CAREX INTUMESCENS Rudge.
CAREX ASA-GRAYI Bailey.   *Carex Grayii* Carey.
CAREX LUPULINA Muhl.
CAREX LURIDA Wahl.
CAREX LURIDA GRACILIS (Boott.) Bailey.
CAREX FRANKII (Kunth.)   *Carex stenolepis* Torr.
CAREX SQUARROSA Dewey.
CAREX STRICTA Lam.
CAREX TORTA Boott.
CAREX PRASINA Wahl.
CAREX CRINITA Lam.
CAREX CRINITA × PRASINA Bailey, Flor. W. Va., 460 (1892).
CAREX VIRESCENS Muhl.
CAREX VIRESCENS COSTATA (Schw.) Dewey.
CAREX TRICEPS HIRSUTA (Willd.) Bailey.
CAREX DEBILIS RUDGEI Bailey.
CAREX VENUSTA MINOR Bœckl.
CAREX GRACILLIMA Schw.
CAREX AMPHIBOLA Steud.   *Carex grisea angustifolia* Boott.
CAREX GLANCODEA Tuck.
CAREX LAXIFLORA Lam.
CAREX LAXIFLORA PATULIFOLIA (Dewey.) Carey.
CAREX ALBURSINA Sheldon.   *Carex laxiflora latifolia* Boott.
CAREX DIGITALIS Willd.
CAREX LAXICULMIS Schw.
Carex platyphylla Carey (*Nuttall*).
CAREX PLANTAGINEA Lam. (*Nuttall*).
Carex Varia Muhl. (*Nuttall*).
CAREX VARIA COLORATA Bailey.
CAREX PENNSYLVANICA Lam.
CAREX PEDICILLATA (Dewey.) Britton.   *Carex communis* Bailey.
CAREX JAMESII Schw.
CAREX LEPTALEA Wahl.   *Carex polytrichioides* Muhl.

CAREX FRASERI And.

The following remarks of Prof. T. C. Porter render it evident that this rare and odd sedge came originally from Randolph or Barbour County, each of which lies between the headwaters of the two Kanawhas:

"Muhlenberg, in his *Descriptio uberior Graminum*, etc., p. 265, under *C. lagopus?* which is *C. Fraseri*, Andrews adds these words: 'Habitat in Tyger-Valley, Pennsylvaniæ, *unde siccam habeo et vivam.*" Kin, the German gardener who collected in Pennsylvania brought it home, and his label reads thus: 'Deigher Walli in der Wilternus.' Dr. Gray has shrewdly conjectured that by 'Deigher Walli,' or Tygert Valley, is meant Tygart's Valley, which lies further south in Virginia." In a foot-note, Professor Porter adds, "A box containing the Carices of Muhlenberg has just been discovered (1877) in the herbarium of the Academy, Philadelphia, and the label attached to the specimens of Kin's collection places Tyger Valley 'prope amnem Kenahway.'"

Mr. Nuttall has found a plentiful station for this species near Nuttallburg in the Great Kanawha region.

CAREX STIPATA Muhl.
CAREX VULPINOIDEA Michx.
CAREX ROSEA Schk.
CAREX ROSEA RADIATA Dewey.
CAREX RETROFLEXA Muhl.   *Carex rosea retroflexa* Torr.
CAREX SPARGANIOIDES Muhl.
CAREX MUHLENBERGII var. Bailey.
CAREX MUHLENBERGII XALAPENSIS (Kth.) Britton.   *Carex Muhlenbergii enervis* Boott.
CAREX CEPHALOPHORA Muhl.
CAREX CANESCENS VULGARIS Bailey.
CAREX TRIBULOIDES Wahl.
CAREX TRIBULOIDES TURBATA Bailey.
CAREX SCOPARIA Schk.
CAREX STRAMINEA Willd.

ARACEÆ.

ARISÆMA TRIPHYLLUM (Linn.) Torr.
ARISÆMA DRACONTIUM (Linn.) Schott.
SPATHYEMA FŒTIDA (Linn.) Raf.
ACORUS CALAMUS Linn. (*Nuttall*).

LEMNACEÆ.

LEMNA MINOR Linn.

COMMELINACEÆ.

COMMELINA VIRGINICA Linn.
TRADESCANTIA VIRGINIANA Linn.
TRADESCANTIA PILOSA Lehm.

JUNCACEÆ.

Juncus effusus Linn.
Juncus setaceus Rostk.
Juncus marginatus Rostk.
Juncus marginatus paucicapitatus Engelm.
Juncus tenuis Willd.
Juncus acuminatus Michx.
Juncus nodosus Linn.
Juncus Canadensis J. Gay.
Juncoides pilosum (Linn.) O. K.· *Luzula pilosa* Willd.
Juncoides campestre (Linn.) O. K. *Luzula cumpestris* DC.

LILIACEÆ.

Asparagus officinalis Linn.
Polygonatum biflorum (Walt.) Ell.
Polygonatum biflorum commutatum (R. & S.) Morong. *Polygonatum commutatum* Dietr.
Streptopus roseus Michx.
Disporum lanuginosum (Michx.) Britton.
Vagnera racemosa (Linn.) Morong. *Unifolium racemosum* Britton.
Unifolium canadense (Desf.) Greene. *Maianthemum Canadense* Desf.
Hemerocallis fulva Linn.
Allium vineale Linn.
Allium tricoccum Aiton.
Allium cernuum Roth.
Allium Canadense Kalm.
Camassia Fraseri (A. Gray) Torr.
Muscari botryoides (Linn.) Mill.
Orinthogallum umbellatum Linn.
Lilium Philadelphicum Linn.
Lilium supurbum Linn. (*Nuttall*).
Lilium Canadense Linn.
Lilium tigrinum Andr.
Erythronium Americanum Ker.
Erythronium albidum Nutt.
    Rich soil, Kanawha region, along Coal and Len's Creeks, Ohio Co., near Mt. de Chantal (*Rev. A. Boutlou*).
Chamælirium leuteum (Linn.) A. Gray.
Uvularia perfoliata Linn.
Uvularia puberula Michx.
    Kate's Mountain, alt. 3,300 ft. (*Small & Vail*).
Uvularia sessilifolia Linn.
Clintonia borealis (Ait.) Raf.
Clintonia umbellulata (Michx.) Torr.

MEDIOLA VIRGINIANA Linn.
TRILLIUM SESSILE Linn.
TRILLIUM ERECTUM Linn.
TRILLIUM ERECTUM ALBUM Pursh.
TRILLIUM ERECTUM DECLINATUM Pursh.
TRILLIUM GRANDIFLORUM (Michx.) Salisb.
TRILLIUM CERNUUM Linn.
TRILLIUM NIVALE Riddell.
TRILLIUM UNDULATUM Willd.   *Trillium erythrocarpum* Michx.
ALETRIS FARINOSA Linn.
MELANTHIUM VIRGINICUM Linn.
MELANTHIUM PARVIFLORUM (Michx.) S. Wats.
VERATRUM VIRIDE Ait. (*Nuttall*).
CHROSPERMA MUSCÆTOXICUM (Walt.) O. K.

SMILACEÆ.

SMILAX HERBACEA Linn.
SMILAX ROTUNDIFOLIA Linn.
SMILAX GLAUCA Walt.
SMILAX PSEUDO-CHINA Linn.
SMILAX HISPIDA Muhl. (*Nuttall*).

AMARYLLIDACEÆ.

HYPOXIS HIRSUTA (Linn.) Coville.   *Hypoxis erecta* Linn.

DIOSCOREACEÆ.

DIOSCOREA VILLOSA Linn.

IRIDACEÆ.

IRIS VERSICOLOR Linn.
IRIS VERNA Linn.
IRIS CRISTATA Ait.
SISYRINCHIUM BERMUDIANA Linn.   *S. angustifolium* Mill.   *S. anceps* Cav.

ORCHIDACEÆ.

ACHROANTHES UNIFOLIA (Michx.) Raf.   *Malaxis unifolia* Michx.
LEPTORCHIS LILIIFOLIA (Linn.) O. K. (*Nuttall*).
APLECTRUM SPICATUM (Walt.) B. S. P.
CORALLORHIZA CORALLORHIZA (Linn.) Karst.   *C. innata* R. Br.
CORALLORHIZA ODONTORHIZA (Willd.) Nutt.
CORALLORHIZA MULTIFLORA Nutt.
GYROSTACHYS CERNUA (Linn.) O. K.
GYROSTACHYS GRACILIS (Biegl.) O. K.
PERAMIUM REPENS (Linn.) Salisb.   *Goodyera repens* R. Br.

PERAMIUM PUBESCENS (Willd.) C. C. Curtis. *Goodyera pubescens* R. Br.
LIMODORUM TUBEROSUM Linn. *Calopogon tuberosus* (Linn.) B. S. P.
POGONIA OPHIOGLOSSOIDES (Linn.) Ker. *Pogonia trianthophora* (Sw.) B. S. P. (*Nuttall*).
ORCHIS SPECTABILIS Linn.
HABENARIA CLAVELLATA (Michx.) Spreng. *H. tridentata* Hook.
HABENARIA FLAVA (Linn.) A. Gray.
HABENARIA ORBICULATA (Pursh) Torr.
HABENARIA CILIARIS (Linn.) R. Br.
HABENARIA LACERA (Michx.) R. Br. *Habenaria peramœna* A. Gray. (*Nuttall*).
HABENARIA PSYCODES (Linn.) A. Gray.
CYPRIPEDIUM PARVIFLORUM Salisb.
CYPRIPEDIUM HIRSUTUM Mill. *C. pubescens* Willd.
  Slope of Kate's Mountain, alt. 3,300 ft. (*Small & Vail*).
CYPRIPEDIUM ACAULE Ait.

SAURURACEÆ.
SAURURUS CERNUUS Linn.

JUGLANDACEÆ.
JUGLANS CINEREA Linn.
JUGLANS NIGRA Linn.
HICORIA OVATA (Mill.) Britton.
HICORIA SULCATA (Willd.) Britton.
HICORIA ALBA (Linn.) Britton.
HICORIA GLABRA (Mill.) Britton.
HICORIA MICROCARPA (Nutt.) Britton.
HICORIA MINIMA (Marsh.) Britton. (*Nuttall.*)

SALICACEÆ.
SALIX NIGRA Marsh.
SALIX NIGRA FALCATA Torr.
SALIX AMYGDALOIDES And.
SALIX ALBA VITELLINA Koch.
SALIX BABYLONICA Tourn.
SALIX DISCOLOR Muhl.
SALIX HUMILIS Marsh.
SALIX SERICEA Marsh.
SALIX CORDATA Muhl.
POPULUS ALBA Linn.
POPULUS TREMULOIDES Michx.
POPULUS GRANDIDENTATA Michx.
POPULUS BALSAMIFERA CANDICANS (Ait.) A. Gray.
POPULUS MONILIFERA Ait.

BETULACEÆ.

BETULA LENTA Linn.

Betula lenta × lutea.
  A number of specimens of this hybrid birch were found in 1892 at Pickens, Randolph Co. In all, the bark forms of each species were intermixed. All the specimens were small saplings about 2 in. in diameter (*Millspaugh*).

BETULA LUTEA Michx. f. (*Nuttall*).
BETULA POPULIFOLIA Marsh.
BETULA NIGRA Linn.
ALNUS VIRIDIS (Chaix.) DC.
ALNUS RUGOSA (Ehrh.) Koch.
CARPINUS CAROLINIANA Walt.
OSTRYA VIRGINIANA (Mill.) Willd.
CORYLUS AMERICANA Walt. (*Nuttall*).
CORYLUS ROSTRATA Ait.

FAGACEÆ.

QUERCUS ALBA Linn.
QUERCUS MINOR (Marsh). Sarg.
QUERCUS MACROCARPA Michx.
QUERCUS PRINUS Linn.
QUERCUS MUHLENBERGII Engelm.
QUERCUS RUBRA Linn.
QUERCUS COCCINEA Wang.
QUERCUS VELUTINA Lam. *Q. tinctoria* Bartr.
QUERCUS PALUSTRIS DuRoi. (*Nuttall*).
QUERCUS DIGITATA (Marsh) Sudw. *Q. cuneata* Wang.
QUERCUS NIGRA Linn.
QUERCUS ILICIFOLIA Wang.
QUERCUS IMBRICARIA Michx.
CASTANEA DENTATA (Marsh.) Sudw. *C. sativa Americana* Wats. & Coult.
CASTANEA PUMILA Mill.
FAGUS ATROPUNICEA (Marsh.) Sudw. *F. ferruginea* Ait.

ULMACEÆ.

ULMUS PUBESCENS Walt. *U. fulva* Michx.
ULMUS AMERICANA Linn.
ULMUS RACEMOSA Thomas.
CELTIS OCCIDENTALIS Linn.

MORACEÆ.

CANNABIS SATIVA Linn.
HUMULUS LUPULUS Linn.
MORUS RUBRA Linn.
MORUS ALBA Linn.

Toxylon pomiferum Raf.   *Maclura aurantiaca* Nutt.
    Banks of the Ohio River, Mason Co., near Point Pleasant. (*Millspaugh*).
PAPYRIUS PAPYRIFERA (Vent.) O. K.   *Broussonetia papyrifera* Vent.

URTICACEÆ.

URTICA GRACILIS Ait.
URTICA URENS Linn.
URTICASTRUM DIVARICATUM (Linn.) O. K.   *Laportea Canadensis* Gaud.
ADICEA PUMILA (Linn.) Raf.   *Pilea pumila* A. Gray.
BOEHMERIA CYLINDRICA (Linn.) Willd.

LORANTHACEÆ.

PHORADENDRON FLAVESCENS (Pursh) Nutt.

SANTALACEÆ.

PYRULARIA PUBERA Michx.
    Also found in Nicholas Co., along Peter Creek. (*Rev. A. Boutlou.*)

ARISTOLOCHIACEÆ.

ASARUM CANADENSE Linn.
ASARUM VIRGINICUM Linn.
ARISTOLOCHIA SERPENTARIA Linn.
ARISTOLOCHIA MACROPHYLLA Lam.   *A. Sipho* L'Her.

POLYGONACEÆ.

ERIGONUM ALLENII Watson, in A. Gray, Man. Ed. 6, 734 (1890).
    Perennial, white tomentose throughout, the tall scape-like stem repeatedly dichotomous above; radical leaves lanceolate, long-petiolate, the upper in whorls of 4 or 5, ovate to ovate-oblong, very shortly petiolate, much reduced above; involucres mostly sessile; flowers glabrous, yellow, the segments elliptical.
    Near White Sulphur Springs, Greenbrier Co. (*Dr. T. F. Allen*).
POLYGONUM ORIENTALE Linn.
POLYGONUM PENNSYLVANICUM Linn.
POLYGONUM PERSICARIA Linn.
POLYGONUM PERSICARIA *forma* ALBIFLORA Millsp. Fl. W. Va. 332 (1892).
POLYGONUM HYDROPIPER Linn.
POLYGONUM PUNCTATUM Ell.   *P. acre* H. B. K.
POLYGONUM HYDROPIPEROIDES Michx.
POLYGONUM VIRGINIANUM Linn.
POLYGONUM AVICULARE Linn.
POLYGONUM ERECTUM Linn.
POLYGONUM TENUE Michx.

Polygonum sagittatum Linn.
Polygonum arifolium Linn.
Polygonum Convolvulus Linn.
Polygonum scandens Linn.   *P. dumetorum scandens* A. Gray.
Fagopyrum Fagopyrum (Linn.) Karst.   *F. esculentum* Mœnch.
Rumex Brittanica Linn.
Rumex crispus Linn.
Rumex obtusifolius Linn.
Rumex crispus × obtusifolius (Meisn.)
Rumex sanguineus Linn.
Rumex conglomeratus Murr.
Rumex acetosella Linn.

CHENOPODIACEÆ.

Chenopodium album Linn.
Chenopodium album viride (Linn.) Moq.
Chenopodium hybridum Linn.
Chenopodium urbicum Linn.
Chenopodium glaucum Linn.
Chenopodium Botrys Linn.
Chenopodium ambrosioides Linn.
Chenopodium anthelminticum Linn.   *C. ambrosioides anthelminticum* A. Gray.

AMARANTHACEÆ.

Amaranthus hybridus Linn.   *A. hypochondriacus* Linn.   *A. chlorostachys* Willd. (*Nuttall*).
Amaranthus hybridus paniculatus (Linn.) Uline & Bray.   *A. paniculatus* Linn.
Amaranthus retroflexus Linn. (*Nuttall*).
Amaranthus albus Linn.
Amaranthus spinosus Linn.

PHYTOLACCACEÆ.

Phytolacca decandra Linn.

AIZOACEÆ.

Mollugo verticillata Linn.

PORTULACACEÆ.

Portulaca oleracea Linn.
Claytonia Virginica Linn.
Claytonia Caroliniana Michx.

CARYOPHYLLACEÆ.

DIANTHUS ARMERIA Linn.
SAPONARIA OFFICINALIS Linn.
SILENE STELLATA (Linn.) Ait.
SILENE VIRGINICA (Linn.)
SILENE ALBA Muhl. *S. nivea* Otth.
SILENE CAROLINIANA Walt. *S. Pennsylvanica* Michx.
    Greenbrier Co., on Kate's Mountain, alt. 3,300 ft. (*Small & Vail*).
SILENE ANTERRHINA Linn.
AGROSTEMMA GITHAGO Linn. *Lychnis Githago* Lam.
CERASTIUM VULGATUM Linn.
CERASTIUM VISCOSUM Linn.
CERASTIUM ARVENSE Linn.
CERASTIUM LONGIPEDUNCULATUM Muhl. *C. nutans* Raf.
ALSINE MEDIA Linn. *Stellaria media* Smith.
ALSINE PUBERA (Michx). Britton. *Stellaria pubera* Michx.
ALSINE LONGIFOLIA (Muhl.) Britton. *Stellaria longifolia* Muhl.
ARENARIA SERPYLLIFOLIA Linn.
SPERGULA ARVENSIS Linn. (*Nuttall*).
ANYCHIA CANADENSIS (Linn.) B. S. P.
Anychia dichotoma Michx.
    This species first appeared in this locality in 1895, at the bottom of a newly excavated railroad cut. Had the seeds been buried and dormant? (*Nuttall*, 1837).
PARONYCHIA DICHOTOMA (Linn.) Nutt.

NYMPHACEÆ.

CASTALIA ODORATA (Dryand) Woodv. & Wood.
NYMPHÆA ADVENA Soland.

MAGNOLIACEÆ.

MAGNOLIA ACUMINATA Linn.
MAGNOLIA TRIPETALA Linn.
MAGNOLIA FRASERI Walt., Fl. Car., 159 (1788).
    Leaves oblong-obovate or spatulate, auriculate at the base, glabrous, 8 to 20 in. long; petals obovate-spatulate, with narrow claws, 4 in. long. Flower more graceful and cone of fruit smaller than in the preceding species.
    Type locality doubtless in the Alleghanies of West Virginia, where it is abundant and in typical form.
LIRIODENDRON TULIPIFERA Linn.

ANONACEÆ.

ASIMINA TRILOBA (Linn.) Dunal.

RANUNCULACEÆ.

CLEMATIS VIRGINIANA Linn.
CLEMATIS VIORNA Linn.
Clematis ovata Pursh.
    Greenbrier Co., in rocky soil high up on Kate's Mountain, near White Sulphur Springs (*N. L. Britton*).
ASTRAGENE AMERICANA Sims.   *Clematis verticillaris* DC.
ANEMONE CYLINDRICA A. Gray.
ANEMONE VIRGINIANA Linn.
ANEMONE CANADENSIS Linn.
ANEMONE QUINQUEFOLIA Linn.
ANEMONE TRIFOLIA Linn.
    Greenbrier Co., in a dry ravine at White Sulphur Springs, alt. about 2,300 ft. (*A. A. Heller*).
HEPATICA HEPATICA (Linn.) Karst.
HEPATICA ACUTA (Pursh.) Britton.
SYNDESMON THALICTROIDES (Linn.) Hoffmg.
SYNDESMON THALICTROIDES *forma* ROSEA Millsp. Fl. W. Va., 319 (1892).
THALICTRUM DIOICUM Linn.
THALICTRUM POLYGAMUM Muhl.
THALICTRUM PURPURASCENS Linn.
THALICTRUM CLAVATUM DC.
TRAUTVETTERIA CAROLINENSIS (Walt.) Vail?   *T. palmata* F. &. M.
RANUNCULUS OBTUSIUSCULUS Raf.   *R. ambigens* Watson.
RANUNCULUS ABORTIVUS Linn.
RANUNCULUS SCELERATUS Linn.
RANUNCULUS RECURVATUS Poir.
RANUNCULUS FASCICULATUS Muhl.
RANUNCULUS SEPTENTRIONALIS Poir.
RANUNCULUS PENNSYLVANICUS Linn f.
RANUNCULUS REPENS Linn.
RANUNCULUS ACRIS Linn.
HELLEBORUS VIRIDIS Linn.
CALTHA PALUSTRIS Linn.
ISOPYRUM TRIFOLIUM (Linn.) Britt.
AQUILEGIA CANADENSIS Linn.
DELPHINIUM TRICORNE Michx. (*Nuttall*).
DELPHINIUM TRICORNE *forma* ALBIFLORA Millsp. Fl. W. Va., 322 (1892).
DELPHINIUM CONSOLIDA Linn.
ACONITUM UNCINATUM Linn.
CIMICIFUGA AMERICANA Michx.
CIMICIFUGA RACEMOSA (Linn.) Nutt.
ACTÆA RUBRA (Ait.) Willd.   *A. spicata rubra* Ait.

ACTÆA ALBA (Linn.) Mill.
HYDRASTIS CANADENSIS Linn.
XANTHORRHIZA APIIFOLIA L'Her.

BERBERIDACEÆ.

BERBERIS CANADENSIS Mill.
BERBERIS VULGARIS Linn.
CAULOPHYLLUM THALICTROIDES (Linn.) Michx.
JEFFERSONIA DIPHYLLA (Linn.) Pers.
PODOPHYLLUM PELTATUM Linn.

MENISPERMACEÆ.

MENISPERMUM CANADENSE Linn.

CALYCANTHACEÆ.

CALYCANTHUS FLORIDUS Linn. *Beurera florida* Ehret.
CALYCANTHUS FERTILIS Walt. *Beurera lævigatus* (Willd.) O.K.

LAURACEÆ.

SASSAFRAS SASSAFRAS (Linn.) Karst. *Sassafras officinale* Nees.
BENZOIN BENZOIN (Linn.) Coult. *Lindera Benzoin* Meisn.

PAPAVERACEÆ.

SANGUINARIA CANADENSIS Linn.
STYLOPHORUM DIPHYLLUM (Michx.) Nutt. (*Nuttall*).
CHELIDONIUM MAJUS Linn.
Glaucium Glaucium (L.) Karst.
    Jefferson Co., near Charlestown, Shenandoah Junction, Spring Mill, and Milltown (*Millspaugh*).
PAPAVER DUBIUM Linn.
ADLUMIA FUNGOSA (Ait). Greene.
BICUCULLA CUCULLARIA (Linn.) Millsp. Fl. W. Va., 327 (1892).
BICUCULLA CANADENSIS (Goldie) Millsp. loc. cit.
BICUCULLA EXIMINA (Ker) Millsp. loc. cit.
CAPNOIDES SEMPERVIRENS (Linn.) Bœrk. (*Nuttall.*)
CAPNOIDES FLAVULUM (Raf.) O.K.
CAPNOIDES AUREUM (Willd.) O.K.
FUMARIA OFFICINALIS Linn.

CRUCIFERACEÆ.

RORIPA NASTURTIUM (Linn.) Rusby. *Nasturtium officinale* R. Br.
RORIPA SYLVESTRIS (Linn.) Bess. *Nasturtium sylvestre* R. Br.
RORIPA OBTUSA (Nutt.) Britton. *Nasturtium obtusum* Nutt.
RORIPA PALUSTRIS (Linn.) Bess. *Nasturtium palustre* DC.

Roripa hispida (Desv.) Britton. *Nasturtium hispidum* DC.
Roripa Armoracia (Linn.) Hitch. *Nasturtium Armoracia* Fries.
Barbarea Barbarea (Linn.) MacM. *B. vulgaris* R. Br.
Barbarea praecox (J. E. Smith) R. Br.
Arabis patens Sulliv.
Arabis laevigata (Muhl.) Poir.
Arabis Canadensis Linn.
Arabis lyrata Linn.
Dentaria diphylla Michx. *Cardamine diphylla* Wood.
Dentaria heterophylla Nutt. *Cardamine heterophylla* Wood.
Dentaria laciniata Muhl. *Cardamine laciniata* Wood.
Dentaria laciniata multifida Muhl.
Cardamine hirsuta Linn.
Cardamine bulbosa (Schreb.) B. S. P.
Cardamine Douglassii (Torr.) Britton.
Cardamine rotundifolia Michx.
Draba ramosissima Desv.
Draba verna Linn.
  Greenbrier Co., on Kate's Mountain, alt. 3,300 ft. (*Small & Vail*).
Hesperis matronalis Linn.
Sisymbrium officinale (Linn.) Scop.
Stenophragma Thaliana (Linn.) Celak. *Sisymbrium Thalianum* (L. Gay).
Erysimum cheiranthoides Linn.
Camelina sativa (Linn.) Crantz.
Brassica nigra (Linn.) Koch.
Brassica sinapistrum Boiss.
Bursa Bursa-pastoris (Linn.) Weber.
Lepidium Virginicum Linn.
Lepidium campestre (Linn.) R. Br.
Raphanus sativus Linn.

CAPPARIDACEÆ.
Cleome spinosa Linn.

DROSERACEÆ.
Drosera rotundifolia Linn.

CRASSULACEÆ.
Sedum pulchellum Michx.
Sedum Nevii A. Gray.
Sedum ternatum (Haw) Michx.
Sedum telephioides Michx.
Sedum Telephium Linn.
Penthorum sedoides Linn.

SAXIFRAGACEÆ.

ASTILBE BITERNATA (Vent.) Britton. *A. decandra* Don.
SAXIFRAGA VIRGINIENSIS Michx.
SAXIFRAGA PENNSYLVANICA Linn.
SAXIFRAGA MICRANTHIDIFOLIA (Haw) B. S. P.
THEROFON ACONITIFOLIUM (Nutt.) Millsp. Fl. W. Va. 361 (1892).
TIARELLA CORDIFOLIA Linn.
MITELLA DIPHYLLA Linn.
HEUCHERA VILLOSA Michx.
HEUCHERA AMERICANA Linn.
HEUCHERA RUGELII Shuttlw.
PARNASSIA GRANDIFOLIA DC.
HYDRANGEA ARBORESCENS Linn.
HYDRANGEA ARBORESCENS KANAWHANA Millsp. Fl. W. Va. 363 (1892).
   Low straggling bush, leaves small, paler beneath, acuminate, somewhat cordate at the base; cymes very open and branching, marginal radiant flowers many, 1 in. broad, fertile flowers nearly glabrous, smaller than in the species. Along the Little Kanawha River from Kanawha Station to Glenville. (*Millspaugh*).
RIBES CYNOSBATI Linn.
RIBES ROTUNDIFOLIUM Michx.
RIBES PROSTRATUM L'Her.
RIBES FLORIDUM L'Her.

HAMAMELIDACEÆ.

HAMAMELIS VIRGINICA Linn.
LIQUIDAMBAR STYRACIFLUA Linn.

PLATANACEÆ.

PLATANUS OCCIDENTALIS Linn.

ROSACEÆ.

PRUNUS AMERICANA Marsh.
   Randolph Co., near Pickens (*Millspaugh*). (*Nuttall*).
PRUNUS ANGUSTIFOLIA Marsh. *P. Chicasa* Michx.
PRUNUS PENNSYLVANICA Linn. f.
PRUNUS VIRGINIANA Linn. (*Nuttall*).
PRUNUS SEROTINA Ehrh.
OPULASTER OPULIFOLIUS (Linn.) O.K.
SPIRÆA CORYMBOSA Raf. *S. betulæfolia* Pall.
SPIRÆA VIRGINIANA Britton, Bull. Torr. Club, 17, 314 (1890).
   "A glabrous shrub, the branches forming long wands, erect or reclining, 1 to 4 ft. long. Leaves oblong or slightly oblanceolate, thin, obtuse or short-pointed at the apex, rounded or cuneate at the base, 1.5 to 2 in. long, 5 to 8 lines wide, green above, pale

beneath, entire or with a few low serrations in the upper half; petioles 2 lines long; pedicels and peduncles pale and glaucous; flowers about 2 lines broad, in terminal compound corymbs 1 to 3 in. across; calyx teeth 5, triangular, blunt, about the length of the short-campanulate tube, distinctly glaucous; petals 5, white ovate-orbicular, obtuse; stamens 15 to 20, persistent; styles 5 to 6; follicles, in the specimens examined, 5 to 6, apparently sterile, included in the persistent calyx."

"On damp rocks along the Monongahela river, Morgantown, West Virginia, collected by Dr. C. F. Millspaugh in flower, June 20, 1890, and in apparently imperfect fruit late in September. Collected also by Mr. G. R. Vasey in the mountains of North Carolina, 1878."

"*Spiræa betulæfolia*, Pall, and *S. corymbosa*, Raf., have much longer follicles exerted beyond the calyx; broader, thicker and dentate leaves, and are different in habit. Rafinesque published a number of species in his New Flora, but none of them can apply to this one."

Spiræa salicifolia Linn. (*Nuttall*).

SPIRÆA TOMENTOSA Linn. (*Nuttall*).

ULMARIA RUBRA Hill. *Spiræa rubra* Britton.

ARUNCUS ARUNCUS (Linn.) Karst. *Spiræa Aruncus* Linn.

PORTERANTHUS TRIFOLIATUS (Linn.) Britton. *Gillenia trifoliata* Linn.
 Greenbrier Co., on Kate's Mountain, alt. 3,300 ft. (*Small & Vail*).

PORTERANTHUS STIPULATUS (Muhl.) Britton. *Gillenia stipulacea* Nutt.

RUBUS ODORATUS Linn.

RUBUS ODORATUS COLUMBIANUS Millsp. Fl. W. Va., 356 (1892).
 Leaves thin, ample, 5 to 7 incised almost to the petiole, divisions oblong-lanceolate, long and taper pointed, sharply and mostly double-serrate. Inflorescence smaller and more compact than in the species. Fruit also smaller and of a more decided musky flavor. Monongalia Co., cool woods of Tibb's Run (*Millspaugh*).

RUBUS STRIGOSUS Michx.

RUBUS OCCIDENTALIS Linn.

RUBUS VILLOSUS Ait.

RUBUS VILLOSUS FRONDOSUS Torr.

RUBUS BAILEYANUS Britton. *R. villosus humifusus* T. & G.

RUBUS MILLSPAUGHI Britton, Bull. Torr. Club, 18:366 (1891).
 "Ascending, wand-like, entirely unarmed or with a very few weak prickles above, glabrous throughout or the younger shoots scurfy pubescent. Stems one and one-half to four meters long; leaves long petioled, pedately 5-foliate or some of those on the twigs 3-foliate; leaflets thin, oval, glabrous on both sides, long-acuminate at the apex, mostly rounded at the base, 12 to 15 cm. long, about 5 cm. wide, sharply, but not deeply serrate; stock of the terminal leaflet 7 to 10 cm. long; inflorescence loosely racemose; bracts linear-lanceolate, acuminate; fruit black, about 10 mm. long" (*Millspaugh*).

"Nearest to *R. villosus*, but evidently a distinct species. Curiously enough there is a leaf of this species glued down on the sheet of *R. Canadensis*, L. in herb Linn., and it appears to have been included in his description of that species—the specimens of which were furnished by Kalm."

Near the summit of Point Mountain in Randolph County at an altitude of 3,500 ft., also along the Gandy in great profusion. Pendleton and Pocahontas, on Little Rich Mountains abundant. The mountaineers claim that it is upon this species that the bears grow fat for their period of hibernation, the fruit being late to ripen and very nutritious.

Mr. John K. Small remarks in his Studies of the Botany of the Southeastern United States, Bull. Torr. Club, 21:19 (1894) in reporting this species: "Grows on the walls of the cañon at Tallulah Falls, Ga. Collected in flower in April, 1893; alt. 1,600 ft. This most likely locates the southern limit of the geographical range of *R. Millspaughi*. Being a typical high mountain species, it is not to be expected much below 1,600 feet, and just south of the above-mentioned locality the Blue Ridge 'runs out' into the plains. Further south the land decreases gradually in altitude until the gulf is reached. According to my observations the above plant thrives most vigorously at altitudes ranging from 4,500 to 6,000 ft. It grows well at lower elevations, but never in such a prolific manner." Mr. Small and Anna M. Vail also give in their "Report of the Botanical Exploration of Southwestern Virginia, 1892," the following additional localities for this species: "Above Fox Creek, on Pine Mountain in deep woods, alt. 3,000 ft. Summit and slopes of Mt. Rodgers, alt. 4,000 to 5,719 ft. Summit of White Top Mountain, alt. 5,678 ft. Slopes and summit of White Rock Mountain, alt. 3,000 to 4,400 ft."

The species was also collected by Mr. T. H. Kearney, Jr., at the summit of Thunderhead (about 6,500 ft.), and on Chilhowee Mountain (at about 1,500 ft.), in Blount Co., Tennessee. Reports of the collection of the species in the mountains of North Carolina, New Hampshire, and northern Michigan have been made.

The species is reported as common in thickets at Wilton and Southport, Maine (*Fernald*); and at Deering, Maine (*Blankinship*).

RUBUS CANADENSIS Linn.

RUBUS CANADENSIS RORIBACCUS Bailey, Am. Gard., 11: 642 (1890).

Dry hillsides, Randolph Co., near Beverly. "Plant larger and stronger than the species; leaflets broad below, usually triangular-ovate, doubly serrate with small teeth, and more or less notched and jagged; peduncles longer, straighter and stouter, habituously more numerous and more conspicuously overtopping the leaves; flowers very large (sometimes two inches across); sepals uniformly larger, some of them much prolonged and leaf-like and conspicuously lobed (sometimes becoming an inch long and wide); fruit much larger."

RUBUS HISPIDUS Linn.
RUBUS TRIVALIS Michx.
DALIBARDA REPENS Linn.
GEUM CANADENSE Jacq.
GEUM VIRGINIANUM Linn. (*Nuttall*).
GEUM VERNUM (Raf.) T. & G.
WALDSTEINIA FRAGARIOIDES (Michx.) Tratt.
FRAGARIA VIRGINIANA Duchesne.
FRAGARIA VESCA Linn.
FRAGARIA INDICA Andr.
POTENTILLA MONSPELIENSIS Linn. *P. Norvegica* Linn.
POTENTILLA CANADENSIS Linn. *P. Canadensis simplex* T. & G.
AGRIMONIA STRIATA Michx. *A. Eupatoria* Linn.
AGRIMONIA PARVIFLORA Soland.
SANGUISORBA CANADENSIS Linn. *Poterium Canadense* A. Gray.
ROSA CAROLINA Linn. (*Nuttall*).
ROSA HUMILIS Marsh.
ROSA LUCIDA Ehrh. *Rosa humilis lucida* Best.
ROSA RUBIGINOSA Linn.
ROSA CANINA Linn.
PYRUS CORONARIA Linn.
PYRUS ANGUSTIFOLIA Ait.
ABRONIA ARBUTIFOLIA (Linn.) Ell. *Pyrus arbutifolia* Linn. f.
ABRONIA NIGRA (Willd.) Britton. *Pyrus melanocarpa* Hook.
SORBUS AMERICANA Marsh. *Pyrus Americana* DC.
CRATEGUS SPATHULATA Michx.
CRATEGUS CORDATA Ait.
CRATEGUS OXYACANTHA Linn.
CRATEGUS APIIFOLIA (Marsh.) Michx.
CRATEGUS COCCINEA Linn.
CRATEGUS MOLLIS (T. & G.) Scheele.
CRATEGUS TOMENTOSA Linn.
CRATEGUS PUNCTATA Jacq.
    Large trees, of the form with bright yellow fruit, plentiful on Channel Ridge, Randolph Co. (*Millspaugh*).
CRATEGUS CRUS-GALLI Linn.
CRATEGUS FLAVA Ait. *C. flexispina* Sarg.
CRATEGUS FLAVA PUBESCENS A. Gray. *C. flexispina pubescens* Sarg.
CRATEGUS UNIFLORA Moench.
Crategus rotundifolia (Ehrh). Bork.
    Greenbrier Co., on Kate's Mountain, alt. 3,300 ft. (*Small & Vail*).
AMELANCHIER CANADENSIS (Linn.) Medic.

LEGUMINOSÆ.

BAPTISIA TINCTORIA (Linn.) R. Br.
BAPTISIA VILLOSA (Walt.) Nutt.
BAPTISIA AUSTRALIS (Linn.) R. Br.
LUPINUS PERENNIS Linn.
MEDICAGO SATIVA Linn.
MEDICAGO LUPULINA Linn.
MELILOTUS OFFICINALIS (Linn.) Lam.
MELILOTUS ALBA Lam.
TRIFOLIUM ARVENSE Linn.
TRIFOLIUM PRATENSE Linn.
TRIFOLIUM REPENS Linn.

Trifolium Virginicum Small, Mem. Torr. Club, 4:112 (1894) Tab. 75.

Perennial from a large and long root, diffusely branched from the summit of the root; branches 2 to 4 cm. long, strictly prostrate, pubescent; leaves 3-foliate, petiole 4 to 8 cm. long; leaflets linear, linear-lanceolate or oblanceolate, 1 to 4 cm. long, acute or cuspidate, serrate-dentate, glabrous above, more or less silky beneath, conspicuously veined; sepals ovate, conspicuous; inflorescence in terminal, globose heads, about 2.5 cm. in diameter; flowers whitish, more or less crowded on slender pedicels, .2 to .4, standard emarginate-mucronate, striate; calyx clothed with long silky hairs, the teeth subulate, nearly half the length of the corolla. Pods and seeds not seen.

Growing on the rocky slopes of Kate's Mountain, Greenbrier Co., in company with *Clematis ovata*.

This species is most closely related to *T. stoloniferum* by its flower, but in all other respects it differs from that and all the other eastern American species.

TRIFOLIUM HYBRIDUM Linn.
TRIFOLIUM AGRARIUM Linn.
TRIFOLIUM PROCUMBENS Linn.
CRACCA VIRGINIANA Linn. *Tephrosia Virginiana* Pers.
Webster Co. on an "island" in Upper Glade (*Millspaugh*).
ROBINIA PSEUDACACIA Linn.
ROBINIA HISPIDA Linn.
ASTRAGALUS CAROLINIANUS Linn.

Astragalus distortus T. & G.

Since the publication of the Preliminary Catalogue, Dr. Gamble has succeeded in securing fruits of this species, reported generically only in that work. This is the farthest eastern extension of the species, which ranges, according to the manual, from Illinois to Iowa, Missouri, Kansas and Texas.

STYLOSANTHES BIFLORA (Linn.) B. S. P.
STYLOSANTHES HAMATA (Linn.) Britton.

MEIBOMIA NUDIFLORA (Linn.) O. K. *Desmodium nudiflorum* DC.
MEIBOMIA GRANDIFLORA (Walt.) O. K. *Desmodium grandiflorum* DC.
MEIBOMIA ROTUNDIFOLIA (Michx.) O. K. *Desmodium rotundifolium* DC.
MEIBOMIA OCHROLEUCA (M. A. Curtiss) O. K. *Desmodium ochroleucum* M. A. Curtis.
MEIBOMIA CANESCENS (Linn.) O. K. *Desmodium canescens* DC.
MEIBOMIA BRACTEOSA (Michx.) O. K. *Desmodium cuspidatum* Hook.
MEIBOMIA DILLENII (Darl.) O. K. *Desmodium Dillenii* Darl.
MEIBOMIA PANICULATA (Linn.) O. K. *Desmodium paniculatum* DC.
MEIBOMIA CANADENSIS (Linn.) O. K. *Desmodium Canadense* DC.
MEIBOMIA RIGIDA (Ell.) O. K. *Desmodium rigidum* DC.
MEIBOMIA OBTUSA (Muhl.) O. K. *Desmodium ciliare* DC.
MEIBOMIA MARILANDICA (L.) O. K. *Desmodium Marilandicum* Britt.
MEIBOMIA LINEATA (Michx.) O. K. *Desmodium lineatum* DC.
LESPEDEZA REPENS (L.) Bart.
LESPEDEZA FRUTESCENS (L.) Britton. *L. Stuvei intermedia* Watson. *Lespedeza reticulata* Pers.
LESPEDEZA VIOLACEA (L.) Pers.
LESPEDEZA VIRGINICA (L.) Britton.
LESPEDEZA STUVEI Nutt.
LESPEDEZA HIRTA (L.) Ell. *Lespedeza polystachya* Michx.
LESPEDEZA CAPITATA Michx.
LESPEDEZA STRIATA (Thumb.) Hook & Arn.
VICIA CAROLINIANA Walt.
 Greenbrier Co., Kate's Mountain White Sulphur Springs, alt. 3,000 ft. (*Small & Vail*).
LATHYRUS VENOSUS Muhl.
 Greenbrier Co., Kate's Mountain, alt. 3,300 ft. (*Small & Vail*).
FALCATA COMOSA (L.) O. K. *Amphicarpœa comosa* Ridd.
APIOS APIOS (L.) MacM. *Apios tuberosa* Moench.
PHASEOLUS POLYSTACHYUS (Linn.) B. S. P.
PHASEOLUS HELVOLUS Linn.
GLEDITSCHIA TRIACANTHOS Linn.
CASSIA MARILANDICA Linn.
CASSIA CHAMÆCHRISTA Linn.
CASSIA NICTITANS Linn.
CERCIS CANADENSIS Linn.
GYMNOCLADUS DIOICUS (Linn.) Koch. *Gymnocladus Canadensis* Lam.

GERANIACEÆ.

GERANIUM MACULATUM Linn.
GERANIUM ROBERTIANUM Linn.
GERANIUM CAROLINIANUM Linn.

OXALIDACEÆ.

OXALIS ACETOSELLA Linn. (*Nuttall.*)
OXALIS VIOLACEA Linn.
OXALIS STRICTA Linn.   *Oxalis corniculata stricta* Sav.
OXALIS RECURVA Ell.

LINACEÆ.

LINUM VIRGINIANUM Linn.
LINUM STRIATUM Walt.
LINUM USITATISSIMUM Linn.

RUTACEÆ.

ZANTHOXYLUM AMERICANUM Mill.
RUTA GRAVEOLENS Linn.
PTELEA TRIFOLIATA Linn.

SIMARUBACEÆ.

AILANTHUS GLANDULOSUS Desf.

POLYGALACEÆ.

POLYGALA VIRIDESCENS Linn.   *Polygala sanguinea* Linn.
POLYGALA VIRIDESCENS ALBIFLORA Wheelock.   *Polygala sanguinea albiflora* Millsp.
POLYGALA MARIANA Mill.
POLYGALA CURTISSII A. Gray.
POLYGALA CRUCIATA Linn.
POLYGALA VERTICILLATA Linn.
POLYGALA AMBIGUA Nutt.
POLYGALA NUTTALLII T. & G.
POLYGALA SENEGA Linn.
POLYGALA PAUCIFOLIA Willd.
  Greenbrier Co., Kate's Mountain, alt. 3,300 ft. (*Small & Vail.*)

EUPHORBIACEÆ.

EUPHORBIA GLYPTOSPERMA PUBESCENS Engelm.
EUPHORBIA MACULATA Linn.
  Mineral Co., opposite Cumberland, Md. (*J. K. Small.*)
EUPHORBIA PRESLII Guss.
EUPHORBIA MARGINATA Pursh.
EUPHORBIA COROLLATA Linn.
EUPHORBIA DENTATA Michx.
EUPHORBIA DARLINGTONII Gray.
EUPHORBIA OBTUSATA Pursh.

PL. VII   RHUS RADICANS Linn.

This species completely covers a half mile of fence alo
river below Morgantown. The growth here is remarkably
very characteristic in all its features.

FIELD COLUMBIAN MUSEUM. BOTANY, PL. VII.

RHUS RADICANS Linn.

EUPHORBIA CYPARISSIAS Linn.
EUPHORBIA COMMUTATA Engelm.
 Greenbrier Co., near White Sulphur Springs (*J. H. Redfield*).
EUPHORBIA LATHYRIS Linn.
ACALYPHA VIRGINICA Linn.
ACALYPHA VIRGINICA INTERMEDIA Muell.

[COREMA CONRADI Torr., (Empetraceæ) mentioned in Botanical Gazette, Vol. II, p. 136, as occurring near Hawk's Nest, Fayette Co., is proven by Professor James to be another species, and should therefore not yet be credited to this state.]

CALLITRICHIACEÆ.
CALLITRICHE HETEROPHYLLA Pursh.

LIMNANTHACEÆ.
FLŒRKEA PROSERPINACOIDES Willd.

ANACARDIACEÆ.
RHUS HIRTA (Linn.) Sudw.   *Rhus typhina* Linn.
RHUS GLABRA Linn.
RHUS COPALLINA Linn.
RHUS VERNIX Linn.   *Rhus venenata* Linn.
RHUS RADICANS Linn.
RHUS AROMATICA Ait.   *Rhus Canadensis* Marsh.

AQUIFOLIACEÆ.
ILEX OPACA Ait.
ILEX MONTICOLA A. Gray.
ILEX MONTICOLA MOLLIS (A. Gray) Britton.   *Ilex mollis* A. Gray.
ILEX VERTICILLATA (Linn.) A. Gray.

CELASTRACEÆ.
EUONYMUS ATROPURPUREUS Jacq.
EUONYMUS AMERICANUS Linn.
Euonymus obovatus Nutt.
 E. Americanus var. obovatus T. & Gray. Of this species Rev. A. Boutlou says: "In Marshall Co., at Board Tree, Cameron, Belton, etc., this is the most common form; while the trailing rooting form I have met almost everywhere I have been in the State."
CELASTRUS SCANDENS Linn.

STAPHYLEACEÆ.
STAPHYLEA TRIFOLIA Linn.

ACERACEÆ.

ACER PENNSYLVANICUM Linn.
   Although in most situations in the State this species is a mere shrub, yet near Welsh in Grant Co. it assumes the proportions of a beautiful tree 20 to 40 ft. high with a strict columnar trunk 5 to 8 inches in diameter (*Millspaugh*). Greenbrier Co., on Kate's Mountain, near White Sulphur Springs, alt. 3,300 ft. (*Small & Vail*).

ACER SPICATUM Lam.

ACER SACCHARUM Marsh.
   In Randolph Co., near Pickens, the sugar maple grows to a diameter of 2 to 4 ft., and a height of 50 to 70 ft. (*Millspaugh*).

ACER NIGRUM Michx. f.   *Acer saccharum* var. *nigrum* Britton.

ACER SACCHARINUM Linn.
   Large trees 2 to 4 ft. in diameter in Randolph Co., near Pickens. At one station in Webster Co., on Buffalo Bull Mountain, nearly every tree of this species is of the Bird's-eye type. (*Millspaugh*).

ACER RUBRUM Linn.

ACER NEGUNDO Linn.   *Negundo aceroides* Mœnch.   (*Nuttall*).

HIPPOCASTANACEÆ.

ÆSCULUS GLABRA Willd.
ÆSCULUS OCTANDRA Marsh.
ÆSCULUS OCTANDRA HYBRIDA (DC.) Sarg.   *Æsculus octandra purpurascens* A. Gray.
ÆSCULUS PAVIA Linn.

BALSAMINACEÆ.

IMPATIENS AUREA Muhl.
IMPATIENS BIFLORA Walt.

RHAMNACEÆ.

RHAMNUS CAROLINIANA Walt.
CEANOTHUS AMERICANUS Linn.

VITACEÆ.

VITIS LABRUSCA Linn.
   An immense specimen of this grape was found in Randolph Co., near Pickens; its trunk measured 22 inches in diameter and its two main branches 8 inches each.   (*Millspaugh*).

VITIS ÆSTIVALIS Michx.
VITIS CORDIFOLIA Michx.
VITIS VULPINA Linn.   *Vitis riparia* Michx.
VITIS RUPESTRIS Scheele.
VITIS ROTUNDIFOLIA Michx.

PARTHENOCISSUS QUINQUEFOLIA (Linn.) Planch. *Vitis quinquefolia* Lam.
AMPELOPSIS CORDATA Michx. *Cissus Ampelopsis* Pers.

TILIACEÆ.
TILIA AMERICANA Linn.
　　Large growths of this species found at Pickens, Randolph Co., with trunk diameters of 26 to 38 inches, and height 60 to 100 feet. (*Millspaugh*), (*Nuttall*).
TILIA HETEROPHYLLA Vent.
　　One specimen cut at Nuttallburg, Fayette Co., had a diameter of 26 inches. (*Millspaugh*), (*Nuttall*).

MALVACEÆ.
ALTHÆA ROSEA Linn.
MALVA ROTUNDIFOLIA Linn.
MALVA MOSCHATA Linn.
SIDA SPINOSA Linn.
SIDA HERMAPHRODITA (Linn.) Rusby. *Sida Napæa* Cav.
ABUTILON ABUTILON (Linn.) Rusby. *Abutilon Avicenne* Gærtn.
HIBISCUS MOSCHEUTOS Linn.
HIBISCUS TRIONIUM Linn.

HYPERICACEÆ.
ASCYRUM HYPERICOIDES Linn. *Ascyrum Crux-Andreæ* Linn.
HYPERICUM PROLIFICUM Linn.
HYPERICUM DENSIFLORUM Pursh.
HYPERICUM VIRGATUM ACUTIFOLIUM Coulter.
HYPERICUM PERFORATUM Linn.
HYPERICUM MACULATUM Walt.
HYPERICUM MUTILUM Linn.
HYPERICUM CANADENSE Linn.
HYPERICUM GENTIANOIDES (Linn.) B. S. P.
HYPERICUM ADPRESSUM Barton.
HYPERICUM ELLIPTICUM Hook.
Hypericum Virginicum Linn. (*Nuttall*).

CISTACEÆ.
HELIANTHEMUM MAJUS (Linn.) B. S. P.
LECHEA MINOR Linn.
LECHEA LEGGETTII Britton & Holl.

VIOLACEÆ.
VIOLA PEDATA Linn.
　　Greenbrier Co., on Kate's Mountain, alt. 3,300 ft., near White Sulphur Springs (*Small & Vail*). Mercer Co., near Bluefield. MacDowell Co., at Fletcher's. (*Millspaugh*).

Viola pedata bicolor Pursh.
   Greenbrier Co., on Kate's Mountain, alt. 3,300 ft. (*Small & Vail*).
Viola palmata Linn.
Viola obliqua Hill.   *Viola cucullata* Ait.
Viola sagittata Ait.
Viola blanda Willd.
Viola primulæfolia Linn.
Viola lanceolata Linn.
Viola rotundifolia Michx.
Viola pubescens Ait.
Viola scabriuscula (T. & G.) Schwein.   *Viola pubescens scabriuscula* T. & G.
Viola hastata Michx.
Viola Canadensis Linn.
Viola striata Ait.
Viola Labradorica Schrank.
   Viola canina var. *Muhlenbergii*, Traut.   Fayette Co., at foot of cliff at Nuttallburg (*Nuttall*).
Viola rostrata Pursh.
Viola tenella Muhl.
Solea concolor (Forst.) Ging.

PASSIFLORACEÆ.

Passiflora lutea Linn.
Passiflora incarnata Linn.

CACTACEÆ.

Opuntia polyacantha Haw.   *Opuntia vulgaris* Linn.

THYMELÆACEÆ.

Dirca palustris Linn.
   Kanawha Co., abundant on Blue Creek (*Rev. A. Boutlou*).

LYTHRACEÆ.

Cuphæa petiolata (Linn.)   Kœhne.

MELASTOMACEÆ.

Rhexia Virginica Linn.

ONAGRACEÆ.

Epilobium spicatum Muhl.
Epilobium coloratum Muhl.
Ludwegia alternifolia Linn.

LUDWEGIA ALTERNIFOLIA LINEARIFOLIA Britton, Bull. Torr. Club, 17: 315 (1890).

"Two or three feet high, divergently branched, the branches ascending. Leaves linear, elongated, 2 to 4 in. long, 1.5 to 4 lines wide, acute; flowers solitary in the axils of the upper leaves or bracts, yellow; sepals ovate-lanceolate acute, narrower than those of L. *alternifolia;* branches and both sides of the leaves somewhat pubescent. Petals apparently remaining on the plant longer than those of L. *alternifolia,* which, as Dr. Millspaugh observes, commonly fall away when the plant is shocked."

"Appearing very distinct from typical L. *alternifolia,* but presumably but a variety of it. From the description it may be the *Rhexia linearifolia* Poir, in Lam. Encyl. vi. 2, said to come from Carolina."

Wood Co., near Lockhart's Run. (*Millspaugh*), (*Nuttall*).

LUDWEGIA PALUSTRIS (Linn.) Ell.
ONAGRA BIENNIS (Linn.) Scop. *Œnothera biennis* Linn. *Œ. biennis grandifolia* Lindl.
ŒNOTHERA* PUMILA Linn.
ŒNOTHERA* FRUTICOSA Linn.
ŒNOTHERA* FRUTICOSA DIFFERTA Millsp. Fl. W. Va., 366 (1892).

Damp meadows, Wood Co., near Lockhart's Run, the most common form.

Stems 1 to 2 ft. high, nearly smooth, branching diffusely from every axil. Flowers profuse, large. Lower leaves ovate. Capsules narrowly winged, very short; apical inflorescence strongly cymose.

ŒNOTHERA* LINEARIS Michx. *Œnothera fruticosa* var. *linearis* Watson.
GAURA BIENNIS Linn.
CIRCÆA LUTETIANA Linn.
CIRCÆA ALPINA Linn.

ARALIACEÆ.

ARALIA SPINOSA Linn.
ARALIA RACEMOSA Linn.
ARALIA NUDICAULIS Linn.
ARALIA HISPIDA Vent.
PANAX QUINQUEFOLIUM Linn. *Aralia quinquefolia* Dec. & Pl.

UMBELLIFERÆ.

HYDROCOTYLE AMERICANA Linn.
ERYNGIUM AQUATICUM Linn.
DAUCUS CAROTA Linn.
DAUCUS CAROTA *forma* ROSEA Millsp. Fl. W. Va., 369 (1892).
ANGELICA CURTISSII Buckley.
ANGELICA VILLOSA (Walt.) B. S. P.

---

*See foot note page 168.

ANGELICA ATROPURPUREA Linn.
OXYPOLIS RIGIDUS (Linn.) Britton. *Tiedemannia rigida* Coult. & Rose.
HERACLEUM LANATUM Michx.
PASTINACA SATIVA Linn.
THASPIUM TRIFOLIATUM (Nutt.) Britton. *Thaspium aureum* Nutt.
Thaspium aureum cordatum Walt.
THASPIUM BARBINODE (Michx.) Nutt.
LIGUSTICUM CANADENSE (Linn.) Britton. *Ligusticum actæfolium* (Michx).
DEERINGIA CANADENSIS (Linn.) O.K.
ZIZIA CORDATA (Walt.) DC.
ZIZIA AUREA (Linn.) Koch.
ZIZIA BEBBII (C. & R.) Britton.
    Greenbrier Co., on Kate's Mountain, alt. 3,300 ft. (*Small & Vail*).
CICUTA MACULATA Linn.
CICUTA BULBIFERA Linn.
CHÆROPHYLLUM PROCUMBENS (Linn). Crantz.
OSMORRHIZA CLAYTONI (Michx.) B. S. P.
OSMORRHIZA LONGISTYLIS (Torr.) DC.
ERIGENIA BULBOSA (Michx.) Nutt.
SANICULA MARYLANDICA Linn.
SANICULA CANADENSIS Linn.

CORNACEÆ.

CORNUS FLORIDA Linn.
    Greenbrier Co., on Kate's Mountain, alt. 3,300 ft. (*Small & Vail*).
CORNUS CIRCINATA L'Her.
CORNUS AMONUM Mill. *Cornus sericea* Linn.
CORNUS CANDIDISSIMA Marsh.
CORNUS ALTERNIFOLIA Linn. f.
NYSSA AQUATICA Linn.
    Nyssa salvatica Marsh. Immense growths of this species at Pickens, Randolph Co., with trunks 3 to 4 ft. in diameter. (*Millspaugh*).

CLETHRACEÆ.

CLETHRA ACUMINATA Michx.

PYROLACEÆ.

CHIMAPHILA UMBELLATA (Linn.) Nutt. *Pseva umbellata* O.K.
CHIMAPHILA MACULATA (Linn.) Pursh. *Pseva maculata* O.K.
MONESES UNIFLORA (Linn.) A. Gray. *Moneses grandiflora* Salisb.
PYROLA ELLIPTICA Nutt.
PYROLA ROTUNDIFOLIA Linn.

MONOTROPACEÆ.

MONOTROPA UNIFLORA Linn.
HYPOPYTIS HYPOPYTIS (Linn.) Small.   *Hypopytis Monotropa* Crantz.

ERICACEÆ.

GAYLUSSACIA DUMOSA (Andr.) T. & G.
GAYLUSSACIA FRONDOSA (Linn.) T. & G.
GAYLUSSACIA RESINOSA (Ait.) T. & G.
OXYCOCCUS MACROCARPUS Pers.
OXYCOCCUS ERYTHROCARPUS Pers.   *Vaccinium erythrocarpon* Michx.
VACCINIUM STAMINEUM Linn.
VACCINIUM PENNSYLVANICUM Lam.
VACCINIUM VACILLANS Soland.
VACCINIUM CORYMBOSUM Linn.
VACCINIUM PALLIDUM Ait.   *Vaccinium corymbosum pallidum* A. Gray.
CHIOGENES HISPIDULA (Linn.) T. & G.
GAULTHERIA PROCUMBENS Linn.
EPIGÆA REPENS Linn.
XOLISMA LIGUSTRINA (Linn.) Britton.   *Andromeda ligustrina* Muhl.
XOLISMA LIGUSTRINA PUBESCENS A. Gray.   *Andromeda ligustrina pubescens* A. Gray.
PIERIS MARIANA (Linn.) Benth & Hook.   *Andromeda Mariana* Linn.
OXYDENDRON ARBOREUM (Linn.) DC.
KALMIA LATIFOLIA Linn.
KALMIA AUGUSTIFOLIA Linn.
MENZIESIA PILOSA (Michx.) Pers.   *Menziesia globularis* Salisb.
RHODODENDRON MAXIMUM Linn.
RHODODENDRON CATAWBIENSE Michx.
AZALEA ARBORESCENS Pursh.   *Rhododendron arborescens* Torr.
AZALEA CANESCENS Michx.   *Rhododendron canescens* Porter.
    Greenbrier Co., Kate's Mountain, alt. 3,300 ft. (*Small & Vail*).
AZALEA VISCOSA Linn.   *Rhododendron viscosum* Torr.
AZALEA VISCOSA GLAUCA Michx.   *Rhododendron viscosum glaucum* A. Gray.
AZALEA VISCOSA NITIDA (Pursh.) Britton.   *Rhododendron viscosum nitidum* A. Gray.
AZALEA NUDIFLORA Linn.   *Rhododendron nudiflorum* Torr.
AZALEA LUTEA Linn.   *Rhododendron calendulaceum* Torr.

DIAPENSIACEÆ.

GALAX APHYLLA Linn.

PRIMULACEÆ.

DODECATHEON MEADIA Linn.
TRIENTALIS AMERICANA Pursh.

STEIRONEMA CILIATUM (Linn.) Baudo.
  Greenbrier Co., on the mountains about White Sulphur Springs, alt. 3,200 ft. (*Small & Vail*).
STEIRONEMA LANCEOLATUM (Walt.) A. Gray.
STEIRONEMA LANCEOLATUM ANGUSTIFOLIUM (Lam.) A. Gray.
LYSIMACHIA QUADRIFOLIA Linn.
LYSIMACHIA TERRESTRIS (Linn.) B. S. P
LYSIMACHIA NUMMULARIA Linn.
NAUMBERGIA THYRSIFLORA (Linn.) Duby.   *Lysimachia thyrsiflora* Linn.
ANAGALLIS ARVENSIS Linn.   (*Nuttall*).
SAMOLUS FLORIBUNDUS H. B. K.   *Samolus Valerandi floribundus* B. S. P.

EBENACEÆ.
DIOSPYROS VIRGINIANA Linn.

STYRACEÆ.
MOHRODENDRON CAROLINUM (Linn.) Britton.   *Halesia tetraptera* Linn.

OLEACEÆ.
FRAXINUS AMERICANA Linn.
  Fine specimens of very large growth in Randolph Co., especially on Channel ridge where the species grows very tall, and at Pickens where specimens were measured from 3 to 6 ft. in diameter. (*Millspaugh*).
FRAXINUS PENNSYLVANICA Marsh.   *F. pubescens* Lam.
FRAXINUS LANCEOLATA Borck.   *F. viridis* Michx. f.
FRAXINUS NIGRA Marsh.   *F. sambucifolia* Lam.
CHIONANTHUS VIRGINICA Linn.
LIGUSTRUM VULGARE Linn.

LOGANIACEÆ.
CYNOCTONUM MITREOLA (Linn.) Britton.   *Mitreola petiolata* T. & G.

GENTIANACEÆ.
SABBATIA ANGULARIS (Linn.) Pursh.
GENTIANA QUINQUEFOLIA Linn.
GENTIANA ANDREWSII Griseb.
GENTIANA SAPONARIA Linn.
GENTIANA LINEARIS Frœl.
OBOLARIA VIRGINICA Linn.

APOCYNACEÆ.
APOCYNUM ANDROSÆMIFOLIUM Linn.
APOCYNUM CANNABINUM Linn.
APOCYNUM CANNABINUM PUBESCENS (R. Br.) A. DC.

ASCLEPIADACEÆ.

ASCLEPIAS TUBEROSA Linn.
ASCLEPIAS RUBRA Linn.
ASCLEPIAS PURPURASCENS Linn.
ASCLEPIAS VARIEGATA Linn.
ASCLEPIAS INCARNATA Linn.
ASCLEPIAS PULCHRA Ehrh. *Asclepias incarnata pulchra* Pers.
ASCLEPIAS SYRIACA Linn. (*Nuttall.*)
ASCLEPIAS EXALTATA (Linn.) Muhl.
ASCLEPIAS QUADRIFOLIA Jacq.
ACERATES VIRIDIFLORA (Raf.) Eaton.
VINCETOXICUM GONOCARPUS LÆVIS (Michx.) Britton. *Gonolobus lævis* Michx.

CONVOLVULACEÆ.

IPOMŒA COCCINEA Linn.
IPOMŒA HEDERACEA Jacq.
IPOMŒA PURPUREA (Linn.) Roth.
    Mineral Co., opposite Cumberland, Md. (*J. K. Small*).
IPOMŒA PANDURATA (Linn.) Meyer.
IPOMŒA LACUNOSA Linn.
CONVOLVULUS SPITHAMÆUS Linn.
CONVOLVULUS SEPIUM Linn. (*Nuttall*).
CONVOLVULUS REPENS Linn. *C. sepium repens* A. Gray.

CUSCUTACEÆ.

CUSCUTA EPITHYMUM Murr. *C. Trifolii* Weihe.
CUSCUTA GRONOVII Willd.
CUSCUTA GLOMERATA Choisy.

POLEMONIACEÆ.

Phlox paniculata Linn. (*Nuttall*).
PHLOX PANICULATA ACUMINATA (Pursh.) Chapm.
PHLOX MACULATA Linn.
PHLOX AMŒNA Sims.
PHLOX REPTANS Michx.
PHLOX SUBULATA Linn.
    Greenbrier Co., dry, stony ledges on Kate's Mountain, alt. 3,300 ft. (*Small & Vail*).
POLEMONIUM REPTANS Linn.
POLEMONIUM VAN BRUNTIÆ Britton. *P. cœruleum* Linn.

HYDROPHYLLACEÆ.

HYDROPHYLLUM MACROPHYLLUM Nutt.
HYDROPHYLLUM VIRGINICUM Linn.

HYDROPHYLLUM CANADENSE Linn.
HYDROPHYLLUM APPENDICULATUM Michx.
PHACELIA BIPINNATIFIDA Michx.
PHACELIA PURSHII Buckley.
PHACELIA DUBIA (Linn.) Small.   *P. parviflora* Pursh.

BORAGINACEÆ.

CYNOGLOSSUM OFFICINALE Linn.
CYNOGLOSSUM VIRGINICUM Linn.
LAPPULA VIRGINIANA (Linn.) Greene.   *Echinospermnm Virginicum* Lehm.
MERTENSIA VIRGINICA (Linn.) DC.
ONOSMODIUM CAROLINIANUM (Lam.) A. DC.
MYOSOTIS PALUSTRIS (Linn.) Relh.
SYMPHYTUM OFFICINALE Linn.
LITHOSPERMUM ARVENSE Linn.
LITHOSPERMUM LATIFOLIUM Michx.
LITHOSPERMUM CANESCENS (Michx.) Lehm.
ECHIUM VULGARE Linn.

VERBENACEÆ.

VERBENA OFFICINALIS Linn.
VERBENA URTICÆFOLIA Linn.
VERBENA HASTATA Linn.
VERBENA ANGUSTIFOLIA Michx.
LIPPIA LANCEOLATA Michx.
PHRYMA LEPTOSTACHYA Linn.

LABIATÆ.

ISANTHUS BRACHIATUS (Linn.) B. S. P.
TEUCRIUM CANADENSE Linn.
COLLINSONIA CANADENSIS Linn.
PERILLA FRUTESCENS NANKINENSIS (Lour.) Britton.   *P. ocymoides crispa* Benth.
MENTHA SPICATA Linn.   *M. viridis* Linn.
MENTHA PIPERITA Linn.
MENTHA SATIVA Linn.
MENTHA CANADENSIS Linn.
LYCOPUS VIRGINICUS Linn.
LYCOPUS SINUATUS Ell.
CUNILA ORIGANOIDES (Linn.) Britton.
KŒLLIA FLEXUOSA (Walt.) Britton.
KŒLLIA VERTICILLATA (Michx.) O. K.   *K. Torreyi* Benth.
KŒLLIA CLINIPODIOIDES (T. & G.) O. K.

KŒLLIA PYCANTHEMOIDES (Leavenw.) O. K.   K. Tullia Benth.
KŒLLIA INCANA (Linn.) O. K.
KŒLLIA MONTANA (Michx.) O. K.
HEDEOMA PULEGIOIDES (Linn.) Pers.
CLINOPODIUM VULGARE Linn.   Calamintha Clinopodium Benth.
MELISSA OFFICINALIS Linn.
SALVIA LYRATA Linn.
MONARDA DIDYMA Linn.
MONARDA FISTULOSA Linn.   M. fistulosa mollis Benth.
MONARDA MEDIA Willd.   M. fistulosa rubra A. Gray.
BLEPHILIA HIRSUTA (Pursh.) Torrey.
VLECKIA NEPETOIDES (Linn.) Raf.   Agastache nepetoides O. K.
MEEHANIA CORDATA (Nutt.) Britton.   Cedronella cordata Benth.
NEPETA CATARIA Linn.
GLECHOMA HEDERACEA Linn.   Nepeta hederacea B. S. P.
SCUTELLARIA LATERIFLORA Linn.
SCUTELLARIA CORDIFOLIA Muhl.   S. versicolor minor Chapm.
SCUTELLARIA SAXATILIS Riddell.
SCUTELLARIA SERRATA Andrews.
SCUTELLARIA INCANA Muhl.   S. canescens Nutt.
SCUTELLARIA PILOSA Michx.
SCUTELLARIA PILOSA HIRSUTA (Short.) A. Gray.
SCUTELLARIA INTEGRIFOLIA Linn.
SCUTELLARIA PARVULA Michx.
SCUTELLARIA GALERICULATA Linn.
SCUTELLARIA GALERICULATA forma ALBIFLORA Millsp. Fl. W. Va. 428 (1892.)
SCUTELLARIA NERVOSA Pursh.
PRUNELLA VULGARIS Linn.   Brunella vulgaris Linn.
PRUNELLA VULGARIS ALBIFLORA (Boggenh.) Britton.
PHYSOSTEGIA VIRGINIANA (Linn.) Benth.
MARRUBIUM VULGARE Linn.
STACHYS PALUSTRIS Linn.
STACHYS ASPERA Michx.
STACHYS ASPERA GLABRA A. Gray.
STACHYS CORDATA Ridd. (Nuttall).
GALEOPSIS TETRAHIT Linn.
LEONURUS CARDIACA Linn.
LAMIUM AMPLEXICAULE Linn.
TRICHOSTEMA DICHOTOMUM Linn.

SOLANACEÆ.

SOLANUM DULCAMARA Linn.
SOLANUM NIGRUM Linn.

SOLANUM CAROLINENSE Linn.
PHYSALIS PHILADELPHICA Lam.
PHYSALIS ANGULATA Linn.
PHYSALIS PUBESCENS Linn.
PHYSALIS VIRGINIANA Mill.
PHYSALIS VISCOSA Linn.
PHYSALIS LANCEOLATA Michx.
PHYSALODES PHYSALODES (Linn.) Britton.
LYCIUM VULGARE (Ait. f.) Dun.
DATURA STRAMONIUM Linn.
DATURA TATULA Linn.
PETUNIA VIOLACEA Lindl.

SCROPHULARIACEÆ.

VERBASCUM THAPSUS Linn.
VERBASCUM BLATTARIA Linn.
VERBASCUM LYCHNITIS Linn.
LINARIA LINARIA (Linn.) Karst.   *L. vulgaris* Mill.
    This species first appeared near Nuttallburg in Fayette Co., this year—1895 (*Nuttall*).
SCROPHULARIA MARILANDICA Linn.   *S. nodosa Marilandica* A. Gray.
COLLINSIA VERNA Nutt.
CHELONE GLABRA Linn.
CHELONE OBLIQUA Linn.
PENTSTEMON HIRSUTUS (Linn.) Willd.
PENTSTEMON PENTSTEMON (Linn.) Britton.   *P. lævigatus* Soland.
PENTSTEMON DIGITALIS (Sweet) Nutt.   *P. lævigatus Digitalis* A. Gray.
Pentstemon canescens Britton.
    Slopes of Kate's Mountain, alt. 3,300 ft., near White Sulphur Springs, Greenbrier Co. (*Small & Vail*).
MIMULUS RINGENS Linn.
MIMULUS ALATUS Soland.
GRATIOLA VIRGINIANA Linn.
GRATIOLA SPHÆROCARPA Ell.
ILYSANTHES GRATIOLOIDES (Linn.) Benth.
LEPTANDRA VIRGINICA (Linn.) Nutt.   *Veronica Virginica* Linn.
VERONICA ANAGALLIS AQUATICA Linn.   *V. Anagallis* Linn.
VERONICA AMERICANA Schw.
VERONICA OFFICINALIS Linn.
VERONICA SERPYLLIFOLIA Linn.
VERONICA PEREGRINA Linn.
VERONICA ARVENSIS Linn.
BUECHNERA AMERICANA Linn.

Dasystoma Pedicularia (Linn.) Benth. *Gerardia Pedicularia* Linn.
Dasystoma Virginica (Linn.) Britton. *Gerardia Virginica* Linn.
Dasystoma flava (Linn.) Wood. *Gerardia flava* Linn.
Dasystoma lævigata Raf. *Gerardia lævigata* Raf.
Gerardia tenuifolia Vahl.
Gerardia auriculata Michx.
Castilleja coccinea (Linn.) Spreng.
Pedicularis Canadensis Linn. (*Nuttall*).
Melampyrum lineare Lam.

OROBANCHACEÆ.

Epiphegus Virginiana (Linn.) Bart.
Conopholis Americana (Linn. f.) Wallr.
Thalesia uniflora (Linn.) Britton. *Aphyllon uniflorum* A. Gray.

BIGNONIACEÆ.

Bignonia crucigera Linn.
   B. cupreolata Linn. Kanawha Co., rich soil between Cannelton and Brownstown, where it grows luxuriantly along the banks of the Great Kanawha River. Its evergreen foliage makes it a conspicuous feature of the winter landscape (*Rev. A. Boutlou*).
Tecoma radicans (Linn.) DC.
Catalpa Catalpa (Linn.) Karst. *C. Bignonioides* Walt.
Catalpa speciosa Warder.
   Mason Co., banks of the Ohio River, near Point Pleasant. (*Millspaugh*.)

ACANTHACEÆ.

Ruellia ciliosa Pursh.
Dianthera Americana Linn.

PLANTAGINACEÆ.

Plantago Major Linn.
Plantago Rugelii Decne.
Plantago lanceolata Linn.
Plantago Virginica Linn.

RUBIACEÆ.

Houstonia cærulea Linn.
Houstonia cærulea *forma* albiflora Millsp. Fl. W. Va. 375 (1892).
Houstonia serpyllifolia Michx. (*Nuttall*).
Houstonia purpurea Linn.
Houstonia purpurea calycosa A. Gray.
Houstonia ciliolata Torr.
Houstonia longifolia Gærtn.

Houstonia tenuifolia Nutt.
Cephalanthus occidentalis Linn.
Mitchella repens Linn.
Diodia teres Walt.
Galium Aparine Linn.
Galium pilosum Ait.
Galium circæzans Michx.
Galium lanceolatum Torr.
Galium latifolium Michx.
Galium trifidum Linn.
Galium tinctorium Linn.   *G. trifidum latifolium* Torr.
Galium concinnum T. & G.
Galium asprellum Michx.
Galium triflorum Michx.

CAPRIFOLIACEÆ.

Sambucus Canadensis Linn.
Sambucus pubens Michx.   *S. racemosa* Linn.
Sambucus pubens albicocca Britt.
Viburnum alnifolium Marsh.   *V. lantanoides* Michx.
Viburnum acerifolium Linn.
Viburnum dentatum Linn.
Viburnum nudum Linn.
Viburnum Lentago Linn.
Viburnum prunifolium Linn.
Triosteum perfoliatum Linn.
Symphoricarpos Symphoricarpos (Linn.) MacM.   *S. orbiculatus* Mœnch.
Lonicera dioica Linn.   *L. glauca* Hill.
Lonicera Japonica Thumb.
Diervilla Diervilla (Linn.) MacM.   *Diervilla trifida* Mœnch.

VALERIANACEÆ.

Valeriana pauciflora Michx.

DIPSACEÆ.

Dipsacus sylvestris Mill.

CUCURBITACEÆ.

Cucurbita ovifera Linn.
Citrullus vulgaris Schrad.
Cucumis Melo Linn.
Micrampelis lobata (Michx.) Greene.   *M. echinata* Raf.
Sicyos angulatus Linn.

CAMPANULACEÆ.

LOBELIA CARDINALIS Linn.
LOBELIA SYPHILITICA Linn.
LOBELIA SYPHILITICA ALBIFLORA Britton.
LOBELIA PUBERULA Michx.
LOBELIA AMŒNA GLANDULIFERA A Gray.
LOBELIA LEPTOSTACHYS A. DC.
LOBELIA SPICATA Lam.
LOBELIA SPICATA PARVIFLORA A. Gray.
LOBELIA INFLATA Linn.
LOBELIA INFLATA SIMPLEX (Raf.) Millsp. Fl. W. Va. 398 (1892).
LEGOUZIA PERFOLIATA (Linn.) Britton.   *Specularia perfoliata* A.DC.
CAMPANULA ROTUNDIFOLIA Linn.
CAMPANULA APARINOIDES Pursh.
CAMPANULA AMERICANA Linn.
CAMPANULA DIVARICATA Michx.

COMPOSITÆ.

ELEPHANTOPUS CAROLINIANUS Willd.
ELEPHANTOPUS TOMENTOSUS Linn.
VERNONIA GIGANTEA (Walt.) Britton.   *V. altissima* Nutt
VERNONIA NOVEBORACENSIS (Linn.) Willd.
VERNONIA GLAUCA (Linn.) Britton.   *V. Noveboracensis latifolia.* A. Gray.
EUPATORIUM PURPUREUM Linn.
EUPATORIUM MACULATUM AMŒNUM (Pursh.) Britton.   *E. purpureum amœnum* A. Gray.
EUPATORIUM HYSSOPIFOLIUM Linn.
EUPATORIUM PUBESCENS Muhl.   *E. rotundifolium pubescens* B. S. P.
EUPATORIUM ALTISSIMUM Linn.
EUPATORIUM SESSILIFOLIUM Linn.
EUPATORIUM PERFOLIATUM Linn.
EUPATORIUM AGERATOIDES Linn. f.
EUPATORIUM AROMATICUM Linn.
EUPATORIUM CŒLESTINUM Linn.
LACINARIA SPICATA (Linn.) O. K.
Lacinaria scariosa squarrulosa (Michx.) Small.
  Greenbrier Co., White Sulphur Springs (*A. Brown*).
CHRYSOPSIS MARIANA (Linn.) Nutt.
SOLIDAGO FLEXICAULIS Linn.   *S. latifolia* Linn.
SOLIDAGO CÆSIA Linn.
SOLIDAGO CURTISSII T. & G.
SOLIDAGO BICOLOR Linn.

Solidago monticola T. & G.
Solidago puberula Nutt.
Solidago speciosa Nutt.
Solidago odora Ait.
Solidago rugosa Mill.
Solidago ulmifolia Muhl.
Soldago Boottii Hook.
Solidago arguta Ait.
Solidago juncea Ait.
Solidago juncea scabrella (T. & G.) A. Gray.
Solidago juncea ramosa Porter & Britton.
Solidago serotina Ait.
Solidago serotina gigantea (Ait.) A. Gray.
Solidago rupestris Raf.
Solidago Canadensis Linn.
Solidago nemoralis Ait.
Euthamia graminifolia (Linn.) Nutt.   *Solidago lanceolata* Linn. (*Nuttall*).
Euthamia Caroliniana (Linn.) Greene.   *Solidago Caroliniana* Linn.
Brachychæta sphacelata (Raf.) Britton.   *B. Cordata* T. & G.
Sericocarpus asteroides (Linn.) B. S. P.
    Greenbrier Co., mountains about White Sulphur Springs, alt. 3,000 ft. (*A. Brown*).
Aster divaricatus Linn.   *A. corymbosus* Ait.
Aster macrophyllus Linn.
Aster patens Ait.
Aster patens phlogifolius (Muhl.) Nees.
Aster lævis Linn.
Aster undulatus Linn.
Aster cordifolius Linn.
Aster Lowrieanus Porter.   *A. cordifolius lævigatus* Porter.
Aster purpuratus Nees.   *A. virgatus* Ell.
Aster ericoides Linn.
Aster ericoides depauperatus Porter.   *A. ericoides pusilus* A. Gray.
Aster ericoides pilosus (Willd.) Porter.   *A. ericoides villosus* T. & G.
Aster lateriflorus (Linn.) Britton.
Aster lateriflorus hirsuticaulis (Lindl.) Porter.
Aster multiflorus Ait.
Aster dumosus Linn.
Aster vimineus Lam.
Aster vimineus foliolosus (Ait.) A. Gray.
Aster paniculatus Lam.
Aster salicifolius Ait.

ASTER NOVI-BELGII Linn.
ASTER PRENANTHOIDES Muhl.
ASTER PUNICEUS Linn.
ASTER UMBELLATUS Mill.
ASTER INFIRMUS Michx.
ASTER ACUMINATUS Michx.
ASTER TENUIFOLIUS Linn.
ASTER LINARIIFOLIUS Linn.
ERIGERON CANADENSIS Linn.
ERIGERON ANNUUS (Linn.) Pers.
ERIGERON RAMOSUS (Walt.) B. S. P.
ERIGERON PULCHELLUS Michx.
ERIGERON PHILADELPHICUS Linn.
ANTENNARIA PLANTAGINIFOLIA (Linn.) Rich.
ANTENNARIA MARGARITACEA (Linn.) Hook. *Anaphalis margaritacea* Benth & Hook.
GNAPHALIUM OBTUSIFOLIUM Linn.
GNAPHALIUM ULIGNOSUM Linn.
GNAPHALIUM PURPUREUM Linn.
INULA HELENIUM Linn.
POLYMNIA CANADENSIS Linn.
POLYMNIA CANADENSIS RADIATA A. Gray.
POLYMNIA UVEDALIA Linn.
SILPHIUM ASTERISCUS Linn.
SILPHIUM TRIFOLIATUM Linn.
    Greenbrier Co., near White Sulphur Springs, alt. 3,000 ft. (*A. Brown*).
CHRYSOGONUM VIRGINIANUM Linn.
PARTHENIUM INTEGRIFOLIUM Linn.
AMBROSIA TRIFIDA Linn.
    Mineral Co., opposite Cumberland, Md. (*J. K. Small*).
AMBROSIA TRIFIDA INTEGRIFOLIA (Muhl.) T. & G.
AMBROSIA ARTEMISIÆFOLIA Linn.
XANTHIUM SPINOSUM Linn.
    Mineral Co., opposite Cumberland, Md. (*J. K. Small*).
XANTHIUM STRUMARIUM Linn.
XANTHIUM CANADENSE Mill.
ECLIPTA ALBA (Linn.) Hassk.
HELIOPSIS SCABRA Dunal.
HELIOPSIS HELIANTHOIDES (Linn.) B. S. P. *H. lævis* Pers.
BRAUNERIA PURPUREA (Linn.) Britton. *Echinacea purpurea* Mœnch.
RUDBECKIA LACINIATA Linn.
RUDBECKIA LACINIATA HUMILIS A. Gray.

RUDBECKIA FULGIDA Ait.
RUDBECKIA TRILOBA Linn.
RUDBECKIA HIRTA Linn.
RUDBECKIA SPECIOSA Wender.
HELIANTHUS LÆTIFLORUS Pers.
HELIANTHUS OCCIDENTALIS Riddell.
HELIANTHUS OCCIDENTALIS DOWELLIANUS T. & G.
HELIANTHUS TOMENTOSUS Michx.
HELIANTHUS GROSSE-SERRATUS Martens.
HELIANTHUS GIGANTEUS Linn.
HELIANTHUS LÆVIGATUS T. & G.
HELIANTHUS DORONICOIDES Lam.
HELIANTHUS MICROCEPHALUS T. & G.   *H. parviflorus* Bernh.
HELIANTHUS DIVARICATUS Linn.
HELIANTHUS HIRSUTUS Raf.
HELIANTHUS STRUMOSUS Linn.
HELIANTHUS TRACHELIIFOLIUS Mill.
HELIANTHUS DECAPETALUS Linn.
VERBESINA OCCIDENTALIS (Linn.) Walt.
VERBESINA ALTERNIFOLIA (Linn.) Britton.   *Ridania alternifolia* O. K.
COREOPSIS LANCEOLATA VILLOSA Michx.
COREOPSIS PUBESCENS Ell.
COREOPSIS AURICULATA Linn.
COREOPSIS MAJOR Walt.   *C. senifolia* Michx.
COREOPSIS MAJOR ŒMLERI (Ell.) Britton.   *C. senifolia stellata* T. & G.
COREOPSIS TRIPTERIS Linn.
BIDENS FRONDOSA Linn.
BIDENS CONNATA Muhl.   *B. connata comosa* A. Gray.
BIDENS LÆVIS (Linn.) B. S. P.
BIDENS BIPINNATA Linn.
BIDENS TRICHOSPERMA (Michx.) Britton.   *Coreopsis trichosperma* Michx.
GALLINSOGA PARVIFLORA Cav.
HELENIUM AUTUMNALE Linn.
ANTHEMIS COTULA Linn.
ANTHEMIS ARVENSIS Linn.
ACHILLEA MILLEFOLIUM Linn.
CHRYSANTHEMUM LEUCANTHEMUM Linn
MATRICARIA MATRICARIOIDES (Less.) Porter.
TANACETUM VULGARE Linn.
SENECIO VULGARIS Linn.
SENECIO AUREUS Linn.
SENECIO OBOVATUS Muhl.   *S. aureus obovatus* T. & G.
SENECIO BALSAMITÆ Muhl.   *S. aureus Balsamitæ* T. & G.

CACALIA SUAVEOLENS Linn.
CACALIA RENIFORMIS Muhl.
CACALIA ATRIPLICIFOLIA Linn.
ERECHTITES HIERACIFOLIA (Linn.) Raf.
ARCTIUM LAPPA Linn.
  Mineral Co., opposite Cumberland, Md. (*J. K. Small*).
ARCTIUM MINUS Schk. *A. Lappa minus* A. Gray.
CARDUUS LANCEOLATUS Linn. *Cnicus lanceolatus* (Willd.)
CARDUUS ALTISSIMUS Linn. *Cnicus altissimus* Willd.
CARDUUS DISCOLOR (Muhl). Nutt. *Cnicus discolor* A. Gray.
CARDUUS VIRGINIANUS Linn. *Cnicus Virginianus* Pursh.
CARDUUS MUTICUS (Michx.) Pursh. *Cnicus muticus* Pursh.
CARDUUS ODORATUS (Muhl.) Porter. *Cnicus odoratus* Muhl.
CARDUUS ARVENSIS (Linn.) Robs. *Cnicus arvensis* Hoffm.
ADOPOGON DANDELION (Linn.) O. K.
ADOPOGON VIRGINICUM (Linn) O. K. *A. amplexicaule* O. K.
CICHORIUM INTYBUS Linn.
HIERACIUM CANADENSE Michx.
HIERACIUM PANICULATUM Linn.
HIERACIUM VENOSUM Linn.
HIERACIUM SCABRUM Michx.
HIERACIUM GRONOVII Linn.
HIERACIUM LONGIPILUM Torr.
PRENANTHES ALTISSIMA Linn.
PRENANTHES ALBA Linn.
PRENANTHES SERPENTARIA Pursh. (*Nuttall.*)
TARAXACUM TARAXACUM (Linn) Karst. *T. officinale* Webb.
LACTUCA SCARIOLA Linn.
LACTUCA CANADENSIS Linn.
LACTUCA PULCHELLA (Pursh.) DC. *L. integrifolia* Nutt.
LACTUCA HIRSUTA Muhl.
LACTUCA SPICATA (Lam.) Hitch. *L. leucophæa* A. Gray.
LACTUCA VILLOSA Jacq.
LACTUCA FLORIDANA (Linn.) Gærtn.
SONCHUS OLERACEUS (Linn.)
SONCHUS ASPER (Linn.) All.
TRAGOPOGON PORRIFOLIUS Linn.

Host Index of the Fungi.*

ABIES BALSAMEA (L.) Miller.
   Peridermium Balsameum.

ABUTILON ABUTILON (L.) Rusby. (*A. Avicenne* Gærtn.)
   Macrosporium Abutilonis.

ACALYPHA VIRGINICA L.
   Cercospora Acalyphæ.

ACER *sp.*
   Daldinia concentrica.
   Helminthosporium persistens.
   Myxosporium seriatum.
   Trametes ambigua.

ACER NEGUNDO L. (*Negundo aceroides* Mœnch.)
   Ceganella Aceris.
   Diplodia atrata.
   Fusarium sarcochroum.
   Phoma negundinicola ramicola.
   Phyllosticta *sp.*
   Tubercularia vulgaris.

ACER PENNSYLVANICUM L.
   Botryodiplodia acerina.
   Cytispora exasperans.
   Phoma Pennsylvanica.
   Phoma samararum.
   Rhytisma punctatum.

ACER RUBRUM L.
   Botryosphæria quercuum.
   Bromella Ravenelii.
   Ceganella Aceris.
   Eutypella rugiella.
   Libertella acerina?
   Phyllosticta acericola.
   Sphæronæma acerinum.
   Steganosporium piriforme.
   Valsa etherialis.
   Valsa pauperata.

---

* Species habiting fallen twigs, bark, branches, trunks, logs, stumps and leaves; soil, ground, sand and rocks; and excrementitious and decaying vegetable and animal substances, etc., etc., are not included in this index.

ACER SACCHARINUM L. (*A. dasycarpum* Ehrh.)
Diaporthe Aceris.
Fomes applanatus.
Libertella acerina?
Phyllosticta acericola.
Scleroderris pallidula.
• Stagonospora collapsa.
Valsa ceratophora.

ACER SACCHARUM Marsh. (*Acer saccharinum* Wang.)
Hypoxylon fuscum.
Pilacre Petersii.

ACTÆA ALBA (L.) Mill.
Urocystis Anemones.

Actinomeris squarrosa see **VERBESINA ALTERNIFOLIA**.

AESCULUS OCTANDRA HYBRIDA (DC.) Sarg. (*Ae. octandra purpurascens* Gr.)
Phyllosticta sphæropsidea.

AGARICUS *sp.*
Nyctalis asterophora.
Sporodinia Aspergillus.

AGRIMONIA STRIATA Michx. (*A. Eupatoria* L.)
Sphærotheca Humuli.
Uredo Agrimoniæ.

ALNUS RUGOSA (Ehrh.) Koch. (*A. serrulata* Willd.)
Cryptospora femoralis.
Diatrypella verruciformis.
Eutypella stellulata.
Glœoporus tremellosus.
Glœosporium Alni. *sp. nov.*
Glœosporium cylindrospermum.
Hypoxylon fuscum.
Phlebia radiata.
Valsa femoralis.

AMALANCHIER CANADENSIS (L.) Medic.
Dimerosporium Collinsii.

AMARANTHUS RETROFLEXUS L.
Cystopus Bliti.

Ampelopsis quinquefolia see **PARTHENOCISSUS QUINQUEFOLIA**.

AMYGDALUS PERSICA L. (*Prunus Persica* Bth. & Hook.)
Cytispora leucostoma.
Cytispora Persicæ.
Exoascus deformans.
Monilia fructigena.
Sterigmatocystis nigra.

Streptothryx atra.
Trichothecium roseum.
Valsa leucostoma.

ANEMONE VIRGINIANA L.
Puccinia Anemones-Virginiana.

Andromeda ligustrina see XOLISMA LIGUSTRINA.

ARALIA SPINOSA L.
Botryosphæria Araliæ.
Diaporthe Araliæ.
Eutypella densissima.
Haplosporella Araliæ.
Hypoderma commune.
Hypoxylon coccineum.
Lecanidion atratum.
Leptothyrium vulgare.
Macrosporium commune.
Nectria cinnabarina.
Nematella nucleata.
Phoma melaleuca.
Phyllosticta Araliæ.
Physarum sinuosum.
Stagonospora petiolorum.
Tubercularia vulgaris.
Valsa ambiens.
Vermicularia petiolorum.

ARCTIUM LAPPA L.
Phyllosticta Lappæ.
Vermicularia Arctii.

ARISÆMA TRIPHYLLUM (L.) Torr.
Uromyces Caladii.

ASCLEPIAS SYRIACA L. (*A. cornuti* Dec.)
Fusarium roseum.
Macrosporium asclepiadeum.
Phoma asclepiadea *sp. nov.*
Phoma *sp.*
Uromyces Howei.

ASIMINA TRILOBA (L.) Dunal.
Anthostoma micrœcium.
Cytispora carphosperma.
Dinemasporium hispidulum.
Dothiorella Asiminæ *sp. nov.*
Macrosporium olivaceum *sp. nov.*
Mucor Mucedo.
Phyllosticta Asiminæ.
Rosellina micrœcium.
Sphæropsis Asiminæ *sp. nov.*
Sphæropsis Asiminæ fructigena *var. nov.*

Tubercularia Asiminæ *sp. nov.*
Ustilago *sp.*
Valsa ambiens.

ASPARAGUS OFFICINALIS L.
Fusarium *sp.*
Gibberella Saubinettii.
Macrosporium commune.
Tilmadoche mutans.
Torula herbarum.
Vermicularia liliacearum.

Aspidium spinulosum see DRYOPTERIS SPINULOSA.

ASTER *sp.*
Thelephora sebacea.

ASTER CORDIFOLIUS L.
Coleosporium Sonchi.
Puccinia Asteris.
Septoria atro-purpurea.

ASTER INFIRMUS Mich.
Fusicladium *sp.*

AVENA SATIVA L.
Epicoccum neglectum.
Ustilago Avenæ lævis.
Ustilago segetum.

AZALEA VISCOSA L.
Sphærographum histricinum.
Pestalozzia Guepini.

BENZOIN BENZOIN (L.) Coulter. (*Lindera Benzoin* Meisn.)
Camorosporum Linderæ *sp. nov.*
Diaporthe sociata.
Diplodia Linderæ.
Phyllosticta lindericola.
Sphæropsis Linderæ.
Valsa Linderæ.

BETA VULGARIS L.
Cercospora beticola.

BETULA *sp.*
Corticium Petersii.
Hypoxylon atroviride?
Hypoxylon multiforme.
Polyporus pubescens.

BETULA LENTA L.
Gelatinosporum betulinum.
Hymenochæte corrugata.
Hymenochæte unicolor.
Polystictus hirsutus.

Poria tomento-cincta.
Septoria microsperma.
Stereum complicatum.
Stereum sericeum.
Stereum versicolor.

BETULA LUTEA Michx. f.
Discosia Artoceras.
Fomes fomentarius.
Lentinus strigosus.

BETULA NIGRA L.
Aposphæria pezizoides.
Cytispora betulina.
Glœosporium betularum.
Melanconium bicolor.
Steganosporium muricatum.

BOEHMERIA CYLINDRICA (L.) Willd.
Cercospora Boehmeriæ.

BOLETUS *sp.*
Sporodinia Aspergillus.

BRASSICA NIGRA (L.) Koch.
Cystopus candidus.
Septoria Brassicæ *sp. nov.*

BRASSICA OLERACEA L.
Botrytis vulgaris.

CARDUUS LANCEOLATUS L.
Puccinia Hieracii.
Puccinia suaveolens.

CALOPTENUS FEMUR RUBRUM (*grasshopper*).
Bacterium *sp.*
Empusa Grylli.

CAREX *sp.*
Puccinia Caricis.

CAREX FRASERI And.
Botrytis torta.
Epidochium melanochlorum?
Stachylidium caricinum.
Trichægum nodulosum.
Zygodesmus graminicola.

CARPINUS CAROLINIANA Walt.
Cytispora leucosperma.
Glœosporium Robergei.
Radulum orbiculare.
Thyrsidium hedericolum Carpini.
Xylaria flabelliformis.

Carya sp., see HIKORIA *sp.*

CASSIA MARILANDIA L.
 Vermicularia Dematium.

CASTANEA DENTATA (Marsh.) Sudw. (*C. sativa Americana* Sarg.)
 Coryneum pustulatum.
 Cryptospora cinctula.
 Diatrype Stigma.
 Discosia Artoceras.
 Glonium parvulum.
 Lenzites corrugata.
 Leptothyrium Castanæ.
 Melanconis modonia.
 Microsphæria Alni.
 Mucronoporus Gilbus.
 Peniophora quercina.
 Phyllactinia suffulta.
 Septoria ochroleuca.
 Sphærella maculiformis.
 Steganosporium Castanæ.
 Stereum versiforme.
 Valsa coronata.

CASTANEA PUMILA Mill.
 Phyllosticta Castanæ.

CATALPA CATALPA (L.) Karst. (*Catalpa Bignonioides* Walt.)
 Epicoccum neglectum.
 Microsphæria elevata.
 Phyllosticta Catalpæ.

CATERPILLARS.
 Empusa Grylli.

CAULOPHYLLUM THALICTROIDES (L.) Michx.
 Cercospora Caulophylli.
 Diaporthe Gladioli?
 Vermicularia compacta.

CELASTRUS SCANDENS L
 Botryosphæria Hibiscii *var.*
 Phyllosticta Celastri *sp. nov.*
 Ramularia Celastri.
 Sphæropsis celastrina.
 Tubercularia Celastri.

CELTIS OCCIDENTALIS L.
 Cytispora Celtidis.
 Haplosporella Celtidis.
 Macrosporium antennæforme.
 Phyllosticta Celtidis.
 Tubercularia hamata.

CEPHALANTHUS OCCIDENTALIS L.
 Discosia Artoceras.

CERCIS CANADENSIS L.
  Cytispora *sp*.
  Diplodia Cercidis.
  Glœosporium *sp*.
  Phyllosticta cercidicola *sp nov*.
  Sarcinella heterospora.

CHENOPODIUM ALBUM VIRIDE (L.) Moq.
  Cercospora dubia.

CHENOPODIUM ANTHELMINTICUM L.
  Cercospora anthelmintica.
  Pyrenophora calvescens.

CHIONANTHUS VIRGINICA L.
  Botryosphæria pyriospora.
  Cercospora Chionanthi *sp. nov*.
  Cytispora *sp*.
  Dermatea Chionanthi.
  Phyllosticta Chionanthi.
  Stagonospora *sp*.
  Valsa Chionanthi.

CICUTA MACULATA L.
  Botrytis oleracea.
  Macrosporium commune.

CIMICIFUGA RACEMOSA (L.) Nutt.
  Leptosphæria Ogilviensis.

CLEMATIS VIRGINIANA L.
  Ascochyta clematidina.

CLINTONIA UMBELLULATA (Michx.) Torr
  Vermicularia liliacearum.

Cnicus lanceolatus Willd see CARDUUS LANCEOLATUS L.

CONVOLVULUS REPENS L. (*Calystegia sepium repens* Gray.)
  Puccinia Convolvuli.
  Puccinia Convolvuli *var*.

CORNUS ALTERNIFOLIA L.f.
  Septoria cornicola.

CORNUS FLORIDA L.
  Aschersonia *sp*.
  Dædalia confragosa.
  Discosia Artoceras.
  Phyllosticta cornicola.
  Phyllosticta globifera *sp. nov*.
  Septoria Corni-Maris.
  Sporodesmium toruloides.
  Tremella virens.
  Valsa ambiens.

CORYLUS AMERICANA Walt.
    Gnomoniella Coryli.

CRATEGUS *sp.*
    Aspergillus glaucus.
    Cylindrosporium Cratægi.
    Gymnosporangium clavariiforme (*Aecid.*)

CRATEGUS OXYACANTHA L.
    Podosphæria Oxyacanthæ.

CUNILA ORIGANOIDES (L.) Britton. (*C. Mariana* L.)
    Puccinia Menthæ.

Cuphœa petiolata see **PARSONSIA PETIOLATA.**

DATURA STRAMONIUM L.
    Macrosporium sp.

DENDROCTONUS FRONTALIS (*Insect.*)
    Cylindrocolla Dendroctoni.

DENTARIA DIPHYLLA Michx.
    Cystopus candidus.

Desmodium paniculatum see **MEIBOMIA PANICULATA.**

Desmodium canescens see **MEIBOMIA CANESCENS.**

DIANTHUS AMERICANA L.
    Cercospora Diantheræ.

Diarrhena Americana see **KORYCARPUS DIANDRUS.**

DIOSCOREA VILLOSA L.
    Phyllosticta Dioscoreæ.
    Leptothyrium vulgare.

DIOSPYROS VIRGINIANA L.
    Fusarium roseum *var.*
    Macrosporium *sp.*
    Podosphæria Oxyacanthæ.
    Valsa Diospyri.

DISPORUM LANUGINOSUM (L.) Morong.
    Discosia maculicola.

DRYOPTERIS SPINULOSA (Retz.) Kuntze. (*Aspidium spinulosum* Sw.)
    Leocarpus fragilis.
    Leptostromella filicina.

ELYMUS CANADENSIS GLAUCIFOLIUS (Willd.) Torr.
    Phyllachora graminis.

EPIGÆA REPENS L.
    Discosia Artoceras.
    Erysiphe Vaccinii.

EQUISETUM ARVENSE L.
Septosporium Equiseti.

ERECHTITES HIERACIFOLIA (L.) Raf.
Sphærotheca Castagnei.

EUPATORIUM AGERATOIDES L.
Cercospora ageratoides.
Erysiphe communis.
Puccinia tenuis.

EUPATORIUM CŒLESTINUM L.
Puccinia conoclinii.

EUPATORIUM PURPUREUM L.
Oidium erysiphoides.
Erysiphe Cichoracearum.

FAGUS ATROPUNICEA (Marsh.) Sudw. (*F. ferruginea* Ait.)
Coryne urnalis.
Cryptosporella compta.
Horomyces fragiformis.
Hydnum coralloides.
Hydnum Erinaceus.
Lachnea scutellata.
Libertella faginea.
Microsphæria erineophila.
Polystictus hirsutus.
Scorias spongiosa.

FRAGARIA *cult.*
Phoma obscurans.
Ramularia Tulasnei.
Septoria aciculosa.

FRAXINUS *sp.*
Aposphæria pezizoides.

FRAXINUS AMERICANA L.
Cucurbitaria Fraxini.
Diplodia infuscans.
Diplodia inquinans.
Fomes applanatus.
Hemiarcyria rubiformis.
Hypholoma sublateritium.
Sphærographum Fraxini.
Sphæropsis phomatella.

FRAXINUS PENNSYLVANICA Mart. (*F. pubescens* Lam.)
Cytispora ceratophora.
Discosia Artoceras.
Glœosporium aridum.

GALAX APHYLLA L.
Asterina Leemingii.
Dimerosporium Galactis.
Phyllosticta Galacis.

GALIUM CIRCÆZANS Michx.
  Septoria pilostega.

GAULTHERIA PROCUMBENS L.
  Hypocrea tenerrima.
  Sphærella Gaultheriæ.

GENTIANA ANDREWSII Griesb.
  Phyllosticta gentianicola.

GEUM CANADENSE Jacq. (*G. album* Gm.)
  Pestalozzia *sp.*
  Phyllosticta *sp.*

Halesia tetraptera see MOHRODENDRON CAROLINUM.

HAMAMELIS VIRGINICA L.
  Corticium leve.
  Gonatobotryum maculiocolum.
  Lecanidion Hamamelidis.
  Leptosphæria Doliolum.
  Phyllosticta Hamamelidis.
  Phyllosticta sphæropsidea.

HELIANTHUS DECAPETALUS L.
  Cylindrocolla flagellaris *sp. nov.*
  Puccinia Helianthi.
  Septoria Helianthi.

HEUCHERA AMERICANA L.
  Septoria Saxifragæ.
  Vermicularia Dematium.

HICORIA *sp.*
  Corticium lilacino-fuscum.
  Scoriomyces Cragini.
  Sphæropsis Caryæ.
  Tremella intumescens.

HICORIA MICROCARPA (Nutt.) Britton. (*Carya microcarpa.*)
  Phyllosticta caryiogena.

HICORIA MINIMA (Marsh.) Britton. (*Carya amara.*)
  Valsa ceratophora.

HICORIA OVATA (Mill.) Britton. (*Carya alba.*)
  Corticium subgiganteum.
  Cytispora caryiogena.
  Dædalia unicolor.
  Diplodia caryiogena.
  Melanoconium pallidum.
  Myxosporium luteum.
  Phyllosticta caryiogena.
  Polyporus adustus.
  Tilmadoche gyrocephala.
  Trichoderma lignorum.

HOLCUS LANATUS L.
Puccinia coronata.

HOUSTONIA CÆRULEA L.
Æcidium Houstonianum.

HOUSTONIA LONGIFOLIA Gærtn.
Æcidium Houstonianum.

HYDNUM *sp.*
Pencillium glaucum.
Stremonites fusca.

HYDRANGEA ARBORESCENS L.
Diaporthe Hydrangæ *sp. nov.*
Hypoderma commune.
Leptosphæria vagabunda.
Tilmadoche gyrocephala.

HYMENOCETUM sp.
Hypomyces rosellus.

HYPERICUM MUTILUM L.
Uromyces Hyperici.

HYPOXYLON COCCINEUM Bull.
Lasiosphæria ovina.

HYPOXYLON RUBIGINOSUM.
Isaria Virginiensis.

HYSTERIX HYSTERIX (L.) Millsp.
Phyllachora graminis.

ILEX OPACA Ait.
Diaporthe cercophora.
Diplodia ilicicola.
Fusicoccum ilicinum.
Heliscus Lugdunensis.
Hypoxylon perforatum.
Leptothyrium foraminulatum.
Leptothyrium *sp.*
Phoma ilicicola.
Phyllosticta opaca *sp. nov.*
Physalospora Ilicis.
Pilacre Petersii.

ILEX VERTICILLATA (L.) Gray.
Phyllosticta Hynaldi.
Rhytisma Prini.
Trichothecium roseum.

IMPATIENS BIFLORA Walt. (*I. fulva.*)
Septoria Nolitangere.
Æcidium Impatientis.

IPOMŒA PANDURATA (L.) Meyer.
Botrytis vulgaris.
Coleosporium Ipomœæ
Pestalozzia funerea.
Phlyctæna Ipomœæ.
Phyllosticta Ipomœæ.
Sphæropsis Ipomœæ.

IRIS CRISTATA Ait.
Vermicularia liliacearum.

JUGLANS CINEREA L.
Dasycypha virginea.
Diplodia Juglandis.
Exidia glandulosa.
Glonium simulans.
Lasiosphæria ovina.
Marsonia Juglandis.
Melanconium oblongum.
Mucronoporus ferruginosus.
Orbilia coccinella.
Propolis Faginea.
Pseudohelotium fibrisedum.
Sphæeronæma infuscans *sp. nov.*
Tapesia fusca.
Tapesia sanguinea.
Valsaria exasperans.

JUNIPERUS VIRGINIANA L.
Gymnosporangium juniperinum (*Teleuto.*)
Gymnosporangium macropus.

KALMIA LATIFOLIA L.
Cercospora Kalmiæ.
Dacryomyces minor.
Hymenochæte unicolor.
Hypocreopsis riccoidea.
Hysterium Kalmiæ?
Poria sinuosa.
Rhabdospora Kalmianum.
Septoria kalmiæcola.

KORYCARPUS DIANDRUS (Michx.) Kuntze. (*Diarrhena Americana.*)
Phyllachora Caricis.

LACHNOCLADIUM SEMIVESTITUM.
Aspergillus flavus.
Aspergillus glaucus oblongisporus *var. nov.*

LACTUCA CANADENSIS L.
Botryosporium pulchrum.
Bremia Lactucæ.

LACTUCA HIRSUTA Muhl.
Bremia Lactucæ.

LESPEDEZA VIOLACEA (L.) Pers.
  Uromyces Lespedezæ.

***Lindera Benzoin* see BENZOIN BENZOIN.**

LIQUIDAMBAR STYRACIFLUA L.
  Aposphæria pezizoides.
  Cytispora *sp.*
  Grandinia crustosa.
  Lophiotrema Nucula.
  Monilia aureo-fulva.
  Propolis faginea.
  Trichia proximella.

LIRIODENDRON TULIPIFERA L.
  Dendrodochium rubellum microsporum.
  Dothiorella minor *sp. nov.*
  Diplodia Liriodendri.
  Eurotium herbariorum.
  Erysiphe Liriodendri.
  Leptothyrium Liriodendri.
  Orbilia rubella.
  Propolis faginea.
  Phoma mixta.
  Phyllosticta liriodendrica.
  Phyllosticta macrospora.
  Polystictus hirsutus.
  Poria corticola.
  Poria Tulipiferæ
  Tubercularia vulgaris.
  Valsa albopuncta *sp. nov.*

LOBELIA CARDINALIS L.
  Septoria Lobeliæ.

LYCOPERSICUM ESCULENTUM L.
  Fusarium Solani.
  Macrosporium Tomato.

MAGNOLIA ACUMINATA L.
  Dendrodochium rubellum microsporum.
  Massaria Magnoliæ *sp nov.*
  Phyllosticta Cookei.
  Sphæronæma Magnoliæ.

MAGNOLIA FRASERI Walt.
  Bombardia fasciculata.
  Botrytis vulgare.
  Calocera viscosa.
  Cladosporium *sp.*
  Collybia conigenoides.
  Corticium leptaleum.
  Corticium scutellare.
  Diatrype platystoma.

Diatrypella verruciformis.
Discosia Artoceras.
Exidia glandulosa.
Helminthosporium macrocarpon.
Helminthosporium septemseptatum.
Hemiarcyria stipata.
Holwaya ophiobolus.
Hymenochæte corrugata.
Hypoxylon Howeanum.
Hypoxylon Nuttallii *sp. nov.*
Hypoxylon perforatum.
Irpex obliquus.
Kneiffia setigera.
Lachnella Virginica.
Leptothyrium petiolorum *var.*
Lycogala epidendrum.
Melanomma Pulvis-pyrius.
Nectria coccinea.
Nectria ditissima.
Nematella nucleata.
Orbilia Xanthostigma.
Peniophora cinerea.
Phlebia merismoides.
Phyllactinia suffulta.
Phoma pedunculi.
Physarum psittacinum.
Pilacre Petersii.
Polyporus *sp.*
Polyporus brunalis.
Poria ferruginosa.
Poria spissa.
Poria tomento-cincta.
Radulum Magnoliæ.
Stagonospora pedunculi.
Stilbum magnum.
Tapesia sanguinea.
Tilmadoche nutans.
Tilmadoche viridis.
Vermicularia subeffigurata.
Xylaria corniformis.

MEIBOMIA CANESCENS (L.) Kuntze. (*Desmodium canescens.*)
Uromyces Hedysari-paniculati.

MEIBOMIA PANICULATA (L.) Kuntze. (*Desmodium paniculatum.*)
Uromyces Hedysari-paniculati.

MENISPERMUM CANADENSE L.
Cercospora Menispermi.
Cladosporium herbarum.
Sphæropsis Menispermi.

MOHRODENDRON CAROLINUM (L.) Britton. (*Halesia tetraptera.*)
Cytispora Halesiæ.
Diaporthe Halesiæ.
Diaporthe Tetrapteræ.
Sirococcus Halesiæ.

MORUS RUBRA L.
Tubercularia *sp.*

MOSS.
Hypocrea tenerrima.
Lycoperdon pedicellatum.
Physarum citrinum.

Nasturtium Armoracia (L.) Fr. see RORIPA ARMORACIA.

NECTRIA VERRUCOSA.
Tubercularia *sp.*

Negundo aceroides see ACER NEGUNDO.

NYSSA AQUATICA L. (*N. sylvatica.*)
Phoma Nyssocarpa.
Sphærella nyssæcola.
Valsa Nyssæ.
Valsa præstans.

Œnothera biennis see next.

ONAGRA BIENNIS (L.) Scop. (*Œnothera biennis.*)
Cercospora Œnotheræ.
Leptothyrium Vulgare.
Phlyctæna arcuata.
Phlyctæna vagabunda.
Phoma herbarum.
Sphæronæma corneum.
Sphæropsis Œnotheræ *sp. nov.*
Vermicularia *sp.*

OPULASTER OPULIFOLIUS (L.) Kuntze. (*Physocarpus opulifolius.*)
Botryosphæria Quercuum.
Didymella Physocarpi.
Pestalozzia Jefferisii.
Phoma *sp.*
Phoma leucostoma.
Phoma Spiræœ.
Sphæronæma Physocarpi.
Sphæropsis Physocarpi.
Sporodesmium moriforme.
Stagonospora Physocarpi.

ORANGE (*decaying.*)
Oospora fasciculata.

OSMORRHIZA CLAYTONII. (Michx.) B.S.P.
　　Puccinia Pimpinellæ.

OSTRYA VIRGINIANA (Mill.) Willd.
　　Thelephora pedicellata.
　　Corticium Oakesii.

OXALIS STRICTA L. (*O. corniculata stricta.*)
　　Microsphæria Russellii.

OXYDENDRON ARBOREUM (L.) DC.
　　Discosia maculicola.
　　Phyllosticta Oxydendri *sp. nov.*
　　Scleroderris pallidula.
　　Tympanis Oxydendri.

PARTHENOCISSUS QUINQUEFOLIA (L.) Planch. (*Ampelopsis quinquefolia.*)
　　Botryosphæria Quercuum.
　　Cercospora Ampelopsidis.
　　Coniothryum Fuckelii.
　　Periconia pycnospora.
　　Phyllosticta Ampelopsidis.
　　Sphæropsis Ampelopsidis.
　　Uncinula Ampelopsidis.

PESTALOZZIA GUEPINI.
　　Dermatea lobata.

PHASEOLUS VULGARIS L.
　　Cercospora columnaris.
　　Colletotrichum Lindemuthianum.
　　Uromyces appendiculatus.

PHLOX AMŒNA Sims.
　　Cercospora omphacodes.
　　Vermicularia phlogina.

PHRYMA LEPTOSTACHYA L.
　　Septoria Leptostachyæ.

Physocarpus opulifolius see OPULASTER OPULIFOLIUS.

PHYLLOSTICTA CARYIOGENA.
　　Discosia rugulosa.

PHYTOLACCA DECANDRA L.
　　Diaporthe aculeata.
　　Leptosphæria clavigera.
　　Macrosporium caudatum.
　　Periconia pycnospora.
　　Phlyctæna septorioides.
　　Phlyctæna vagabunda.
　　Phoma Phytolaccæ.

PICEA MARIANA (Mill.) BSP.
　　Fomes carneus.

Lenzites sepiaria.
Polystictus versicolor.
Scleroderma vulgare.

PINUS ECHINATA Mill. (*P. mitis.*)
Coleosporium Senecionis (*Æcid.*)
Hyphoderma Desmazieri.

PINUS RIGIDA Mill.
Amphisphæria pinicola.
Dasycypha Ellisiana.
Lophiodermium pinastri.
Pleosphæria corticola.
Stictis fimbriata.

PINUS STROBUS Linn.
Dacryomyces deliquescens.

PINUS VIRGINIANA Mill. (*P. inops.*)
Amphisphæria pinicola.
Botryosphæria Quercuum.
Corticium scutellare.
Cytispora Curreyi.
Fomes volvatus.
Mollisia pinastri.
Polystictus abietinus.
Poria Xantha.
Rosellina abietina trichota.
Speira minor.
Stictis fimbriata.
Stereum Pini.
Tremella aurantia.

PLATANUS OCCIDENTALIS L.
Aposphæria pezizoides.
Cytispora Platani.
Dacryomyces Syringæ.
Dendrophoma Therryana.
Eutypella Platani.
Glœosporium nervisequum.
Helminthosporium macrocarpon.
Hendersonia Desmazieri.
Myxosporium platanicolum.
Phoma scabra.
Rosellinia millegrana.
Stilbum flavipes.

POA PRATENSIS L.
Erysiphe graminis.
Oidium monilioides.

PODOPHYLLUM PELTATUM L.
Puccinia Podophylli.

POLYGONATUM BIFLORUM (Walt.) Ell.
    Cladosporium herbarum.

POLYGONUM AVICULARE L.
    Cercospora avicularis.

POLYGONUM ERECTUM L.
    Uromyces Polygoni.

POLYGONUM HYDROPIPER L.
    Septoria Polygonorum.

POLYMNIA UVEDALIA L.
    Helotium herbarum.
    Leptosphæria Doliolum.
    Macrosporium *sp*.
    Periconia pycnospora.
    Pleurotus cyphelliformis.
    Septoria Polymnæ.

POLYPORUS PERGAMENUS.
    Calicium tigillare.
    Cephalothecium roseum.

POLYPORUS VARIUS Fr.
    Cladosporium epimyces.
    Pencillium glaucum.

POLYSTICTUS VERSICOLOR.
    Dactylium dendroides.

PORIA SPISSA.
    Orbilia vinosa.

PORTULACCA OLERACEA L.
    Cystopus Portulacæ.

POTENTILLA CANADENSIS L.
    Phragmidium Potentillæ (*Uredo.*)

POTENTILLA MONSPELIENSIS L. (*P. Norvegica.*)
    Mollisia Dehnii.

PRENANTHES SERPENTARIA Pursh.
    Septoria Nabali.

PRUNUS *cult.* "Cherry."
    Libertella faginea.
    Monilia fructigena.
    Plowrightia morbosa.
    Podosphæria Oxyacanthæ.
    Podosphæria tridactyla.
    Polystictus cinnabarinus.
    Volutella ciliata.

PRUNUS DOMESTICA L.
    Cytispora leucostoma.

Exoascus Pruni.
Monilia fructigena.
Plowrightia morbosa.

Prunus Persica see AMYGDALUS PERSICA.

PRUNUS SEROTINA Ehrh.
Merulius ambiguus.
Polyporus nidulans.
Poria vaporaria.
Sphæropsis cerasina.

PYRUS COMMUNIS L.
Entomosporium maculatum.
Micrococcus amylovorus.

PYRUS CORONARIA L.
Gymnosporangium macropus (*Æcid.*)
Plowrightia morbosa

PYRUS MALUS L.
Fusicladium dendriticum,
Phyllosticta Pirina.
Polystictus hirsutus.
Schizophyllum commune.

QUERCUS *sp.*
Asterostoma cervicolor.
Botryosphæria Quercuum.
Chlorosplenium Schweinitzii.
Cryptospora trichospora.
Guepinia spathularia.
Hemiarcyria clavata.
Hypoxylon atroviride?
Hypoxylon stigmatum.
Nummularia punctulata.
Rosellinia corticium.
Stereum pustulosum.
Stereum versicolor.

QUERCUS ALBA L.
Bactridium flavum.
Coryne urnalis.
Fomes applanatus.
Hemiarcyria rubiformis.
Hemiarcyria clavata.
Lachnella erinaceus.
Lachnea scutellata.
Marsonia Martini.
Merulius tremellosus.
Merulius rubellus.
Phyllosticta phomiformis.
Polystictus versicolor.
Schizophyllum commune.
Stereum sulphuratum.

QUERCUS PALUSTRIS DuRoi.
Erysiphe quercina.
Fomes applanatus.
Lycoperdon pyriforme.
Trichopeziza capitata.

QUERCUS PRINUS L.
Botryodiplodia *sp*.
Cyathicula quisquillaris.
Marsonia Martini.
Phyllosticta phomiformis.
Phyllosticta Quercus-Prini.
Polyscytalum sericeum.
Pseudovalsa sigmoidea.
Stereum complicatum.

QUERCUS RUBRA L.
Fomes applanatus.
Leptothyrium dryinum.

QUERCUS VELUTINA Lam. (*Q. tinctoria*.)
Marsonia Martini.

RESEDA ODORATA L.
Cladosporium herbarum fasciculare.
Pyrenopeziza lacerta.

RHODODENDRON CATAWBIENSE Michx.
Pestalozzia Guepini.

RHODODENDRON MAXIMUM L.
Exobasidium Rhodedendri.
Grandinia crustosa.
Heliotium castaneum.
Hypocrea Virginiensis.
Hypoxylon colliculosum.
Lophiodermium Rhododendri.
Pestalozzia Guepini.
Sporocybe Azaleæ.
Stereum triste.
Tremella frondosa.

RHUS COPALLINA L.
Aponectria inaurata.
Calospora aculeans.
Polyporus pocula.
Sporocybe Rhois.
Stereum sericeum.

RHUS HIRTA (L.) Sudw. (*R. typhina*)
Calospora aculeans.
Calospora Rhoina.
Cladosporium herbarum.
Cytispora Rhoina.
Cytispora Rhois-hirtæ *sp. nov*.

Irpex lacteus.
Myxosporium Rhois.
Polyporus adustus.
Sphæropsis Sumachi.
Sporocybe Rhois.
Torula dimidiata.
Tubercularia vulgaris.

RHUS RADICANS L. (*R. toxicodendron.*)
Cylindrosporium Toxicodendri.
Macrosporium commune.
Pestalozzia Toxica.
Phyllosticta roicola.
Uromyces Terebinthi.
Vermicularia Toxica *sp. nov.*

RIBES *cult.*
Phyllosticta Ribis *sp. nov.*

ROBINIA PSEUDACACIA L.
Cladosporium epiphyllum.
Cladosporium nigrellum.
Cucurbitaria elongata.
Cytispora coccinea.
Cytispora orthospora.
Diaporthe oncostoma.
Dothiorella glandulosa.
Epicoccum Duriæanum.
Eutypella stellulata.
Fomes rimosus.
Hypoxylon rubiginosum.
Libertella *sp.*
Nectria ditissima.
Rosellinia subiculata.
Tubercularia vulgaris.
Vermicularia petiolorum.

RORIPA ARMORACIA (L.) Hitch. (*Nasturtium Armoracia.*)
Cercospora Armoraciæ.

ROSA *cult.*
Actinonema Rosæ.
Oidium leucoconium.

ROSA HUMILIS Marsh.
Phragmidium subcorticium.
Phyllosticta Rosæ.

RUBUS BAILEYANUS Britt. (*R. villosus humifusus.*)
Hypoderma virgultorum.
Scleroderris rhabarbarina.

RUBUS CANADENSIS L.
Cercospora Rubi.

Cercospora septorioides *sp. nov.*
Phyllosticta *sp*.
Septoria Rubi.

RUBUS *culi.*
Botryosphæria Quercuum *var.*
Diplodia Rubi.
Hainesia Rubi.

RUBUS HISPIDUS L.
Uredo (*Cæoma*) nitens.

RUBUS ODORATUS L.
Diaporthe rostellata.
Oidium erysiphoides.
Pericornia pycnospora.
Pyrenopeziza lacerata.
Vermicularia compacta.

RUBUS STRIGOSUS Michx.
Glœosporium rubicolum *sp. nov.*
Glœosporium venetum

RUBUS VILLOSOS Ait.
Diaporthe obscura.
Teichospora nitida.
Uredo (*Cæoma*) nitens.

RUMEX ACETOSELLA L.
Coniosporium harknessioides.

RUMEX OBTUSIFOLIUS L.
Glœosporium Rumicis *sp. nov.*
Macrosporium commune.

SALIX NIGRA Marsh.
Corticium salicinum.
Cytispora Salicis.
Diplodia Salicina.
Melampsora farinosa.
Trimmatostroma Americana.

SALIX NIGRA FALCATA Torr.
Aposphæria pezizoides.
Hendersonia Lirella.
Lophidium compressum.

SAMBUCUS CANADENSIS L.
Cercospora despazeoides.
Corticium scutellare.
Microsphæria Grossulariæ.
Phyllosticta Sambuci.

SAMBUCUS PUBENS Michx. (*S. racemosus.*)
Tubercularia Sambuci.
Tubercularia vulgaris.

SANGUINARIA CANADENSIS L.
Glœosporium Sanguinariæ.
Phyllosticta Sanguinariæ

SAPONARIA OFFICINALIS L.
Macrosporium Saponariæ.

SASSAFRAS SASSAFRAS (L.) Karst. (*S. officinale.*)
Athostoma microplacum.
Colletotrichum *sp.*
Cytispora Sassafras *sp. nov.*
Discosia Artoceras.
Glonium stellatum.
Hypoxylon Sassafras.
Phyllosticta Sassafras.
Sphæropsis Sassafras.
Valsa subclypeata.

SCLERODERMA VULGARE.
Boletus parasiticus.

SCROPHULARIA MARILANDICA L.
Septoria Scrophulariæ.

Smilacina racemosa see **VAGNERA RACEMOSA.**

SMILAX *sp.*
Myicoporon Smilacis.

SMILAX GLAUCA Walt.
Cercospora smilacina.
Puccinia Smilacis (*Uredo.*)

SMILAX ROTUNDIFOLIA L.
Cercospora Smilacis.
Discosia maculicola.
Phoma smilacina.
Phyllosticta Smilacis subeffusa.

SOLANUM TUBEROSUM L.
Phytophthora infestans.

SOLIDAGO CANADENSIS L.
Coleosporium Solidaginis.

SPERGULA ARVENSIS L.
Peronospora obovata.

SPHÆROPSIS ASIMINÆ.
Macrosporium olivaceum.

STEREUM *sp.*
Hypomyces aurantinus.

TARAXACUM TARAXACUM(L.) Karst. (*Taraxacum officinale* Web.)
Puccinia Hieracii.
Ramularia Taraxaci.

TECOMA RADICANS (L.) DC.
  Physalospora *sp.*
  Septoria Tecomæ.

THALICTRUM POLYGAMUM Muhl.
  Leptostroma vulgare.

TIARELLA CORDIFOLIA L.
  Puccinia Heuchera.

TILIA HETEROPHYLLA Vent.
  Hercospora Tiliæ.

TILIA AMERICANA L.
  Phyllosticta Tiliæ.

TRAUTVETTERIA CAROLINENSIS (Walt.) Vail. (*T. palamata.*)
  Botrytis vulgaris.
  Pericornia *sp.*
  Sarcinella heterospora.
  Septoria Trautvetteriæ.
  Vermicularia *sp.*

TRIFOLIUM PRATENSE L.
  Uromyces Trifolii.

TRIFOLIUM REPENS L.
  Polythrincium Trifolii.

TRIOSTEUM PERFOLIATUM L.
  Cladosporium Triostei.

TRITICUM VULGARE L.
  Fusarium culmorum.
  Hymenula cerealis.
  Puccinia Rubigo-vera.
  Tilletia Tritici.
  Ustilago segetum.

TSUGA CANADENSIS Carr.
  Coryneum cupulatum.
  Corticium albo-flavescens.
  Corticium ochraceum.
  Cytispora Curreyi.
  Dacryomyces stellatus.
  Dacryomyces corticioides.
  Fomes lucidus.
  Fomes pinicola.
  Lenzites abietina.
  Lenzites sepiaria *forma.*
  Leocarpus fragilis.
  Lindbaldia effusa.
  Merulius Molluscus.
  Microcera erumpens.
  Odontia farinaceum.

Otidea onotica ochracea.
Panus dorsalis.
Peridermium Peckii.
Polystictus abietinus.
Sphærella conicola
Sporodesmium *sp.*
Stereum sangiunolentum.
Tapesia fusca.
Tremellodon gelatinosum.
Valsa Abietis.

ULMUS PUBESCENS Walt. (*U. fulva.*)
Corticium incarnatum.
Dothidella Ulmiæ.
Mucronoporus Everhartii.
Nectria vulpinia?
Phyllosticta Ulmi?

UREDO (*Cæoma*) NITENS.
Tuberculina persicina.

VAGNERA RACEMOSA (L.) Morong. (*Smilacina racemosa.*)
Septoria Smilaciniæ.
Vermicularia liliacearum.

VERBENA URTICÆFOLIA L.
Septoria Verbenæ.

VERNONIA NOVEBORACENSIS (L.) Willd.
Cercospora oculata.
Cercospora Vernoniæ.
Coleosporium Sonchi.
Coleosporium Vernoniæ.
Ophiobolus porphyrogonus.
Ophiobolus fulgidus.
Phlyctæna vagabunda.

VIOLA BLANDA Willd.
Puccinia Violæ (*Uredo.*)

VIOLA HASTATA Michx.
Puccinia Violæ (*Æcid.*)

VIOLA OBLIQUA Hill. (*V. cucullata.*)
Cercospora granuliformis.
Cercospora Violæ.

VIOLA PRIMULÆFOLIA L.
Septoria hyalina.

VIOLA ROTUNDIFOLIA Michx.
Puccinia Violæ (*Uredo.*)

VIOLA SAGITTATA Ait.
Septoria Violæ.

VITIS *sp.*
    Asterostoma corticolum.
    Botryosphæria Quercuum.
    Corticium Petersii.
    Diplodia viticola.
    Phialea virgultorum.
    Valsa Vitis.

VITIS ÆSTIVALIS Michx.
    Phyllosticta Labruscæ.

VITIS CORDIFOLIA Michx.
    Phyllosticta Labruscæ.
    Saccidium Vitis *sp. nov.*
    Uncinula Americana.

VITIS *cult.* "Concord."
    Dermatella viticola.
    Lophidium nitidum.
    Phoma uvicola.
    Phyllosticta Labruscæ.
    Uncinula Ampelopsidis.

VITIS LABRUSCA L.
    Plasmopara viticola.

VITIS RUPESTRIS Scheele.
    Phyllosticta Labruscæ.
    Trematosphæria vitigena *sp. nov.*

WEEDS (*in shade.*)
    Arcyria cinerea.

XANTHIUM CANADENSE Mill.
    Botrytis vulgaris.
    Erysiphe Cichoracearum.

XANTHORRHIZA APIIFOLIA L'Her.
    Phyllosticta Xanthorrhizæ *sp. nov.*
    Vermicularia Dematium.

XOLISMA LIGUSTRINA (L.) Britton. (*Andromeda ligustrina.*)
    Rhytisma decolorans.

YUCCA FILAMENTOSA L.
    Coniothyrum concentricum.
    Macrosporium caudatum.
    Vermicularia subeffigurata scapincola.

ZEA MAYS L.
    Colletotrichum lineola.
    Coniophora *sp.*
    Diplodia Maydis.
    Helminthosporium folliculatum.
    Leptosphæria orthogramma.

Macrosporium Maydis.
Ophiobolus acuminatus.
Puccinia Sorghi (*Teleut.*)
Ustilago Maydis.

ZIZIA CORDATA (Walt.) DC.
Oidium erysiphoides.

Local Plant Names.*

Bee-weed	Aster Lowrieanus
Blue Devil	Echium vulgare
Blue-stem	Echium vulgare
Blue Thistle	Echium vulgare
Blue-weed	Echium vulgare
Blister Pine	Abies balsamea
Broom Sedge	Andropogon scoparius
Buck-horn Plantain	Plantago lanceolata
Bull's-eye	Chrysanthemum Leucanthemum
Catawba	Catalpa Catalpa
Colic-root	Asarum Canadense
Coon-root	Sanguinaria Canadensis
Crowd-weed	Brassica sinapistrum. Lepidium campestre
Cuckle-burr	Xanthium Canadense
Cut-paper	Papirius papyrifera
Deer's-tongue	Panicum clandestinum
Devil's Flax	Linaria vulgaris
Devil's Grandmother	Elephantopus tomentosus
Devil's Grass	Chondrilla juncea
Devil's Iron-weed	Lactuca pulchella
Devil's Plague	Daucus Carota
Devil's-weed	Lactuca Canadensis
Dog Burr	Cynoglossum officinale
Eve's Thread	Hemerocallis fulva
Fall Aster	Aster Lowrieanus
Farewell Summer	Aster lateriflorus hirsuticaulis
Feather Grass	Holcus lanatus
Federal-weed	Xanthium spinosum
Fire Cherry	Prunus Pennsylvanica
Gipsy-weed	Veronica officinalis
Glade Lily	Lilium Philadelphicum

*The significations of most of these names are given in the "Preliminary Flora," or in "Weeds of West Virginia."

GLENN PEPPER	Lepidium campestre
GLENN-WEED	Lepidium campestre
HIVE VINE	Meibomia rotundifolia
HOG BITE	Chondrilla juncea
HUTTON-WEED	Dipsacus sylvestris
IMPUDENT LAWYER	Linaria vulgaris
INDICATOR	Botrychium Virginianum
KILL COW	Eleocharis tenuis
KRAUT-WEED	Brassica sinapistrum
NAIL ROD	Aster lateriflorus hirsuticaulis
NAKED-WEED	Chondrilla juncea
NIGGER HEAD	Rudbeckia hirta
OLD FIELD SWEET	Aster lateriflorus hirsuticaulis
OLD VIRGINIA STICK-WEED	Aster lateriflorus hirsuticaulis
OLD WHITE-TOP	Holcus lanatus
PINK BLOOM	Sabbatia angularis
POPPLE	Populus tremuloides
POVERTY GRASS	Eleocharis tenuis. Juncus tenuis
QUEEN-WEED	Pastinaca sativa
QUILL-WORT	Eupatorium purpureum
RAMPS	Allium tricoccum
RIPPLE	Plantago lanceolata
RADICAL-WEED	Solanum Carolinense
RED-WEED	Rumex acetosella
RHEUMATISM-WEED	Apocynum Canadense
SEEDY BUCKBERRY	Xolisma ligustrina
SEEDY DEERBERRY	Vaccinium corymbosum
SHERIFF PINK	Chrysanthemum Leucanthemum
SHITTIM WOOD	Mohrodendron Carolinum
SHOO FLY	Baptisia tinctoria
SINK-FIELD	Potentilla Canadensis
SKELETON-WEED	Chondrilla juncea
SPRUCE PINE	Picea Mariana
STICK-WEED	Aster Lowrieanus
ST. JOHN	Hypericum perforatum
TAR-WEED	Parsonsia petiolata
TOBACCO-WEED	Elephantopus tomentosus
WALLINK	Veronica Americana
WATER THISTLE	Dipsacus sylvestris
WHITE SPRUCE	Picea Mariana
WHITE TOP	Erigeron annuus
WILD BEET	Œnothera fruticosa

Wild Cotton	Apocynum cannabinum
Wild Sweet Potato	Ipomœa pandurata
Wire-weed	Aster lateriflorus hirsuticaulis
Wool-mat	Cynoglossum Virginicum
Yellow Daisy	Rudbeckia hirta
Yellow Lin	Magnolia acuminata
Yellow Tip	Solidago juncea
Yew Pine	Picea Mariana

Index.

	PAGE.
Abies	192
Abronia	211
Abutilon	217
Acalypha	215
ACANTHACEÆ	227
Acanthostigma	142
Acer	216
Acerates	223
Achillea	232
Achnanthes	85
Achroanthes	199
Aconitum	205
Acorus	197
Actæa	205
Actinonema	116
Adiantum	190
Adicea	202
Adlumia	206
Adopogon	233
Æcidum	130
Æsculus	216
AGARICACEÆ	156
Agaricus	160
Agastache	225
Agrimonia	211
Agrostemma	204
Agrostis	194
Agyrium	182
Ailanthus	214
AIZOACEÆ	203
Aletris	199
Alisma	192
ALISMACEÆ	192
Allium	198
Alnus	201
Alsine	204
Althæa	217
Amalanchier	211
Amanita	156
Amanitopsis	157
AMARANTHACEÆ	203
Amaranthus	203
AMARYLLIDACEÆ	199
Amblystegium	188
Ambrosia	231
Ampelopsis	217
Amphicarpæa	213
Amphisphæria	141
ANACARDIACEÆ	215
Anagallis	222
Anaphalis	231
Andromeda	221
Andropogon	193
Anemone	205
Aneura	184
Angelica	219
Anomodon	188
ANONACEÆ	204
Antennaria	231
Anthemis	232
Anthostoma	135
Anychia	204
Aphyllon	227
Apios	213
Aplectrum	199
APOCYNACEÆ	222
Apocynum	222
Aponectria	144
Aposphæria	108
AQUIFOLIACEÆ	215
Aquilegia	205
Aralia	219
ARALIACEÆ	219
Arabis	207
ARACEÆ	197
Archilejunea	183
Arctium	233
Arcyria	86
Arisæma	197
Aristida	193
Aristolochia	202
ARISTOLOCHIACEÆ	202
Arrhenatherum	194
Arthonia	181

	PAGE.		PAGE.
Aruncus	209	Bombardia	135
Asarum	202	BORAGINACEÆ	224
Aschersonia	120	Botrychium	190
ASCLEPIADACEÆ	223	Botryodiplodia	116
Asclepias	223	Botryosphæria	138
ASCOBOLACEÆ	152	Botryosporium	88
Ascobolus	152	Botrytis	88
Ascochyta	116	Bovista	81
Ascophanus	152	Bovistella	82
Ascyrum	217	Brachychæta	230
Asimina	204	Brachyelytrum	194
Asparagus	198	Brassica	207
Aspergillus	88	Brauneria	231
Aspidium	190	Bremia	83
Asplenium	190	Bromus	195
Aster	230	Broomella	145
Asterina	132	*Broussonetia*	202
Asterostoma	171	*Brunella*	225
Astilbe	208	BRYACEÆ	186
Astragalus	212	Bryum	186
Astragene	205	Buechnera	226
Astrophyllum	185	Buellia	181
Azalea	221	Bulgaria	154
		BULGARIACEÆ	153
Baccillus	83	Bursa	207
Bactridium	100	Buxbaumia	185
Bæomyces	180		
BALSAMINACEÆ	216	Cacalia	233
Baptisia	212	CACTACEÆ	218
Barbarea	207	Calamagrostis	194
Barbula	186	CALICIACEÆ	182-155
Bartramia	185	Calicium	182-155
BARTRAMIACEÆ	185	CALLITRICHIACEÆ	215
Bazzania	183	Callitriche	215
Bellincinia	183	Calocera	172
Belonidium	152	*Calopogon*	200
Benzoin	206	Calospora	142
BERBERIDACEÆ	206	Caltha	205
Berberis	206	CALYCANTHACEÆ	206
Betula	201	Calycanthus	206
BETULACEÆ	201	Camarosporium	117
Biatora	180	Camassia	198
Bicuculla	206	Camelina	207
Bidens	232	Campanula	229
Bignonia	227	CAMPANULACEÆ	229
BIGNONIACEÆ	227	Camptosorus	190
Blepharostoma	183	Campylium	189
Blephila	225	Cannabis	201
Boehmeria	202	Cantharellus	158
Boletus	161	Capnoides	206

CAPPARIDACEÆ	207
CAPRIFOLIACEÆ	228
Cardamine	207
Carduus	233
Carex	196
Carpinus	201
CARYOPHYLLACEÆ	204
Cassia	213
Castalia	204
Castanea	201
Castilleja	227
Catalpa	227
Caulophyllum	206
Ceanothus	216
Cedronella	225
CELASTRACEÆ	215
Celastrus	215
Celtis	201
Cenangella	153
Cenchrus	193
Cephalanthus	228
Cephalothecium	89
Cephalozia	183
Cerastium	204
Ceratium	98
Ceratodon	188
Cercis	213
Cercospora	93
Cetraria	175
Chærophyllum	220
Chamælirium	198
Chamæraphis	193
Cheilanthes	190
Chelidonium	206
Chelone	226
CHENOPODIACEÆ	203
Chenopodium	203
Chlorosplenium	150
Chimaphila	220
Chiogenes	221
Chionanthus	222
Chrosperma	199
Chrysanthemum	232
Chrysogonum	231
Chrysopsis	229
Cichorium	233
Cicuta	220
Cimicifuga	205
Cinna	194
Circæa	219
Cissus	217
CISTACEÆ	217
Citrullus	228
Cladonia	179
CLADONIACEÆ	179
Cladosporium	91
Clasterosporium	92
Clavaria	172
CLAVARIACEÆ	172
Claytonia	203
Clematis	205
Cleome	207
Clethra	220
CLETHRACEÆ	220
Climacium	189
Clinopodium	225
Clintonia	198
Clitocybe	157
Clitopilus	160
Cnicus	233
Coleosporium	129
Collema	177
COLLEMEÆ	177
Colletotrichum	124
Collinsia	226
Collinsonia	224
Collybia	157
Comatricha	86
Commelina	197
COMMELINACEÆ	197
COMPOSITÆ	229
CONIFERACEÆ	192
Coniophora	172
Coniosporium	90
Coniothyrium	114
Conocyphalum	184
Conopholis	227
CONVOLVULACEÆ	223
Convolvulus	223
Coprinus	161
Corallorhiza	199
Cordyceps	145
Coreopsis	232
CORNACEÆ	220
Cornus	220
Corticium	170
Corycarpus	194
Corylus	201
Coryne	154
Coryneum	125

	PAGE.		PAGE.
Cracca	212	*Desmodium*	213
CRASSULACEÆ	207	Diachæa	85
Crategus	211	Dianthera	227
Cribraria	86	Dianthus	204
Crucibulum	81	DIAPENSIACEÆ	221
CRUCIFERACEÆ	206	Diaporthe	139
Cryptospora	144	DIATOMACEÆ	84
Cryptosporella	138	Diatrype	135
Cucumis	228	Diatrypella	135
Cucurbita	228	Dicksonia	191
CUCURBITACEÆ	228	Dicranella	188
Cucurbitaria	143	DICRANIACEÆ	186
Cunila	224	Dicranodontium	186
Cuphea	218	Dicranum	187
Cuscuta	223	Didymella	139
Cyathicula	150	Didymium	85
Cylindrocolla	99	Diervilla	228
Cylindrosporium	124	Dimerosporium	132
Cylindrothecium	189	Dinemasporium	122
Cymbella	84	Diodia	228
Cynoctonum	222	Dioscorea	199
Cynogolossum	224	DIOSCOREACEÆ	199
CYPERACEÆ	195	Diospyros	222
Cyperus	195	Diphyscium	185
Cypripedium	200	Diplodia	115
Cystopteris	191	Diplophyllum	183
Cystopus	82	Dipsacus	228
Cytispora	11	DIPSACEÆ	228
		Dirca	218
Dacryomyces	173	Discosia	121
Dactylis	194	Disporum	198
Dactylium	89	Ditrichum	188
Dactyloctenium	194	Dodecatheon	221
Dædalia	165	DOTHIDEACEÆ	146
Daldinia	137	Dothidella	146
Dalibarda	211	Dothiorella	110
Danthonia	194	Draba	207
Dasyscypha	151	Drosera	207
Dasystoma	227	DROSERACEÆ	207
Datura	226	Dryopteris	190
Daucus	219	Dulichium	195
Deeringia	220	Durella	155
Delphinium	205		
DEMATIACEÆ	90	Eatonia	194
Dendrodochium	98	EBENACEÆ	222
Dendrophoma	109	*Echinacea*	231
Dentaria	207	*Echinospermum*	224
Dermatea	153	Echium	224
DERMATEACEÆ	152	Eclipta	231
Dermatella	152	Eleocharis	195

	PAGE.
Elephantopus	229
Eleusine	194
Elodea	192
Elymus	195
Empusa	83
Endocarpon	182
Entodon	189
ENTOMOPHTHORACEÆ	83
Entomosporium	122
Epicoccum	101
Epidochium	101
Epigæa	221
Epilobium	218
Epiphegus	227
EQUISITACEÆ	191
Equisetum	191
Eragrostis	194
Erechtites	233
ERICACEÆ	221
Erigenia	220
Erigeron	231
Erigonum	202
Erinella	152
Eriophorum	196
Eryngium	219
Erysimum	207
Erysiphe	131
Erythronium	198
Euonymus	215
Eupatorium	229
Euphorbia	214
EUPHORBIACEÆ	214
Eurotium	131
Euthamia	230
Eutypa	134
Eutypella	134
EXCIPULACEÆ	122
Exidia	173
EXOASCUS	155
Exobasidium	172
FAGACEÆ	201
Fagopyrum	203
Fagus	201
Falcata	213
Favolus	165
Festuca	195
FILICINÆ	190
Fimbristylis	195
Fissidens	185

	PAGE.
FISSIDENTACEÆ	185
Fistulina	162
Flœrkea	215
Fomes	163
Fragaria	211
Fraxinus	222
Frullania	183
Fumaria	206
Funaria	186
FUNARIACEÆ	186
Fusarium	100
Fusicladium	91
Fusicoccum	111
Galax	221
Galeopsis	225
Galium	228
Gallinsoga	232
Gaultheria	221
Gaura	219
Gaylussacia	221
Geaster	81
Gelatinosporum	120
Gentiana	222
GENTIANACEÆ	222
Geocalyx	183
Geopyxis	148
Georgia	185
GEORGIACEÆ	185
GERANIACEÆ	213
Geranium	213
Gerardia	227
Geum	211
Gibberella	145
Gillenia	209
Glaucium	206
Glechoma	225
Gleditschia	213
Glœosporium	122
Glœoporus	166
Glonium	155
Gnaphalium	231
Gnomoniella	138
Gonatobotryum	90
Goodyera	199
GRAMINACEÆ	193
Grandinia	168
GRAPHIDACEÆ	181
Graphis	181
Gratiola	226

	PAGE.
GRIMMIACEÆ	188
Guepinia	174
GYMNOASCACEÆ	155
Gymnocladus	213
Gymnosporangium	129
Gyromitra	147
Gyrostachys	199
Habenaria	200
Hainesia	122
Halesia	222
HAMAMELIDACEÆ	208
Hamamelis	208
Haplosporella	114
Harpanthus	184
Hedeoma	225
Hedwegia	189
Helenium	232
Helianthemum	217
Helianthus	232
Heliopsis	231
Heliscus	100
Helleborus	205
Helminthosporium	92
Helotiella	151
Helotium	149
Helvella	147
HELVELLACEÆ	147
Hemiarcyria	87
Hemorocallis	198
Hendersonia	116
Hepatica	205
Heracleum	220
Herbertia	183
Hercospora	139
Herpotrichia	142
Hesperis	207
Heuchera	208
Hibiscus	217
Hicoria	200
Hieracium	233
HIPPOCASTANACEÆ	216
Hirneola	173
Holcus	194
Holwaya	154
Homalocenchrus	193
Horomyces	174
Houstonia	227
Humaria	148
Humulus	201

	PAGE.
HYDNACEÆ	167
Hydnum	167
Hydrangea	208
Hydrastis	206
HYDROCHARITACEÆ	192
Hydrocotyle	219
HYDROPHYLLACEÆ	223
Hydrophyllum	223
Hygrophorus	158
Hylocomium	188
Hymenochæte	169
Hymenula	99
HYPERICACEÆ	217
Hypericum	217
Hyphelia	102
Hyphoderma	80
Hypholoma	160
HYPHOMYCETACEÆ	87
HYPNACEÆ	188
Hypnum	188
Hypocrea	144
HYPOCREACEÆ	144
Hypocreopsis	145
Hypoderma	156
Hypomyces	144
Hypopytis	221
Hypoxylon	136
HYSTERIACEÆ	155
Hysterium	155
Hysterix	195
Hysterographium	156
Ilex	215
Illosporium	99
Ilysanthes	226
Impatiens	216
Inula	231
Ipomœa	223
IRIDACEÆ	199
Iris	199
Irpex	167
Isanthus	224
Isaria	97
Isopyrum	205
Ithyphallus	81
Jeffersonia	206
Jubula	183
JUGLANDACEÆ	200
Juglans	200

	PAGE.
JUNCACEÆ	198
Juncoides	198
Juncus	198
Jungermannia	184
JUNGERMANNIACEÆ	183
Juniperus	192
Kalmia	221
Kantia	183
Kneiffia	168
Kœllia	224
Korycarpus	194
Kyllingia	195
LABIATÆ	224
Lachnea	148
Lachnella	151
Lachnocladium	173
Lacinaria	229
Lactarius	158
Lactuca	233
Lamium	225
Lamproderma	85
Laportea	202
Lappula	224
Lasiosphæria	142
Lathyrus	213
LAURACEÆ	206
Lecanora	178
LECANOREÆ	178
Lecanidion	155
Lechea	217
Lecidea	181
LECIDEÆ	180
Leersia	186
Legouzia	229
LEGUMINOSÆ	212
Lejunea	183
Lemna	197
LEMNACEÆ	197
Lentinus	159
Lenzites	160
Leocarpus	85
Leonurus	225
Leotia	153
Lepidium	207
Leptandra	226
Leptobryum	186
Leptogium	177
Leptorchis	199

	PAGE.
Leptosphæria	141
Leptostromella	122
Leptothyrium	121
LEPTROSTOMACEÆ	121
Lespedeza	213
Leucobryum	186
Leucodon	189
Libertella	125
Ligusticum	220
Ligustrum	222
LILIACEÆ	198
Lilium	198
LIMNANTHACEÆ	215
Limodorum	200
LINACEÆ	214
Linaria	226
Lindbaldia	86
Linum	214
Lippia	224
Liquidambar	208
Liriodendron	204
Lithospermum	224
Lobelia	229
LOGANIACEÆ	222
Lolium	195
Lonicera	228
Lophidium	146
LOPHIOSTOMACEÆ	146
Lophiotrema	146
Lophodermium	156
LORANTHACEÆ	202
Ludwegia	218
Lupinus	212
Luzula	198
Lycium	226
Lycogala	86
LYCOPERDACEÆ	81
Lycoperdon	82
LYCOPODIACEÆ	191
Lycopodium	191
Lycopus	224
Lysimachia	222
LYTHRACEÆ	218
Maclura	202
Macrosporium	95
Magnolia	204
MAGNOLIACEÆ	204
Maianthemum	198
Malva	217

	PAGE.
MALVACEÆ	217
Marasmius	159
Marchantia	184
MARCHANTIACEÆ	184
Marrubium	225
Marsonia	125
Marsupelia	184
Massaria	141
Matricaria	232
Medicago	212
Mediola	199
Meehania	225
Meibomia	213
Melampsora	127
Melampyrum	227
MELANCONIACEÆ	122
Melanconis	139
Melanconium	125
Melanomma	142
Melanthium	199
MELASTOMACEÆ	218
Melica	194
Melilotus	212
Melissa	225
MENISPERMACEÆ	206
Menispermum	206
Mentha	224
Menziezia	221
Mertensia	224
Merulius	166
Metzgeria	184
Micrampelis	228
Microcera	101
Micrococcus	84
Microsphæria	131
MICROTHYRIACEÆ	146
Mimulus	226
Mitchella	228
Mitella	208
Mitremyces	81
Mitrula	147
MNIACEÆ	185
Mohrodendron	222
Mollia	186
Mollisia	150
Mollugo	203
Monarda	225
Moneses	220
Monilia	87
Monotropa	221

	PAGE.
MONOTROPACEÆ	221
MORACEÆ	201
Morchella	147
Morus	201
Mucor	82
Mucronoporus	164
Muhlenbergia	194
Muscari	198
Mycena	157
Myicoporon	146
Myosotis	224
Myriadoporus	165
Myriangium	179
MYXOMYCETEÆ	85
Myxosporium	123
Næmatella	173
NAIDACEÆ	192
Nasturtium	206
Naumbergia	222
Navicula	84
NECKERACEÆ	189
Neckeria	189
Nectria	144
NECTROIDACEÆ	120
Negundo	216
Nepeta	225
NIDULARIACEÆ	81
Nitzschia	85
Nummularia	138
Nyctalis	159
NYMPHACEÆ	204
Nymphæa	204
Nyssa	220
Obolaria	222
Odontia	168
Odontochisma	183
Œnothera	219
Oidium	87
OLEACEÆ	222
Omphalia	158
Onagra	219
ONAGRACEÆ	218
Onoclea	191
Onosmodium	224
Oospora	87
Opegrapha	181
Ophiobolus	143
OPHIOGLOSSACEÆ	190

	PAGE.
Ophioglossum	190
Opulaster	208
Opuntia	218
Orbilia	153
ORCHIDACEÆ	199
Orchis	200
Orinthogallum	198
OROBANCHACEÆ	227
Orthotrichum	188
Osmorrhiza	220
Osmunda	191
Ostropa	156
Ostrya	200
Otidea	148
OXALIDACEÆ	214
Oxalis	214
Oxycoccus	221
Oxydendron	221
Oxypolis	220
Panax	219
Panæolus	161
Panicularia	195
Panicum	193
Pannaria	177
PANNARIEÆ	177
Panus	159
Papaver	206
PAPAVERACEÆ	206
Papyrius	202
Parmelia	176
PARMELIEÆ	176
Parnassia	208
Paronychia	204
Parthenium	231
Parthenocissus	217
Passiflora	218
PASSIFLORACEÆ	218
Paspalum	193
Pastinaca	220
PATELLARIACEÆ	155
Pedicularis	227
Pellæa	190
Pellia	184
Peltigera	177
PELTIGERIEÆ	177
Pencillum	88
Peniophora	171
Penthorum	207
Pentstemon	226

	PAGE.
Peramium	199
Periconia	90
Peridermium	130
Perilla	224
PERISPORIACEÆ	130
Peronospora	83
PERONOSPORACEÆ	82
Pertusaria	179
Pestalozzia	125
Petunia	226
Peziza	148
PEZIZACEÆ	148
Phacelia	224
PHACIDIACEÆ	154
Phalaris	193
PHALLACEÆ	81
Phaseolus	213
Phegopteris	190
Phialea	149
Phlebia	168
Phleum	194
Phlox	223
Phlyctæna	120
Phoma	106
Phoradendron	202
Phragmidium	129
Phryma	224
Phyllachora	146
Phyllactinia	130
Phyllosticta	102
Physalis	226
Physalodes	226
Physalospora	138
Physarum	85
Physcia	176
Physcomitrium	186
Physostegia	225
Phytolacca	203
PHYTOLACCACEÆ	203
Phytophthora	83
Picea	192
Pieris	221
Pilacre	97
Pilea	202
Pinus	192
Placodium	178
Plagiochila	184
Plagiothecium	189
PLANTAGINACEÆ	227
Plantago	227

Plasmopara	83
PLATANACEÆ	208
Platanus	208
Pleonectria	145
Pleurotus	158
Plowrightia	146
Poa	194
Podophyllum	206
Podosphæria	130
Pogonia	200
Polygala	214
POLYGALACEÆ	214
POLYGONACEÆ	202
Polygonatum	198
Polygonum	202
Polymnia	231
POLEMONIACEÆ	223
Polemonium	223
Polypodium	190
POLYPORACEÆ	161
Polyporus	162
Polyscytalum	87
Polystictus	163
Polythrincium	91
POLYTRICHIACEÆ	185
Polytrichum	185
Populus	200
Porella	183
Poria	164
Porothelium	166
Porteranthus	209
Portulaca	203
PORTULACACEÆ	203
Potamogeton	192
Potentilla	211
Poterium	211
Prenanthes	233
PRIMULACEÆ	221
Propolis	154
Prunella	225
Prunus	208
Psathyrella	161
Pseudohelotium	149
Pseudovalsa	142
Ptelea	214
Pteris	190
Ptilium	189
Puccinia	128
Pyrenopeziza	150
Pyrenophora	143
Pyrenula	182
Pylaisia	189
Pyrola	220
PYROLACEÆ	220
Pyrularia	202
Pyrus	211
Quercus	201
Radula	183
Radulum	167
Ramalina	175
Ramularia	90
RANUNCULACEÆ	205
Ranunculus	205
Raphanus	207
Reticularia	86
Rhabdospora	120
Rhamnus	216
RHAMNACEÆ	216
Rhexia	218
Rhizina	148
Rhododendron	221
Rhus	215
Rhynchospora	196
Rhytisma	154
Ribes	208
Ridania	232
Rinodia	170
Robinia	212
Roripa	206
Rosa	211
ROSACEÆ	208
Rosellinia	135
RUBIACEÆ	227
Rubus	209
Rudbeckia	231
Ruellia	227
Rumex	203
Russula	158
Ruta	214
RUTACEÆ	214
Sabbatia	222
Saccharomyces	84
SACCHAROMYCETACEÆ	84
Sacidium	121
Sagittaria	192
SALICACEÆ	200
Salix	200

	PAGE.
Salvia	225
Sambucus	228
Samolus	222
Sanguinaria	206
Sanguisorba	211
Sanicula	220
SANTALACEÆ	202
Saponaria	204
Sarcinella	97
Sarcoscypha	148
Sassafras	206
SAURURACEÆ	200
Saururus	200
Saxifraga	208
SAXIFRAGACEÆ	208
Scapania	183
SCHIZOMYCETACEÆ	83
Schizophyllum	160
Scirpus	196
Scleroderma	82
Scleroderris	153
Sclerotina	149
Scorias	132
Scoriomyces	100
Scrophularia	226
SCROPHULARIACEÆ	226
Scutellaria	225
Sedum	207
Selaginella	191
SELAGINELLACEÆ	191
Senecio	232
Septoria	117
Septosporium	96
Sericocarpus	230
Sicyos	228
Sida	217
Sieglingia	194
Silene	204
Silphium	231
SIMARUBACEÆ	214
Sirococcus	109
Sisymbrium	207
Sisyrinchium	199
SMILACEÆ	199
Smilax	199
SOLANACEÆ	225
Solanum	225
Solea	218
Solenia	166
Solidago	229

	PAGE.
Sonchus	233
Sorbus	211
SPARGANIACEÆ	192
Sparganium	192
Spartina	193
Spathularia	147
Spathyema	197
Specularia	229
Speira	95
Spergula	204
Sphærella	138
SPHÆRIACEÆ	132
Sphærocephalus	185
Sphærographium	120
SPHÆROIDACEÆ	102
Sphæronæma	109
SPHÆROPSIDEÆ	102
Sphæropsis	113
Sphærotheca	130
SPHAGNACEÆ	189
Sphagnum	189
Spirillum	84
Sporocybe	98
Sporodinia	82
Sporodesmium	95
Spiræa	208
Stachylidium	91
Stachys	225
Stagonospora	116
STAPHYLACEÆ	215
Staphylea	215
Stauroneis	84
Steganosporium	126
Steironema	222
Stellaria	204
Stenophragma	207
Stereodon	189
STEREODONTACEÆ	188
Stereum	168
Sterigmatocystis	88
Sticta	177
STICTACEÆ	154
Stictis	154
STILBACEÆ	97
Stremonitis	86
Streptococcus	84
Streptopus	198
Streptothryx	90
Strobilomyces	162
Stropharia	160

Stylosanthes	212	Tricholoma	157
Stylophorum	206	Trichopeziza	151
STYRACEÆ	222	Trichosphæria	138
Symphoricarpos	228	Trichostema	225
Symphytum	224	Trichothecium	89
Syndesmon	205	Trientalis	221
Synedra	85	Trifolium	212
		Trillium	199
Tanacetum	232	Trimmatostroma	102
Tapesia	150	Triosteum	228
Taraxacum	233	Tripsacum	193
Taxus	192	Trogia	159
Tecoma	227	Trypethelium	182
Teichospora	143	Tsuga	192
Tephrosia	212	Tubercularia	98
Teucrium	224	TUBERCULARIACEÆ	98
Thalesia	227	Tuberculina	99
Thalictrum	205	Tubulina	86
Thaspium	220	Tylostoma	81
Thelephora	168	Tympanis	153
THELEPHORACEÆ	168	Typha	192
Thelia	188	TYPHACEÆ	192
Theloschistes	175		
Thelotrema	179	Udora	192
Therofon	208	ULMACEÆ	201
Thuidium	188	Ulmaria	209
Thuja	192	Ulmus	201
THYMELEACEÆ	218	Ulocolla	173
Thyrsidium	125	UMBELLIFERÆ	219
Tiarella	208	Umbilicaria	176
Tiedmannia	220	UMBILICARIÆ	176
Tilia	217	Uncinula	131
TILIACEÆ	217	Unifolium	198
Tilletia	127	Uniola	194
Tilmadoche	85	Uredo	130
Tortula	186	Urnula	152
TORTULACEÆ	186	Urocystis	127
Torula	90	Urtica	202
Toxylon	202	URTICACEÆ	202
Tragopogon	233	Urticastrum	202
Trametes	165	USNACEÆ	175
Trautvetteria	205	Usnea	175
Trematosphæria	142	USTILAGINACEÆ	126
Tremella	173	Ustilago	126
TREMELLINACEÆ	173	Ustulina	136
Tremellodon	167	Uvularia	198
Trichægum	96		
Trichia	86	Vaccinium	221
Trichocolea	183	Vagnera	198
Trichoderma	88	Valeriana	228

	PAGE.		PAGE.
VALERIANACEÆ	228	VITACEÆ	216
Valsa	132	Vitis	216
Valsaria	141	Vleckia	225
Veratrum	199	Volutella	100
Verbascum	226	Volvaria	160
Verbena	224		
VERBENACEÆ	224	Waldstenia	211
Verbesina	232	Weissia	188
Vermicularia	109	Woodsia	191
Vernonia	229		
Veronica	226	Xanthium	231
VERRUCARIACEÆ	182	Xanthorrhiza	206
Verticillium	89	Xolisma	221
Vibrissea	147	Xylaria	136
Viburnum	228		
Vicia	213	Zanthoxylum	214
Vincetoxicum	223	Zizia	220
Viola	217	Zygodesmus	90
VIOLACEÆ	217		

www.ingramcontent.com/pod-product-compliance
Lightning Source LLC
Chambersburg PA
CBHW021833230426
43669CB00008B/956